MW00810060

Delegation in Contemporary Democracies

Delegation is a ubiquitous social phenomenon linked with the growing differentiation of modern societies. It is one of several different modes of organization that exist to make collective action successful, but has been overlooked and under-researched.

Using a rational choice institutional analysis and principal-agent models, this book constitutes the most comprehensive study to date of political delegation. The well known American and European specialists bring existing literature on delegation; bureaucracy; the electorate and legislature and government within representative democracy together with research on new forms of delegation such as non-majoritarian institutions, to provide a more complete and synthetic analysis of delegation in political systems.

With a broad and comparative approach, this volume paves the way to a richer study of this important aspect of democratic institutions. It will be of strong interest to advanced students, researchers and professionals concerned with delegation in the areas of public policy, public administration and democratic theory.

Dietmar Braun is a Professor of Political Science at the University of Lausanne, Switzerland. **Fabrizio Gilardi** is a lecturer in Political Science at the University of Lausanne, Switzerland.

Routledge/ECPR studies in European political science

Edited by Thomas Poguntke
University of Birmingham, UK
and

Jan W. van Deth
University of Mannheim, Germany, on behalf of the European Consortium for Political Research

The Routledge/ECPR Studies in European Political Science series is published in association with the European Consortium for Political Research – the leading organization concerned with the growth and development of political science in Europe. The series presents high-quality edited volumes on topics at the leading edge of current interest in political science and related fields, with contributions from European scholars and others who have presented work at ECPR workshops or research groups.

Also available from Routledge in association with the ECPR:
Sex Equality Policy in Western Europe, edited by Frances Gardiner; **Democracy and Green Political Thought**, edited by Brian Doherty and Marius de Geus; **The New Politics of Unemployment**, edited by Hugh Compston; **Citizenship, Democracy and Justice in the New Europe**, edited by Percy B. Lehning and Albert Weale; **Private Groups and Public Life**, edited by Jan W. van Deth, **The Political Context of Collective Action**, edited by Ricca Edmondson; **Theories of Secession**, edited by Percy Lehning; **Regionalism across the North/South Divide**, edited by Jean Grugel and Wil Hout

Delegation in Contemporary Democracies

Edited by Dietmar Braun and Fabrizio Gilardi

LONDON AND NEW YORK

First published 2006
by Routledge
2 Park Square, Milton Park, Abingdon, Oxon OX14 4RN

Simultaneously published in the USA and Canada
by Routledge
270 Madison Ave, New York, NY 10016

Routledge is an imprint of the Taylor & Francis Group

Transferred to Digital Printing 2009

Typeset in Baskerville by Wearset Ltd, Boldon, Tyne and Wear

British Library Cataloguing in Publication Data
A catalogue record for this book is available from the British Library

Library of Congress Cataloging in Publication Data
A catalog record for this book has been requested

ISBN10: 0-415-35343-2 (hbk)
ISBN10: 0-415-54356-8 (pbk)

ISBN13: 978-0-415-35343-4 (hbk)
ISBN13: 978-0-415-54356-9 (pbk)

Contents

Illustrations

Figures

Tables

Contributors

Torbjörn Bergman is Senior Lecturer in Political Science at Umeå University, Sweden.

Dietmar Braun is Professor of Comparative Political Science at the Institut d'Etudes Politiques et Internationales, University of Lausanne, Switzerland.

Peter Munk Christiansen is a Professor in the department of Political Science, University of Southern Denmark, Odense, Denmark.

Patrick Dumont is Researcher at the University of Luxembourg and member of the Comparative Politics Centre, Université catholique de Louvain, Belgium.

David Epstein is a Professor in the Department of Political Science, Columbia University, New York NY.

Fabio Franchino is Lecturer in Political Science and Director of the Master's in European Policy at University College London, UK.

Fabrizio Gilardi is Lecturer in Political Science at the University of Lausanne, Switzerland.

Víctor Lapuente Giné is PhD candidate at Nuffield College, University of Oxford, UK.

Wolfgang C. Müller is a Professor at the University of Mannheim, Germany.

Asbjørn Sonne Nørgaard is a Professor in the Department of Political Science, University of Southern Denmark, Odense.

Sharyn O'Halloran is a Professor in the Department of Political Science, Columbia University, New York NY.

Gül Sosay is Assistant Professor in the Department of Political Science and International Relations, Bogaziçi University, Istanbul, Turkey.

Kaare Strøm is Professor of Political Science at the University of California, San Diego CA.

Frédéric Varone is a Professor in the Department of Political and Social Science, the Université catholique de Louvain, Belgium.

Series editor's preface

Thomas Poguntke

Starting from the observation that 'delegation is an ubiquitous social phenomenon' in complex societies, the editors and authors of this volume combine a detailed discussion of the 'standard chain of delegation' with an exploration of a hitherto under-researched field, namely delegation to independent agencies. Using principal–agent theory as a common conceptual baseline, democracy is understood as a chain of delegation, and the transfer of powers to independent regulatory agencies is seen as a fifth step in this chain of delegation that has so far not been given adequate attention in the literature. Another label that is frequently used for these institutions captures their essential nature better: calling them 'non-majoritarian institutions' highlights the fact that they are neither directly accountable to voters nor elected politicians. Furthermore, they are, at least partially, outside the conventional chain of principal–agent relationships in that they are, to varying degrees, deliberately removed from institutional mechanisms which could tie their actions to the preferences of their principals. To use an obvious example: politicians control the appointment of central bank governors or constitutional judges, but once they have assumed office, they assume a great deal of institutionally guaranteed independence. Those are, of course, the obvious – and historically grown – examples of non-majoritarian institutions while many more have developed over the past years.

The first section of the book lays the foundations for capturing the peculiarities of such non-majoritarian institutions by focusing at the standard chain of delegation. Kaare Strøm, Wolfgang C. Müller and Torbjörn Bergman discuss the '(moral) hazards of parliamentary democracy' which, arguably, suffers from the fact that parties are not agents for controlling governments and the essential mechanism of accountability lies with electoral competition (Chapter 2). Patrick Dumont and Frédéric Varone explore the impact of the size of a polity on the functioning of the chain of democratic delegation and conclude that MPs in small constituencies may be more accountable to voters but less efficient in controlling government (Chapter 3) while David Epstein and Sharyn O'Halloran discuss the origins of delegation to bureaucracy (Chapter 4). The next chapter deals with the related problem of trust in principal–agent relationships concerning the bureaucracy, which can be violated by the principal as well as the agent. Political credibility is a crucial problem here and the inherent problem of whether or not principal (i.e. politicians) will be sufficiently long in office to reward agents (i.c. bureaucrats) can be overcome by delegating the power of promotion to independent institutions, as Víctor Lapuente Giné argues (Chapter 5).

The next chapters deal specifically with independent agencies and Fabrizio Gilardi shows that their proliferation in OECD countries is directly related to the neo-liberal agenda of privatization, while there is considerable variation as regards their exact nature and competences, depending on the sectors concerned (Chapter 6). Dietmar Braun analyses the distributive agencies and looks at research funding councils where target groups are included in the delegation mechanism. The general conclusion to be drawn from this analysis is that one needs to go beyond the standard binary conceptualization of delegation relationships (Chapter 7). Gül Sosay discusses problems of legitimating delegation arrangements. While she remains sceptical because of potential contradictions between efficiency and democracy (Chapter 8), mass publics may worry less than academic analysts and turn to (perceived) output legitimacy: the German Bundesbank and Constitutional Court are famous examples of non-majoritarian institutions enjoying significantly higher levels of legitimacy than any of the elected institutions of the Federal Republic. The chapter by Peter Munk Christiansen and Asbjørn Sonne Nørgaard addresses the role of interest organizations as agents providing information to governments through their participation in policy-proposing commissions which may allow minority governments to shape the legislative process according to their own preferences (Chapter 9). The volume concludes with an analysis of different patterns of delegation in the European Union and Fabio Franchino finds that the decision rules in the Council influence whether policy authority is delegated to the Commission or to national institutions.

There is not a general conclusion to be drawn form this volume. Rather, as the editors Dietmar Braun and Fabrizio Gilardi argue, a number of themes emerge which warrant more conceptual work and empirical investigation, namely the importance of institutional contexts, the relevance and political contexts and power strategies, and the need to broaden the conceptualization of delegation relationships beyond binary models and beyond the standard chain of delegation. They are, however, cautious to point out that the growth of delegatory institutions over the past years need not be irreversible, and governments may attempt to recapture direct control.

Acknowledgements

This volume has its origins in a workshop organized at the ECPR Joint Sessions 2003 in Edinburgh, where most of the chapters were originally presented. The workshop provided an excellent opportunity to discuss delegation as a political phenomenon in a friendly and stimulating environment, which motivated us to put together this collective work in published form. Many people have helped us in finalizing this project. In particular, we would like to thank Thomas Poguntke, who warmly welcomed our proposal as editor of the Routledge/ECPR series, Rachel Astle for editing the manuscript and Bashkim Iseni for preparing it for the publisher. The generous financial support of the Fondation du 450ème anniversaire de l'Université de Lausanne is also gratefully acknowledged.

Dietmar Braun and Fabrizio Gilardi
Melbourne and Lausanne

1   Introduction

Dietmar Braun and Fabrizio Gilardi

Delegation is a ubiquitous social phenomenon linked to the growing differentiation of modern societies. With the division of labour and specialization, the multiplication of 'social circles' (cf. Simmel) and the genesis of functional systems and subsystems, the power and capacity of individuals to realize objectives on their own account fall into question. The realization of objectives depends to an increasing degree on what other individuals do and, thus, is subject to collective action. Different modes of organization exist to make collective action, which is often plagued by 'opportunism' and non-coordination, successful: hierarchy, markets, networks and delegation. While the former modes have been elaborated in detail in the literature, delegation has remained somewhat the stepchild of political theory.

While hierarchy depends on command, markets on unplanned coordination by prices, and networks on the will to cooperate on an equal base, delegation can be considered as an 'extension of self' (Coleman, 1990) by transmitting authority in the form of property rights to someone who is considered to have capacities that the 'delegator' – or in terms of rational choice theory, the principal – doesn't have but wants to make use of in order to improve his well-being. Delegation is, therefore, a form of collective action where we find a principal (the 'delegator') and an agent (the 'delegated') who combine forces in order to realize the objectives of the principal. In doing so, the sphere of action of the principal is extended. In contrast to hierarchy, delegation does not use commands but contracts and incentives, which the agent voluntarily accepts. In contrast to the market, the coordination in delegation is conscious and based on explicit contracts. While actors in networks deal with each other from an equal base of power, the delegation relationship is asymmetric; the agent is supposed to work for the principal to realize their aims.

Forms of delegation have been a subject in political science for quite some time, though a profound theoretical controversy on the main components and rationales of delegation as a mode of collective action is lacking.

The most obvious political phenomenon is *democratic representation*, which was initially discussed in Montesquieu's and Burke's treatises on the relationship between the citizen and his representative in parliament. Burke demanded – in opposition to Rousseau, who wanted the direct binding of the representative to the will of the citizen – the delegation of authority from the citizen to the deputy, who then deliberates with other deputies in order to define the 'common will' (Burke, 1863). More recently and more in detail, Hannah Pitkin has elaborated on the different forms of democratic representation and their rationales (Pitkin, 1961). Her work can be considered as one of the early contributions to a then not yet existing theory of delegation as representation.

In the 1920s, Max Weber and his disciple Robert Michels attacked another obvious delegation phenomenon, i.e. the *role of party leaders and their followers*. The 'iron law of oligarchy', pronounced by Michels, demonstrates one of the main problems of delegation, the seemingly inevitable growing autonomy and estrangement of the delegated from the delegators (Michels, 1911).

One can consider in general the political literature on *elites* and their relationship with the 'masses' and citizens respectively, dealt with for example in the work of classical authors like Pareto, Mosca, Schumpeter and C. Wright Mills and modern authors like Putnam (Putnam, 1976) and Bourdieu (Bourdieu, 1981, 1984), as a potential contribution to a theory on delegation.

Whenever – and this is not necessarily only the case in democracies citizens transfer some of their rights of sovereignty to delegates on the political level, a delegation relationship is established.

While this literature discussed delegation as representation, delegation may also be found on the executive side of policy making. An obvious example would be the role of *bureaucrats* in public policy making. Though Max Weber was certainly among the first to have scrutinized this phenomenon, his discussion does not analyse the relationship between politician and bureaucrat in terms of delegation. According to his studies, bureaucrats are engaged in a hierarchical relation with politicians and have no leeway for action. Hierarchy is, however, different from delegation as stipulated above. It was Niskanen in the 1960s who made it clear that bureaucrats have their own will and room to manoeuvre (Niskanen, 1971). The relationship should not be considered hierarchical. When politicians transfer some of their property rights to bureaucrats, they must be aware that the logic of bureaucrats' actions can fundamentally differ from pure execution of governments' orders.

Corporatism, especially in the form of 'state corporatism' (Schmitter, 1979), is another example of delegation on the executive side. The delegation of important functions of the political system such as the organization of industrial relations or social security to corporate actors in society clearly manifests the willingness of policy makers to transfer some of their property rights to societal actors in order to reduce transaction costs and forgo information problems.

The more recent studies on the role of 'independent agencies', most notably in regulatory policies, prominently put forward by Majone's considerations of a shift from the redistributive to the regulatory state (Majone, 1997), can be regarded as a last domain where political scientists are boarding the 'train of delegation'. Independent agencies can be considered as a particular form of execution, similar to bureaucratic action but with more discretion than is usually attributed to the bureaucrat. This raises particular problems that are dealt with in the literature.

Although we find a large number of political phenomena that can be scrutinized under the denominator of 'delegation', a theory of delegation embracing and synthesizing all these different approaches is still lacking. Recently, *principal–agent theory*, a strand of rational choice theory, has become prominent in studies dealing with delegation and has become a unifying paradigm in the building of a theory of delegation. What are the basic components of principal–agent theory with respect to delegation?

Principal–agent theory

Principal–agent theory is based on an economic theory of choice and behaviour. It assumes that actors are interest-maximizing and opportunistic. Although phenomena of sympathy and identification can occur within an agency relationship (Coleman, 1990: 157–162), rarely is there complete harmony of interests between the principal and his agent. This means that most of the time there is, at least potentially, a conflict of interests between these two actors, which is frustrating because the very *raison d'être* of the agent is that of fulfilling the principal's interests. Given this configuration, the principal's problem is motivating his agent. In particular, the problem is to establish an incentive structure that leads the agent to maximize the principal's interest. In fact, since actors behave opportunistically, an immediate implication of the conflict of interests is that the agent will systematically try to maximize his own interest instead of that of the principal, in other words, the agent will tend to *shirk*.

Another important assumption is that information is asymmetrically distributed between the two actors, typically being in favour of the agent, who knows more about himself than the principal does. This causes two main problems for the principal: two different kinds of opportunistic behaviour, one known as *adverse selection* (or *ex ante* opportunism, or hidden information) and the other as *moral hazard* (or *ex post* opportunism, or hidden action). Adverse selection occurs whenever the principal cannot be sure that he is selecting the agent who has the most appropriate skills or preferences. Moral hazard occurs whenever the agent's actions cannot be perfectly monitored by the principal. These are general problems inherent not only in agency relationships but more generally in all contractual and hierarchical relationships (Moe, 1984: 755).

These problems could be mitigated if the agreement between the principal and the agent could be fixed in perfect, complete contracts. Such contracts, however, would have very demanding requirements (Milgrom and Roberts, 1992: 127–132). Due to the fact that actors are only rationally bounded, actual contracts will always suffer from incompleteness. In actual contractual relations, 'contingencies inevitably arise that have not been planned for and, when they do, the parties must find way to adapt' (Milgrom and Roberts, 1992: 128). This has the effect of worsening the problems of opportunistic behaviour rather than mitigating them.

Given these informational and motivational constraints, the principal's problem is to prevent the agent from shirking. It is thus not surprising that scholars, especially in economics, have mainly directed their efforts to understanding what kind of incentive structure the principal should (and, since he is assumed to be rational, will) set up in order to minimize the agent's shirking. Hence, an extensive amount of the economic literature deals with optimal incentive structure issues (e.g. Mirrlees, 1976; Glover, 1994). In political science, however, principal–agent models have also been used to investigate more substantial issues such as delegation in political settings. In particular, on the basis of principal–agent theory both legislative and executive relationships in parliamentary democracies have been subject to a reconceptualization in terms of delegation.

The chain of delegation in parliamentary democracies

Democracies have been conceptualized as chains of delegation by Kaare Strøm (2000, 2003; Strøm *et al.*, 2003). The idea is that the influence of democratic principals, i.e. citizens, on policies is shaped by the different formal institutions that separate them from the final decision. These institutions can be seen as delegation steps, as principals give instructions to agents and thus delegate to them decision-making authority. In the first place, citizens delegate authority to their representatives, who usually sit in parliaments, and in presidential systems also in the presidential chair. Then, in parliamentary systems, the parliament delegates some of its authority to the government, which, as a whole, further delegates to the individual ministers. Next, the government typically delegates policy implementation to the bureaucracy. Strøm thus identifies four main links in the delegation chain. As will be shown below, delegation to independent agencies can be seen as a fifth step, which seems to be neglected in this literature.

The ideal-typical chains of delegation in parliamentary and presidential democracies can be differentiated on the basis of the complexity of the chain. Parliamentary democracies are characterized by the *singularity principle*, according to which each principal employs a single agent (or a set of non-competing agents), as well as by indirect delegation, as few agents (members of parliament) are directly elected by citizens, and most agents (ministers and bureaucrats) are indirectly appointed, often through several stages. Presidential democracies, on the other hand, feature a more complex chain that, however, ensures a more direct link between citizens and agents. Most notably, the government is directly elected by citizens in presidential systems, but not in parliamentary ones. Different institutional arrangements lead to different consequences, and thus agency losses and control mechanisms follow from the structure of the delegation chain. In particular, the fact that in parliamentary democracies (in contrast to presidential systems) there is less reliance on checks and balances implies that *ex post* controls are weak and *ex ante* controls are strong. The more important role of parties in parliamentary democracy leads to effective screening devices that mitigate adverse selection of agents.

Equipped with this overview of the main features of the delegation chain, we can now turn to the single steps.

Delegation from voters to elected representatives

The first step of delegation is from voters to legislators. Mitchell (2000) argues that this agency relationship is framed by two sets of rules, namely party methods of candidate selection and electoral laws, which are best thought of as control mechanisms intended to control agency losses. Electoral laws and candidate selection by parties constitute *ex ante* means to avoid adverse selection, whereas *ex post* controls are based mainly on monitoring and reporting by third parties such as interest groups and the press, but also on institutional checks. More specifically, agency losses are more likely to occur when legislators' careers do not directly depend on the preferences of voters, because in that case incentive compatibility between the former and the latter tends to be lower. Müller (2000), on the other hand, considers legislators as agents not of voters, but of the extra-parliamentary party organization. The question here is how can the party control its representatives standing for or already in public office through the standard *ex ante* (contract design, screening and selection) and *ex post* (reporting requirements and monitoring, institutional checks) control mechanisms? (Müller, 2000: 322–329).

Delegation from legislators to the executive

The second link of the chain of delegation in parliamentary systems is that between members of parliaments and governments. Saalfeld (2000) identifies two key elements of legislative organization that are likely to affect the nature of the agency relationship between parliament and government. First, he stresses that the delegation process from members of parliaments to the government is mediated and controlled by political parties. Second, he argues that committee specialization is a response to the growing information asymmetry between parliament and government, but is also a new source of agency problems, namely between committee members and non-members.

Delegation from the governmental cabinet to individual ministries

The third link of the parliamentary chain of delegation involves cabinet and ministers. The agency relationship deriving from this link, however, is fundamentally different from the others. In fact, in this case 'the principal is made up of its own agents' (Andeweg, 2000: 377); the government delegates to ministers, yet it is also composed of them. This, it is argued, opens up significant potential for agency losses. Andeweg (2000) makes the point that the nature of the agency relationship between the government and its ministers varies along two dimensions of government decision making, namely whether it is organized hierarchically or collegially, and whether it is strongly departmentalized (that is, each ministers enjoys considerable autonomy in its own legislature) or, rather, decisions are taken collectively. Agency losses are more likely when ministers are more autonomous and when the government is organized collegially. In that case the prime minister does not have the right of supervision over the ministers' activities, and the government is departmentalized, so that each minister has nearly complete autonomy in his own legislature. Conversely, agency losses are less likely when the government is hierarchical and the decisions are taken collectively.

Delegation from the government to the bureaucracy

Delegation to bureaucracy is the fourth link in the chain of delegation and, especially in the United States, was the first area where principal–agent models were applied in political science. American scholars have spent a good deal of time and effort in debating the extent to which the bureaucracy is autonomous from Congress and/or the President (for an overview, see Moe, 1987; Huber and Shipan, 2000). Consistent with the assumption of the principal–agent model, they have looked for and identified several mechanisms through which politicians can minimize bureaucratic drift, i.e. the difference between the policy chosen by the enacting coalition and that implemented by the bureaucracy. As Weingast (1984: 154) puts it, 'specialized institutions evolve to mitigate agency shirking'.

In addition to 'fire alarm' and 'police patrols' (McCubbins and Schwartz, 1984), the role of administrative procedures as *ex ante* control mechanisms has been studied in depth (McCubbins *et al.*, 1987, 1989). By limiting the agent's range of feasible actions, it is argued that procedures mitigate both general informational asymmetries and specific moral hazard problems. Administrative procedures have two main effects. First, they counterbalance informational asymmetries by forcing the bureaucracy to disclose relevant information about both planned and implemented actions. Further, procedures determine the nature of the information available to the agency, as well as the extent to which decisions must be based on such information. Second, they cope with a problem discussed by Horn and Shepsle (1989) as 'legislative drift' and that Moe (1990) has subsequently defined as 'the problem of political uncertainty', namely the fact that political property rights, unlike economic ones, are not guaranteed. This means that what is created by a coalition today can be subverted or even completely destroyed by another tomorrow without any sort of compensation. To avoid this problem today's coalition will try to establish 'an institutional structure to create pressures on agencies that replicate the political pressures applied when the relevant legislation was enacted' (McCubbins *et al.*, 1987: 255). In addition to solving these two problems, procedures have the advantage of being nearly costless, as well as of adapting automatically to changes in the preferences of the enacting coalition's constituency (what the authors call 'the auto-pilot function').

More recently, the literature on delegation to the bureaucracy in the United States has been advanced by the work of David Epstein and Sharyn O'Halloran (Epstein and O'Halloran, 1999). They focus on the relationship between Congress and the executive, and conceptualize delegation as the choice of the principal (Congress) to give discretion to agents (executive agencies) by not specifying the details of policy in legislation and/or by not setting up control mechanisms. Their explanation is grounded in a political transaction-cost approach. While they have not been the first to apply to politics concepts from transaction-cost economics (e.g. Weingast and Marshall, 1988; Kiewiet and McCubbins, 1989; Horn, 1995; Moe, 1990), the strength of their contribution is to be found in their combination of formal modelling and extensive empirical analysis. Their theory argues that Congress will choose the mode of policy production that is most efficient (i.e. specifying it in detail or delegating the task to the executive). However, efficiency is not used as a technical term, but rather as a political one, meaning that policy making will be delegated to maximize the chances of re-election and not necessarily to improve the quality of policies. Their results show that two factors are particularly important in explaining the decision to delegate. First, Congress is less willing to grant discretion under divided government, because the President has greater power over appointments in executive agencies and thus has the possibility to express his preference. Under these conditions, divided government can be associated with greater distance between the preferences of the principal (Congress) and the agent (executive agencies), and the former thus has incentives to keep control over policy. The second factor is information and is linked to the complexity of policies. Legislators have limited time and skills and thus have incentives to delegate in more complex (or 'informationally intensive') policy areas.

The limit of Epstein and O'Halloran's work is that it remains focused almost exclusively on the United States, although it has been very influential well beyond the United States, and their theory has been applied to the context of EU decision-making (Franchino, 2000a, b). Analyses of delegation to bureaucracy that are explicitly comparative have been carried out by John Huber and Charles Shipan (Huber and Shipan, 2002). They develop and empirically test a formal model showing that four factors affect delegation, two of which are related to the incentives to delegate and the other two to the capacity to do so. Delegation is conceptualized as the extent to which policy details are specified in statutes, thus leaving less discretion to bureaucrats. The first factor, affecting incentives to delegate, is policy conflict between principals (legislators) and agents (bureaucrats). Of course, delegation is less likely when there is policy conflict. The second factor, also affecting incentives to delegate, is the presence of non-statutory factors enhancing control on the bureaucracy. If such factors are present, then the need to increase the precision of legislation as a means of control is less acute. The other two factors are related to the ability to draft detailed statutes. The first is legislative capacity and is related to the professionalism of legislators. The authors stress that since in parliamentary democracies the initiators of legislation are ministers, the professionalism of members of parliament is relevant only under minority government. Under majority government, a better proxy for legislative capacity is the expectations of ministers about turnover in cabinet. Finally, the bargaining environment also affects the ability to create detailed legislation, which is lower when the two chambers of the legislatures are controlled by different parties. In parliamentary contexts, the bargaining environment is less relevant and not taken into account by Huber and Shipan.

Delegation to non-majoritarian institutions

As discussed above, the standard chain of delegation is composed of four steps, linking in turn voters to legislators, legislators to government, government to individual ministers and ministers to the bureaucracy. For each link there is a good selection of literature, particularly for delegation to bureaucracy which has been extensively studied. However, the literature neglects an additional step of delegation that has become increasingly important since the 1990s, especially in Europe. Sometimes, policy makers decide to set up institutions that enjoy considerable independence from elected officials. These can be conceptualized as non-majoritarian institutions (NMIs). Non-majoritarian institutions can be defined as 'those governmental entities that (a) possess and exercise some grant of specialized public authority, separate from that of other institutions, but (b) are neither directly elected by the people, nor directly managed by elected officials' (Thatcher and Stone Sweet, 2002: 2). The concept was made popular by Giandomenico Majone (1997, 2001a), who argued that many public institutions share the characteristic of not being directly account-able either to voters or to elected politicians and can thus be called 'non-majoritarian', since their insulation from the will of the majority as expressed in the legislature can effectively protect the rights of minorities. Non-majoritarian institutions are at odds with a strict majoritarian view of democracy, which maintains that majorities should be able to control all governmental activity, but fit in well with the Madisonian model, where it is important to disperse, share and limit power so as to impede the rise of a tyranny of the majority.

Such institutions are not new. Courts (Stone Sweet, 2002), independent administrative agencies (Christensen and Pallesen, 2001), and the European Commission (Majone, 2001b, 2002; Tallberg, 2002) are all cases in point. The ideal-typical example, however, is independent central banks, about which there is an enormous literature (for a thorough review see Berger *et al.*, 2001). The peculiarity of central banks, and by extension of most NMIs, is that, in opposition to what principal–agent theory predicts, they are not designed to implement the 'ally principle' (Bendor *et al.*, 2001), according to which the principal tries to choose agents as similar to itself as possible so as to prevent moral hazard. In the case of central banks, principals, in addition to not applying the ally principle, also purposely give up some of the control mechanisms they could use to control the actions of the agent. Thus, in many countries central banks are given an explicit mandate to fight inflation, are selected to be more 'conservative' (i.e. inflation-averse) than the government, and are insulated from the influence of elected politicians. Empirical evidence shows that independent central banks do contribute to keeping inflation low, although it depends on a series of contextual factors (Franzese, 1999).

The example of central banks therefore indicates that delegation to NMIs has, in principal–agent terms, some extraordinary features. Governments delegate important powers to agents, such as central banks, that are known to have different preferences and they also remove some of the institutional mechanisms they could use to control their actions. However, despite these counter-intuitive choices, the government is likely to be better off, as shown by the positive impact of central bank independence on inflation. To explain this paradox, Majone (2001a, b) has suggested that delegation to NMIs does not correspond to an agency relationship but, rather, to a fiduciary relationship. In this model, political property rights over policy are fully transferred to the delegate, who is thus subject to duties exceeding the normal duties of an agent. Independent central banks, but also examples such as the European Commission, would then be best characterized as fiduciaries. Thus the distinction between agency and fiduciary relationship points to a qualitative difference between delegation types. While it surely deepens our understanding of delegation, more work is needed to refine the concept and apply it empirically.

Independent regulatory agencies

Independent regulatory agencies (IRAs) are NMIs with regulatory competences. They are the main institutional feature of the regulatory state, and
constitute a major institutional change in regulation. They can be defined
as public organizations with regulatory powers that are neither directly
elected by the people, nor directly managed by elected officials. Examples
include the British Office of Communications (Ofcom), the German Bun-
deskartellamt, the French Autorité des marchés financiers (AMF), and the
Italian Autorità per l'energia elettrica e il gas, to name a few. Although
IRAs are a relatively recent phenomenon in Europe, in just over a decade
they have become extremely common. An indication of this is the fact that
the OECD, in one of its latest reports on regulatory reforms, writes that
'[o]ne of the most widespread institutions of modern regulatory governance is the so-called independent regulator or autonomous administrative agency with regulatory powers' (OECD, 2002: 91).

Given this popularity among policy makers, IRAs have recently
attracted much academic interest. The literature on IRAs was initially
focused on their consequences rather than their origins. Thatcher (1994)
showed that differences in the expansion of competition in the telecommunications industry in the early 1990s in France and United Kingdom
were due to differences in the institutional aspects of regulation in the two
countries. Most notably, while the United Kingdom set up an IRA for
telecommunications in 1984, in France the ministry remained the regulator. IRAs were also found to have significant effects on the regulation of
utilities in general. In Britain, IRAs have had a profound impact on the
nature of regulation, as they have used their powers to take action in many
fields, sometimes outside and beyond their intended scope of action, and
have developed a 'conceptual framework' emphasizing the promotion of
competition and the protection of consumers (Thatcher, 1998). Other
studies have addressed the consequences of IRAs on aspects other than
regulation itself. Thatcher (2002a) stresses that these consequences are
often unexpected. The relationship between IRAs and elected politicians
is a case in point, as the former initially conformed to national patterns of
policy making, where typically government maintained control, but have
subsequently acquired considerable autonomy and power, often in ways
that were not foreseen in the statute. Thatcher (2002b) has empirically
examined the relationship between IRAs and elected politicians, and has
shown that formal powers to overturn regulators' decision have not often
been used by ministers, thus suggesting that their *de facto* independence
has become quite high. Similarly, Wilks and Bartle (2002) argue that
competition authorities have become important players over time,
although they were established for symbolic reasons and were originally
not expected to play a very active role in policy development and implementation. However, the most important consequence of the establish-

ment of IRAs has probably been on legitimacy. In fact, it has been argued that the regulatory state in general suffers from legitimacy problems (Majone, 1998, 1999; Scott, 2000), but these are mainly related to the fact that non-majoritarian institutions such as IRAs, which are outside the chain of delegation and democratic accountability (for central banks see Elgie, 2002; Stiglitz, 1998), have been established. There are reasons to believe that independence and accountability can be reconciled. The legitimacy of IRAs, like that of other NMIs, has a substantive and a pro-cedural component (Majone, 2001a: 77). Substantive legitimacy depends on the capacity of IRAs to deliver good policy output. According to Majone, 'the democratic legitimacy of non-majoritarian institutions depends on their capacity to engender and maintain the belief that they are the most appropriate ones for the functions assigned to them' (Majone, 2002: 389). This largely corresponds to Scharpf's 'output legiti-macy' (Scharpf, 1997: 153–155, 1999), where political choices are legitim-ate if they promote common welfare. Procedural legitimacy, on the other hand, means that IRAs must be accountable for their actions. This, in turn, corresponds to Scharpf's 'input legitimacy' (Scharpf, 1997: 153–155, 1999), where political decisions are legitimate if they are based on the agreement of those who are asked to comply.

Independent distributive agencies

Concurrently, but independently from this literature, several authors were working on another kind of independent agency, situated not in regula-tory policy, but in distributive policies directed to the promotion of research. Observations in this field resembled the findings about IRAs. Policy makers were prepared to create research councils and funding agencies dedicated to the promotion of research projects. Authority to spend money on research was delegated to these agencies where policy makers often have an influence only 'at a distance'. The statutes of research councils are in many ways comparable to those of IRAs. Prin-cipal–agent theory has become a dominant approach in this field for understanding the main problems in research policies as well as the underlying dynamics.

The contributions to this volume

This overview demonstrates not only the variety of topics recent discus-sions of delegation have addressed, but also that principal–agent can be a useful and interesting tool for understanding the structure and dynamics of delegation in a parsimonious way. The problem is that there is seldom cross-referencing between the various studies of different 'parts' of the chain, particularly between the 'chain of delegation' literature and the 'independent agencies' literature, though both have developed a

considerable number of studies and reached a certain degree of sophistication. In bringing together political science scholars from all fields of
delegation study (representation, bureaucracy, independent agencies) we
hope to overcome this artificial and unintended gap and, hence, achieve a
synthesized theoretical view on delegation topics. In this book the main
components and problems of the principal–agent approach appear, such
as the difficulties with 'incomplete contracts', the antinomy between autonomy and control, the risk of adverse selection and moral hazard, the
attempt to increase the credibility of the principal, the problem of trust,
and information problems. The application of these components and
problems to the different fields of study in this volume allows us not only
to speak in a common language but also to understand whether and to
what degree these components and problems are articulated in these
fields. Do we find major differences in, for example, the relationship
between the elector and his representative and between the Congress
representative and an administrator? Are funding agencies subject to the
same problems as independent regulatory agencies? The answers to these
and other questions allow us to come to a more encompassing and integ-
rative view of delegation phenomena in the political field.

The contributions to this book are grouped in two parts. In the first,
the authors have examined the standard chain of delegation, which, as
was noted above, extends from citizens to bureaucracy via parliaments and
governments. The second part, in contrast, is focused on what may be
called the 'next steps' of delegation, which include independent agencies,
interest organizations and the European Union.

The standard chain of delegation

In Chapter 2 Kaare Strøm, Wolfgang Müller and Torbjörn Bergman refor-
mulate the complex relationships in representative democracy in terms of
principal–agent theory. According to them, one should understand
parliamentary democracy, most notably Westminster democracy which is
their main focus, as a long chain of sequential delegation relationships.
This is in contrast to presidential systems where multiple 'agents' are participating in legislation. It is this characteristic of a linear and sequential
chain of delegation which creates particular 'agency losses' in parliamentary democracy. Their main proposition is that parliamentary democracy is
well equipped to deal with adverse selection, but not with the other typical
problem linked to delegation, the moral hazard of democratic representatives. One explanation is that structures such as parties fail to provide a
controlling function. Parties in parliamentary democracies are able to
solve the information problem voters have with regard to the choice of
their representatives, but they exacerbate the accountability problem once
representatives have been elected. It is mainly party discipline, which has a
negative impact on the behaviour of representatives.

Not only are accountability problems generated within parliamentary democracies but so are control problems. Representatives of the parliamentary majority bound by party discipline and dependent on the electoral success of governmental parties have no incentives to control the government, and representatives from opposition parties do not have sufficient influence to do so.

Though the problems of party democracy are well known in the literature, the study offers new insights in that it stresses the difficulties the Westminster model has in maintaining accountability to their voters. The problems of delegation can be clearly seen; in parliamentary systems where the government has all the power to realize its promises, there are no mechanisms to force the government to keep its promises or to control what it actually does. Such 'agency losses' cause legitimacy problems.

The main merit of Chapter 2 is that it highlights that different democratic regimes have different kinds of agency losses. The Westminster system is better at avoiding adverse selection and enabling voters to make well informed choices. But it exposes agents to less constraint from other agents than the checks-and-balances system in the United States does. No system, they state, manages to ensure there are no agency losses; '[d]emocratic agency problems are stubborn and come in different forms', they are invariably there whatever institutional solutions are chosen.

In Chapter 3, Patrick Dumont and Frédéric Varone analyse the 'chain of delegation' from an interesting point of view. They consider the extent to which the *size* of a country may influence the organization of delegation within the chain, as well as the problems Strøm Müller and Bergman mention such as democratic accountability. The 'size of democracy', which means considering how small countries work, was raised as a topic some time ago by Dahl and Tufte (1973). Small countries also play the main role in Katzenstein's observations on corporatism (Katzenstein, 1984, 1985). It seems intuitively right to assume that smallness has implications for delegation, as it leads to frequent contact between a small number of actors. It also influences how the link between voters and the different institutions in the political system is organized. The authors develop a research programme by distinguishing three size-related variables (smallness, proximity and short cuts) that are rigorously discussed in turn, using the chain of delegation in Luxembourg as an illustration.

As an example we can mention here the relationship between MPs and government. The authors demonstrate that the size of the electorate (as the main and foremost principal), which is expressed in the small size of constituencies, has implications for the control capacity of MPs. Small constituencies imply more intense and frequent contact with voters and, hence, less time for representatives to control the government. In addition, less specialization is possible in small parliaments as MPs are required to attend several parliamentary commissions and do not have the time or opportunity to deepen their knowledge of special topics. This causes a shortage of information, which could otherwise be used for controlling the government. In short, governments in small democracies often have more leeway than governments in larger countries, as governments in small democracies are less constrained by control and, hence, less accountable. The smallness of a democracy therefore exacerbates the moral hazard problem Strøm *et al.* sketch in Chapter 2.

The authors consider a large number of such points that play a role in the discussion of delegation in the parliamentary chain. They convincingly conclude that smallness might be one of the rare independent variables that has an influence on all parts of the chain of delegation. They are also aware that much further clarification and empirical research is needed and they make useful suggestions for future research.

In Chapter 4, David Epstein and Sharyn O'Halloran start by raising the question when is it worth while to delegate and what kind of constraints might one expect when delegating. They discuss these questions in the context of the relationship of the parliament and the executive. Their 'positive theory of political delegation' is mainly derived from observations in the United States but, as they claim, may be used also in the context of parliamentary systems.

In the beginning, legislators must decide whether to use internal experts to receive adequate information or whether to delegate decision making to some external agency (government, bureaucratic or independent agencies) and if so, with what level of discretion. Legislators may opt for a combination of both. By including the distance of preference points between the internal and external agents on the one hand and the legislators on the other, and by taking into account uncertainty, they develop a trade-off space which tells us when it is most likely that legislators will delegate certain policy areas.

The main outcome of their model is, in contrast to other studies, that administrative control procedures are important, but that it is impossible to gain perfect control of executive agencies. In addition, the more complex and uncertain the environment of legislators is, the more delegation becomes attractive.

These points have already been raised in several other publications by the authors. The interesting point they add in Chapter 4 is the discussion of how their theory can be helpful in also highlighting delegation problems in other democratic regimes. The authors are convinced that their theory is applicable in all cases despite the different role of MPs in different democratic regimes. There are, of course, different dynamics at work in different regimes. In the United States the system of checks and balances gives the Congress incentives to delegate 'and thereby blur the distinctions between legislation and implementation'. In parliamentary systems, however, where the cabinet is strong and dominant, the parliament might want to have independent internal experts to counterbalance the government. If the parliament has little policy-making expertise and is fractured, then there will instead be an incentive to delegate legislation to cabinets and bureaucracy in order to develop the 'intricate details of complex policy'. If the parliament has 'distinct policy goals from the cabinet' it might establish competing centres of legislative power and oversight.

One might therefore find completely different incentives in presidential and parliamentary regimes, which adds insights to the article of Strøm *et al.* in this book. Both studies are good entry points for more empirically oriented comparative studies of the implications of delegation.

In Chapter 5, Víctor Lapuente Giné develops a general theory to explain different levels of bureaucratization in countries which have both autocratic and democratic regimes. He starts from the assumption that politicians need loyal and efficient public employees to stay in office. Instead of assuming adversarial relationships or opportunism, as is usually done in principal–agent theory, he refers, like Braun in this book, to a theoretical perspective that treats delegation as a relationship of mutual gain and includes the notion of trust. Thus it is possible to see that not only the agent, but also the principal, may shirk or violate trust.

The main problem in the relationship between policy makers and bureaucrats is for the principal, i.e. the policy maker, to be sure that public employees work hard and that they are loyal, while employees must be sure that their effort and loyalty are rewarded. The first aspect is jeopardized by moral hazard and the second by political credibility; if the government changes, the policy makers may not be able to fulfil promises given to employees in terms of promotion, etc.

In order to solve this commitment problem, politicians have to choose whether to retain authority to use incentives and sanctions for the effort of public employees for themselves, delegate it to an independent bureaucratic organization or install binding commitments to their intervention by law.

The merit of Lapuente's approach is to embed this choice into a comparative institutional context. On the one hand, we have regimes with concentrated powers where it is easy for policy makers to use their powers and where they have no incentive to delegate powers to independent agencies. This creates a problem where the effort of public employees may be suboptimal because they fear that policy makers will break their promises. On the other hand, this is different in 'separation of power' systems with multiple veto players. Only in that case is the credible commitment of policy makers possible, as such a system creates trust by binding the principal. Bureaucratization, which Lapuente considers equivalent to delegating sanctioning powers to independent committees, is not necessary. The delegation of powers to such committees is, however, a solution in systems with concentrated powers because in that case it strengthens the credible commitment of policy makers vis-à-vis their employees.

The discussion of two fundamental types of political systems is, without a doubt, the strength of Lapuente's article. It demonstrates that institutions and institutional regimes shape the incentives of actors and that it leads to different solutions in the principal–agent design.

The next steps in delegation: independent agencies, interest organizations, and the European Union

In Chapter 6, Fabrizio Gilardi considers the more recently developed strand in delegation theory on independent regulatory agencies. Although such agencies are not new, there has been a significant increase in numbers since the end of the 1980s. Gilardi attempts to answer two questions with respect to these institutions: why have they proliferated and why do we find such an astonishing variation in the set-up of these agencies, i.e. in terms of their discretion?

Using a quantitative, cross-national comparison, he finds that liberalization and privatization embraced by governments since the 1980s have engendered an increasing need for credible commitment of policy makers, particularly when there are few veto players or, in the words of Lapuente, when a system has concentrated powers. In such a concentration of powers system, delegation is a way to maintain policies in the long run, which also helps counter the political uncertainty problem derived from changes in government. However, this is not sufficient to understand the widespread diffusion of delegation. In addition, Gilardi mentions the European Union as an actor that actively promotes this standard as well as effects of 'taken-for-grantedness', which have been described by sociological institutionalism.

Variation in discretion depends on – and this adds a new perspective to the discussion so far – the sector of regulation. Some sectors have more need for credible commitment than others. Together with high 'replacement risks' of government and a low number of veto players, this explains the higher occurrence of such agencies in such sectors.

Although there has been an increase in IRAs, Gilardi asserts, there is no evidence to suggest they will stay. Changes in the need for credible commitment or the attractiveness of new institutional devices can impact on the eagerness of policy makers to use independent regulatory agencies. The legitimacy problem Sosay mentions in this book might be another factor that leads to a downturn. The trend towards the 'regulatory state' (Majone) may pass away.

In Chapter 7, Dietmar Braun demonstrates that independent agencies are also a well known phenomenon in other policy areas than the regulatory one. He discusses, with reference to Lowi's famous typology, the distributive policy arena and therein research policies to ascertain the extent to which we find commonalities and differences in the set-up and working of independent agencies in the regulatory policy arena.

Braun points to the necessity to include target groups in the equation of delegation and to consider delegation as a triad between political principals, target groups and independent agencies. He stipulates, however, that this emphasis on target groups may be a peculiar feature of distributive policies, where target groups have a particularly strong role in policy making. He attempts to conceptualize the triad by first dealing with the relationship between policy makers and target groups as the basic relationship in which delegation to independent agencies is embedded. It appears that this relationship has a number of elements similar to the logic of delegation because of the 'risk investments' involved but can best be characterized by trust relationships. The main reason to delegate is the uncertainty of policy makers about the trustworthiness of scientists.

Embedding delegation into a larger framework of trustor–trustee relationship in research policy – and this is a new perspective – has consequences for the position of independent agencies. They become dependent on both policy makers and scientists in choosing their ideal preference points. The position, though, is somewhat different for the various types of funding agencies. This is a useful addition by Braun to the ongoing discussion on delegation and is similar to the point made by Gilardi, who emphasized the importance of sector characteristics of policy fields for the decision on discretion. In contrast, Braun asserts that characteristics of the whole policy field play an important role in reaching such a decision. In research policies, however, we find variations in discretion *within one policy field* because of different degrees of uncertainties that are linked to the funding of basic, strategic and applied research.

Further research might be needed to identify whether and how the structure of the policy field influences delegation systematically, which in the words of Lowi is another way of saying that 'policies influence politics'.

In Chapter 8, Gül Sosay discusses the 'other side' of independent regulatory agencies. She does not deal with 'positive' questions such as why delegate, what are probable agency losses or how much discretion should be given to such agencies, but instead asks how these agencies are embedded in the democratic system in terms of legitimacy. Usually, the 'efficiency-enhancing capacity' of such agencies is used as an argument to legitimate their existence. For Sosay this doesn't appear to be sufficient explanation, as efficiency is an economic rationale, not a democratic one. Thus the question becomes: can independent agencies be defended on the grounds of efficiency?

This is a particular problem for independent agencies because, while bureaucratic agencies have similar features, they are indirectly linked to democratic accountability through the policy makers, as principals, who are themselves responsible to the public. This is not the case with independent agencies that are set apart and are deliberately exempt from participating in the 'chain of delegation'. She discusses two possible scenarios to legitimate independent agencies.

In the first scenario independent agencies can be defended on the grounds of substantive legitimacy (output legitimacy). According to her, this leads to a bureaucratic/technocratic type of rule as developed by Weber, Schumpeter and von Hayek. All these authors developed arguments that can defend institutions that are exempted from 'procedural legitimacy', i.e. democratic participation. Independent agencies are adequate institutions that are necessary in the process of rationalization. Sosay argues, though, that this output legitimacy causes problems, for two reasons. This kind of legitimacy depends on the argument that independent agencies pursue collective welfare for all and that they are not involved in redistributive matters, which are typically subject to democratic participation. For her this argument does not suffice, because collective welfare cannot be defined in an unequivocal way and is always subject to political struggle. And efficiency policies also have redistributive impacts, which, according to Majone, can be neglected only if there are no losers in the redistribution game. However, this is not often the case. According to Sosay, then, defending independent agencies on the grounds of output legitimacy is dangerous and does not provide an answer to the debate on the legitimacy of such agencies.

In the second scenario, independent agencies are anchored in procedural legitimacy, i.e. the direct participation of the people in the working of the agencies. Sosay suggests that such participation is not excluded, but it depends on the definition of procedural legitimacy. Obligatory requirements to keep in close contact with the public can be easily integrated into the procedural requirements of independent agencies, but she doubts that this can be realized in a practical way. In principle, this would only open the doors to agency capture. The majority of the public will not bear the transaction and information costs of participating. Therefore, independent agencies will by default continue to function without the public.

Given these considerations her conclusions are pessimistic. Whichever way one turns, it will be difficult to raise enough legitimacy for the existence of independent regulatory agencies. To continue in the same way as before is to embark on technocratic rule with the elitist outlook that we recognize from the work of Schumpeter. To open up these institutions will not be possible without transforming them so completely that in the end they can no longer function efficiently. It seems that a conflict exists between efficiency and democracy in the management of modern societies that is not easily solved.

In Chapter 9, Peter Munk Christiansen and Asbjørn Sonne Nørgaard present a fresh look at relations between government and interest organizations, a relationship often described in terms of corporatism or, as the authors say, in terms of a political exchange perspective. The reasoning of the authors is based on principal–agent theory; interest organizations are agents in the sense that they are able to provide information to meet either the government or opposition party needs.

The delegation perspective helps to show that policy-proposing commissions are not just a forum for exchange but can be used by government as a strategic device to maintain power in the context of minority governments. Participation in such commissions can convert otherwise obstructive organizations linked to the opposition into agents that deliver information to the government and are bound by the agreements in the commission. In this way, the authors are able to demonstrate that even in minority government systems there seems to be more power for governments than in the US system. Minority governments can actively shape the legislative process to their advantage.

To treat policy-proposing commissions and participating interest organizations in terms of delegation adds an additional dimension to the 'democratic chain of delegation', which the literature has not dealt with to date. It is worth continuing to think in this direction and scrutinize other parliamentary or presidential regimes under this perspective.

In Chapter 10, Fabio Franchino looks at a special case, the European Union, which is often considered as an *objet non-identifié* because of its combination of territorial and functional power distribution elements and its 'hybrid' status between confederation and federation. The main problems in this case are the transfer of power (from member states to the supranational or federal institutions) and discretion (how much discretion should be given to national administrations when they implement the EU legislation).

The application of delegation theory to the European Union is not new. Franchino summarizes a number of previous studies that have already dealt with the challenge of transferring authority to supranational institutions. Two alternative explanations are offered in the literature for why member states delegate and to what extent. One explanation stresses political credibility and the other makes a link between decision procedures in the European Council and the transfer of power. The Council delegates greater policy authority to the Commission when acts are adopted by qualified majority voting or when they require greater managerial skill at the supranational level and it delegates more discretion to national institutions if the European legislation is adopted on the basis of unanimity. Franchino tests which proposition has greater explanatory power or, more precisely, whether the 'decision rule hypothesis may add significant additional information to the commitment argument or if it can be subsumed by the latter'. He finds that the decision rule model better explains the degree of discretion granted to national administrations than the commitment argument. With regard to the discretion granted to the European Commission discretion, both models have their independent explanatory powers.

The second part of Franchino's article treats the degree of discretion the European Parliament is willing to confer to national administrations. His main argument here is that discretion depends on the availability of control strategies, i.e. 'statutory control' (reliance on statutes to ensure correct execution) and 'ongoing non-statutory oversight' (these are other instruments to ensure bureaucratic compliance, e.g. a legislative veto). The availability of such non-statutory means can make statutory control superfluous. Hence, more discretion can be given if there are additional means for control. Then Franchino suggests that MPs in the European Parliament have a structural disadvantage in comparison with the European Council, as they cannot exert ongoing control, as they only have standard tools, such as hearings. This forces the Parliament to rely on statutory control while the national governments in the Council with their *ex post* oversight possibilities can rely on non-statutory control. One can therefore expect that the Council will be inclined – independent of conflicts between the Council and the Parliament – to develop less detailed legislation, while the Parliament will try, within the codecision procedure, to correct this and introduce more detailed legislation. Based on empirical results, Franchino confirms this expectation.

The 'delegation look' puts conflicts between the European Parliament and the Council in perspective. Instead of seeing fundamental conflicts in opinions between both institutions, the delegation perspective demonstrates that often the tension is based on a difference in the institutionalized access to control mechanisms.

In the concluding chapter, we show that even though no consistent theory of political delegation emerges from this collective effort, a number of important transversal themes are developed. The first is linked to the incentives to delegate. While principal–agent theory gives a prominent place to the need for information and expertise, most chapters emphasize that the political context and strategies of power. The willingness to embark on long-term commitments and to stabilize trust relationships with target groups also plays an important role for delegation. Another major theme is the importance of the institutional context, which most contributors show to be a crucial factor in shaping delegation arrangements. In contrast to what basic principal–agent models suggest, this book demonstrates that delegation patterns are influenced by the characteristics of the institutional framework within which principals and agents interact. A further aspect that emerges throughout this volume is that delegation relationships need not be binary. In many cases, delegation involves several actors, and should thus be understood as compound relationships.

In conclusion, the main contribution of this book is to give a view of delegation that is broader than the perspectives of most existing studies, which are either focused on single delegation steps or on the standard chain of delegation. By re-examining the latter and investigating delegation arrangements that go beyond it, this volume avoids many of the biases that may derive from the selection of specific delegation arrangements and/or countries, and thus paves the way for a richer and more comprehensive study of political delegation.

References

Andeweg, R. B. (2000) 'Ministers as Double Agents? The Delegation Process between Cabinet and Ministers', *European Journal of Political Research*, 37 (3): 377–395.

Bendor, J., Glazer, A. and Hammond, T. (2001) 'Theories of Delegation', *Annual Review of Political Science*, 4: 235–369.

Berger, H., Haan, J. de and Eijffinger, S. C. W. (2001) 'Central Bank Independence. An Update of Theory and Evidence', *Journal of Economic Surveys*, 15 (1): 3–40.

Bourdieu, P. (1981) 'La représentation politique. Eléments pour une théorie du champ politique', *Actes de la recherche en sciences sociales*, 36–37: 3–24.

Bourdieu, P. (1984) 'La délégation et le fétichisme politique', *Actes de la recherche en sciences sociales*, 52–53: 49–55.

Burke, E. (1863) 'Mr. Burke's speech to the electors at Bristol', in F. and C. Revington, *The Works of the Right Honourable Edmund Burke* III, London.

Christensen, J. G. and Pallesen, T. (2001) 'Institutions, Distributional Concerns, and Public Sector Reform', *European Journal of Political Research*, 39: 179–202.

Coleman, J. S. (1990) *Foundations of Social Theory*, Cambridge MA: The Belknap Press of Harvard University Press.

Dahl, R. and Tufte, E. R. (1973) *Size and Democracy*, Stanford CA: Stanford University Press.

Downs, A. (1967) *Inside Bureaucracy*, Boston MA: Little Brown.

Elgie, R. (2002) 'The Politics of the European Central Bank. Principal–Agent Theory and the Democratic Deficit', *Journal of European Public Policy*, 9 (2): 186–200.

Epstein, D. and O'Halloran, S. (1999) *Delegating Powers. A Transaction Cost Politics Approach to Policy Making under Separate Powers*, Cambridge: Cambridge University Press.

Franchino, F. (2000a) 'The Commission's Executive Discretion, Information and Comitology', *Journal of Theoretical Politics*, 12 (2): 155–181.

Franchino, F. (2000b) 'Control of the Commission's Executive Functions. Uncertainty, Conflict and Decision Rules', *European Union Politics*, 1 (1): 63–92.

Franzese, R. J. (1999) 'Partially Independent Central Banks, Politically Responsive Governments, and Inflation', *American Journal of Political Science*, 43 (3): 681–706.

Gilardi, F. and Braun, D. (2002) 'Delegation aus der Sicht der Prinzipal–Agent Theorie. Ein Literaturbericht', *Politische Vierteljahresschrift*, 43 (1): 147–161.

Glover, J. (1994) 'A Simpler Mechanism that stops Agents from Cheating', *Journal of Economic Theory*, 62: 221–229.

Horn, M. J. (1995) *The Political Economy of Public Administration. Institutional Choice in the Public Sector*, Cambridge: Cambridge University Press.

Horn, M. J. and Shepsle, K. (1989) 'Commentary on "Administrative Arrangements and the Political Control of Agencies": Administrative Process and Organizational Form as Legislative Responses to Agency Costs', *Virginia Law Review*, 75: 499–508.

Huber, J. D. and Shipan, C. R (2000) 'The Costs of Control. Legislators, Agencies, and Transaction Costs', *Legislative Studies Quarterly*, 25 (1): 25–52.

Huber, J. D. and Shipan, C. R. (2002) *Deliberate Discretion? The Institutional Foundations of Bureaucratic Autonomy*, Cambridge: Cambridge University Press.

Katzenstein, P. J. (1984) *Corporatism and Change*, Ithaca NY: Cornell University Press.

Katzenstein, P. J. (1985) *Small States in World Markets. Industrial Policy in Europe*, Ithaca NY and London: Cornell University Press.

Kiewiet, D. R. and McCubbins, M. (1989) 'Parties, Committees, and Policymaking in the US Congress. A Comment on the Role of Transaction Costs as Determinants of the Governance Structure of Political Institutions', *Journal of Theoretical and Institutional Economics*, 145: 676–685.

Majone, G. (1997) 'From the Positive to the Regulatory State. Causes and Consequences of Changes in the Mode of Governance', *Journal of Public Policy*, 17 (2): 139–167.

Majone, G. (1998) 'Europe's "Democratic Deficit". The Question of Standards', *European Law Journal*, 4 (1): 5–28.

Majone, G. (1999) 'The Regulatory State and its Legitimacy Problems', *West European Politics*, 22 (1): 1–24.

Majone, G. (2001a) 'Nonmajoritarian Institutions and the Limits of Democratic Governance. A Political Transaction-Cost Approach', *Journal of Theoretical and Institutional Economics*, 157: 57–78.

Majone, G. (2001b) 'Two Logics of Delegation. Agency and Fiduciary Relations in EU Governance', *European Union Politics*, 2 (1): 103–121.

Majone, G. (2002) 'The European Commission. The Limits of Centralization and the Perils of Parliamentarization', *Governance*, 15 (3): 375–392.

McCubbins, M. D., Noll, R. G. and Weingast, B. R. (1987) 'Administrative Procedures as Instruments of Political Control', *Journal of Law, Economics, and Organisation*, 3 (2): 243–277.

McCubbins, M. D., Noll, R. G. and Weingast, B. R. (1989) 'Structure and Process, Politics and Policy. Administrative Arrangements and the Political Control of Agencies', *Virginia Law Review*, 75: 431–482.

Michels, R. (1911) *Zur Soziologie des Parteiwesens in der modernen Demokratie. Untersuchungen über die oligarchischen Tendenzen des Gruppenlebens*, Leipzig: Klinkhardt.

Milgrom, P. and Roberts, J. (1992) *Economics, Organization and Management*, Englewood Cliffs NJ: Prentice-Hall.

Mirrlees, J. A. (1976) 'The Optimal Structure of Incentives and Authority within an Organization', *Bell Journal of Economics*, 7 (1): 105–131.

Mitchell, P. (2000) 'Voters and their Representatives. Electoral Institutions and Delegation in Parliamentary Democracies', *European Journal of Political Research*, 37 (3): 335–351.

Moe, T. M. (1984) 'The New Economics of Organization', *American Journal of Political Science*, 28: 739–777.

Moe, T. M. (1987) 'An Assessment of the Positive Theory of "Congressional Dominance"', *Legislative Studies Quarterly*, 12 (4): 475–520.

Moe, T. M. (1990) 'Political Institutions. The Neglected Side of the Story', *Journal of Law, Economics, and Organisation*, 6, Special Issue: 213–53.

Müller, W. C. (2000) 'Political Parties in Parliamentary Democracies. Making Delegation and Accountability Work', *European Journal of Political Research*, 37 (3): 309–333.

Niskanen, W. A. (1971) *Bureaucracy and Representative Government*, Chicago: Aldine.

OECD (2002) *Regulatory Policies in OECD Countries. From Interventionism to Regulatory Governance*, Paris: Organisation for Economic Co-operation and Development.

Pitkin, H. F. (1961) *The Theory of Representation*, Berkeley CA: University of California Press.

Putnam, R. (1976) *The Comparative Study of Political Elites*, Englewood Cliffs NJ: Prentice Hall.

Saalfeld, T. (2000) 'Members of Parliament and Government in Western Europe. Agency Relations and Problems of Oversight', *European Journal of Political Research*, 37 (3): 353–376.

Scharpf, F. W. (1997) *Games Real Actors Play. Actor-centred Institutionalism in Policy Research*, Boulder CO: Westview Press.

Scharpf, F. W. (1999) *Governing in Europe. Effective and Democratic?* Oxford: Oxford University Press.

Schmitter, P. C. (1979) 'Still the Century of Corporatism?', in P. C. Schmitter and L. Gerhard (eds) *Trends toward Corporatist Intermediation*, Beverly Hills CA and London: Sage.

Scott, C. (2000) 'Accountability and the Regulatory State', *Journal of Law and Society*, 27 (1): 38–60.

Stiglitz, J. (1998) 'Central Banking in a Democratic Society', *Economist*, 146 (2): 199–226.

Stone Sweet, A. (2002) 'Constitutional Courts and Parliamentary Democracy', *West European Politics*, 25 (1): 77–100.

Strøm, K. (2000) 'Delegation and Accountability in Parliamentary Democracies', *European Journal of Political Research*, 37: 261–289.

Strøm, K. (2003) 'Parliamentary Democracy and Delegation', in K. Strøm, W. Müller and T. Bergman (eds) *Delegation and Accountability in Parliamentary Democracies*, Oxford: Oxford University Press.

Strøm, K., Müller, W. C. and Bergman, T. (eds) (2003) *Delegation and Accountability in Parliamentary Democracies*, Oxford: Oxford University Press.

Tallberg, J. (2002) 'Delegation to Supranational Institutions. Why, How, and with What Consequences?', *West European Politics*, 25 (1): 23–46.

Thatcher, M. (1994) 'Regulatory Reform in Britain and France. Organizational Structure and the Extension of Competition', *Journal of European Public Policy*, 1 (3): 441–464.

Thatcher, M. (1998) 'Institutions, Regulation, and Change. New Regulatory Agencies in the British Privatised Utilities', *West European Politics*, 21 (1): 120–147.

Thatcher, M. (2002a) 'Delegation to Independent Regulatory Agencies: Pressures, functions and Contextual Mediation', *West European Politics*, 25 (1): 125–147.

Thatcher, M. (2002b) 'Regulation After Delegation. Independent Regulatory Agencies in Europe', *Journal of European Public Policy*, 9 (6): 954–972.

Thatcher, M. and Stone Sweet, A. (2002) 'Theory and Practice of Delegation to Non-majoritarian Institutions', *West European Politics*, 25 (1): 1–22.

Weingast, B. R. (1984) 'The Congressional-Bureaucratic System. A Principal–Agent Perspective (With Applications to the SEC)', *Public Choice*, 44: 147–191.

Weingast, B. R. and Marshall, W. J. (1988) 'The Industrial Organization of Congress; or, Why Legislatures, Like Firms, Are Not Organized in Markets', *Journal of Political Economy*, 96 (1): 132–163.

Wilks, S. and Bartle, I. (2002) 'The Unanticipated Consequences of Creating Independent Competition Agencies', *West European Politics*, 25 (1): 148–172.

Part I

The standard chain of delegation

2 The (moral) hazards of parliamentary democracy

*Kaare Strøm, Wolfgang C. Müller and
Torbjörn Bergman*

Introduction[1]

While the twentieth century witnessed some of the greatest political atrocities in human history, it was also the century in which democracy was gradually established and consolidated in large parts of the world. At the end of the millennium, there were more stable democracies than ever, and there was no continent to which democracy was entirely foreign (Lijphart, 1999; Przeworski *et al.*, 2000). Democracy may take many forms, but contemporary exemplars are predominantly *representative*. Parliamentary government, which we define below, is the most common way to organize such democratic representation. Of the thirty-six stable democratic states covered by Lijphart (1999), today only five – the United States, Switzerland, Colombia, Costa Rica, and Venezuela – are not parliamentary.[1] In fact, about a third of the world's population live under this regime form, a larger proportion than under any other system of government. Although the states that feature parliamentary constitutions span all continents, Europe remains the heartland of parliamentarism. In Western Europe (leaving aside microstates such as the Vatican), only Switzerland is not parliamentary. And, by and large, the great majority of European citizens accept their parliamentary constitutions as legitimate vehicles for popular representation.

Unlike US federalism or presidentialism, parliamentary government was not the product of deliberate institutional design. Rather, it evolved gradually in several locations and over several centuries. Britain was the birthplace of parliamentary government, and the roots of parliamentary government can be traced back as far as 1688 (Norton, 1981: 12) or 1693 (Lowell, 1896: 3), when the King first appointed a government out of the majority party (the Whigs) in the House of Commons. Although as early as the eighteenth century there were precursors of parliamentary and party government elsewhere,[2] it is first and foremost through the British influence that this form of government has spread throughout the world. And although it no longer (if it ever did) reflects the realities of British politics, the Westminster model of parliamentary democracy (which we shall discuss and define below) is analytically crucial.

The European 'tidal wave' of parliamentarism did not occur until the late nineteenth and early twentieth centuries. The 1920s and 1930s, on the other hand, witnessed the demise of many democracies, and disproportionately parliamentary ones (Shugart and Carey, 1992: 39–41). After another growth season for parliamentarism in the early years after World War II, the 1970s brought a wave of concern about government overload and adversary politics in such political systems. Confidence in political institutions began to slip (Crozier *et al.,* 1975; Rose, 1980), and levels of electoral volatility began to rise and have continued to do so. Although contemporary parliamentary democracies are evidently robust, they are not without their perils.

This chapter discusses both the appeal and the hazards of parliamentary democracy. We ask two main questions. What are the key governance problems facing different regimes of democratic representation, and particularly parliamentary democracies? And how effectively do these institutions respond to such challenges? Our answers can be succinctly stated. First, any form of democratic representation faces the perennial problems of adverse selection and moral hazard. Second, parliamentary democracy in its typical form is comparatively well equipped to deal with adverse selection, but less capable of dealing with moral hazard. These strengths and weaknesses are in turn tied in with the accountability mechanisms that typify parliamentary democracy, and specifically with the key role of political parties. To understand the merits and demerits of parliamentary democracy, we therefore have to grasp the functions of political parties in such regimes.

In order to make and explain this argument, we employ agency theory, or the principal–agent approach (see, e.g. Moe, 1984; Pratt and Zeckhauser, 1985; Furubotn and Richter, 1997). We thus consider representative democracy to consist of a web of delegation relationships. In such relationships, a principal (in whom authority is originally vested) conditionally authorizes an agent to act in his or her name and place.[3] The same person or organization may be a principal in one relationship and an agent in another. Popular sovereignty, however, implies that voters are the ultimate principal.

The principal–agent approach builds on a number of ontological and epistemological assumptions. We thus assume that the political community is given and bounded, that the preferences of principals as well as agents are exogenously given (i.e. not explained within our models), that all principals and agents act rationally on the information available to them, that principals face important information scarcities, and that politics is hierarchical, in such a way that the principal's preferences are analytically and normatively privileged (for a further discussion, see Strøm *et al.*, 2003, especially pp. 59–61).

Such assumptions are, of course, a stylization. Like all analytical devices, delegation models simplify and distort reality. Yet there are three reasons, we believe, why that may be a price worth paying. One is that principal–agent models give us a general framework by which a variety of apparently unrelated representation issues can be understood. Indeed, we see parliamentary democracy as a bundle of political agency relationships between ordinary citizens and the various politicians that serve them. Hence, the same analytical framework can be used to answer questions that have hitherto often been studied in mutual isolation, by different scholarly communities, and in needlessly diverse sets of terms. A second virtue of this framework is its simplicity and parsimony, which permits us to spend less time on definitional debates and more on empirical application. Finally, the principal–agent approach lends itself to rigorous and precise theoretical reasoning.

The rest of this chapter is organized as follows. In the next section we look at the essential institutional characteristics of parliamentary government and parliamentary democracy. We next discuss democratic delegation and two critical problems to which this can give rise, namely adverse selection and moral hazard. In the section that follows, we discuss different institutional solutions (accountability mechanisms) to these problems in representative democracies. Turning specifically to parliamentary democracies, we explain why they tend to foster strong and cohesive political parties, which can be critical actors in the democratic chain of delegation and accountability (see also Cox, 1987). We show that while parliamentary constitutions provide suitable controls against adverse selections, they are often poorly equipped to deal with moral hazard. Finally, we discuss the implications of this institutional bias and the inevitable trade-offs involved in democratic institutional design.

Parliamentary government and parliamentary democracy

Before we engage in a more substantive discussion of these themes, however, we need to clarify our use of the key terms *parliamentarism*, *parliamentary government*, and *parliamentary democracy*. Let us first consider the term *parliamentary government*, which conventionally focuses on the institutional relationship between parliament and the core executive (the cabinet).

There have been many attempts to identify parliamentary government, some providing comprehensive descriptions and others minimal definitions. We favour the latter. What characterizes parliamentary government, in our conception, is simply that the cabinet must be tolerated by the parliamentary majority (see Strøm *et al.*, 2003; also Strong, 1963; Steffani 1979). Most authoritative definitions of parliamentarism contain this component, but then often add the stipulation that the cabinet also is appointed by (or 'emerges' from) the legislature (Epstein, 1968; Lijphart, 1999: 117–118; Sartori, 1997: 101), or that the executive has the authority to dissolve parliament (Mainwaring and Shugart, 1997: 14–15; Stepan and

Skach, 1993: 3). In contrast, we do not assume that in parliamentary systems the parliament plays any decisive role in cabinet selection, or that the prime minister can dissolve parliament before the end of its regular term. Neither investiture requirements nor provisions for early dissolution are universal features of politics conventionally categorized as parliamentary, and neither institution is in our opinion critical to the dynamics of this regime type.[4] Thus, in our minimal definition, *parliamentary government (or simply, parliamentarism) is a system of government in which the prime minister and his or her cabinet are accountable to any majority of the members of parliament and can be voted out of office by the latter, through an ordinary or constructive vote of no confidence.*[5]

Although this definition of parliamentary government achieves some conceptual simplification, it does not give us a very rich understanding of the dynamics or merits of parliamentary systems. For example, in this minimal sense parliamentary government is conceivable without full universal suffrage and indeed without full democracy as this is currently understood. Therefore, we need to introduce a more configurative conception of parliamentary democracy.

Representative democracy

The core value of democracy is popular sovereignty, the principle that ultimate authority rests with ordinary citizens. Ordinary citizens in democratic societies rarely exercise this authority directly, however. Just as they may delegate important tasks in their private lives to specialists (e.g. their medical treatment to physicians and the education of their children to teachers), they rely on politicians to help them with most community decision-making tasks. Thus, citizens delegate sovereignty to various representatives, such as individual politicians and organizations, in particular political parties.

As has been frequently noted, political representation has a number of political meanings. Pitkin (1967) differentiates between a 'formalistic' view of representation as authorization and a second conception of representation as accountability. In the former sense, a representative is one who has been given authority to act, whereas in the latter sense a representative is one who has to account for his or her actions. We build on both these conceptions.[6] To us, then, representation means that popular sovereignty is exercised through a process of *delegation* from citizens to politicians and civil servants. Citizens delegate political authority for reasons of capacity or competence, or to get round problems of preference aggregation, coordination, or collective action (see Strøm *et al.*, 2003).

In democratic societies, citizens delegate to politicians first and foremost through free and fair elections.[7] Yet democratic elections are only a first step. The need for further delegation has long been recognized by many (though not all) democratic theorists. In a classic formulation, John Stuart Mill stressed the need for parliamentary delegation to the cabinet. Since 'no body of men ... is fit for action', parliaments 'ought not to administer' (1984: 249), 'or to dictate in detail to those who have the charge of administration' (1984: 250). Hence, parliament should not make administrative decisions, select ministers (or civil servants), or even legislate in a substantive sense.

> Instead of the function of governing, for which it is radically unfit, the proper office of a representative assembly is to watch and control the government: to throw the light of publicity on its acts: to compel a full exposition and justification of all of them which any one considers questionable; to censure them if found condemnable, and, if the men who compose the government abuse their trust, or fulfil it in a sense which conflicts with the deliberate sense of the nation, to expel them from office, and either expressly or virtually appoint their successors.
>
> (1984: 258)

Mill thus favoured a system in which parliament delegates extensively and limits itself to the tasks of controlling the executive and serving as an arena for public debate.

Contemporary parliamentary democracies tend to be structured according to Mill's vision. Thus, the directly elected representatives of the people delegate extensively to members of the executive branch. Yet, although political delegation may be ubiquitous, it is no panacea. Democratic delegation may be neither sufficient nor necessary to solve such challenges as coordination and collective action problems. Collective agents may face the same problems of preference aggregation, collective action, and coordination as their principals. Delegation can also be jeopardized by constraints on the agent. This is when, for reasons beyond his own abilities or preferences, the agent cannot satisfy the principal's demands. Even if we ignore constraints that arise from the mortality of human beings, the scarcities of life on earth, or the laws of physics, agents may be politically constrained by rules that prohibit certain forms of agency or that force agents into behaviour that neither they nor their principals would have freely chosen.

For example, although parliamentarians or cabinet members may indeed consider themselves to be agents of their voters, they also have other constitutionally prescribed roles to play. Many constitutions, for example the German (Article 38) and Italian (Article 67) ones, explicitly designate parliamentarians as representatives of all citizens, not simply those that elected them. And politicians do tend to embrace this conception of their agency (Wessels, 1999).[8] Such broad constitutional accountability can at least give elected officials a normative justification for ignoring their voters' preferences. Moreover, democratic constitutions may disallow the representation of certain popular preferences (e.g. for racial discrimination, cruel punishment, or confiscatory government takings) or insist on certain principles, such as the sovereignty or indivisibility of the nation, that were particularly dear to their framers. In such cases, government officials represent not only their voters and other superiors, but also the constitutional founders or some set of rights and liberties to which the constitution is committed. Thus, office-holders in democracies are constrained and frequently common agents, with manifold responsibilities and accountabilities.

The chain of delegation

There are many ways in which the citizens can delegate to politicians, and politicians among one another. Yet, we can use the delegation language to spell out an ideal-typical definition of parliamentary democracy – a configurative model from which we can most easily understand how this form of government differs from alternative constitutions, and particularly presidentialism. In its ideal-typical form, then, parliamentary democracy is a chain of delegation, from the voters to the ultimate policy makers, in which we can identify at least four discrete steps:

1   from voters to their elected representatives;
2   from legislators to the core executive, specifically to the head of government (the prime minister);
3   from the prime minister to the heads of different executive departments;
4   from the heads of different executive departments to their respective civil servants.

Though different political regimes mean different vehicles of delegation, all representative democracies feature some such chain. In a parliamentary system, however, this chain of delegation has the following characteristics:

1   It is indirect, in that voters (the ultimate principals) directly elect only their parliamentary representatives. All other agents are only indirectly elected by and accountable to the citizens.
2   Parliamentary democracy means a particularly simple form of delegation.[9] In each link of the parliamentary chain, a single principal delegates to a single agent (such as the respective members of a parliament).[10] Voters in a presidential system, in contrast, typically elect multiple competing agents (such as, for example, a president and the members of two separate legislative chambers).
3   In a similar fashion, under parliamentary democracy agents are accountable to a single principal (although not necessarily an indi-

vidual person or a principal unique to that agent). Cabinet ministers, for example, report to a single master (the prime minister). Likewise, civil servants have a single principal, their respective cabinet minister. In a presidential system, on the other hand, agents may have multiple principals. Civil servants, for example, may report to the president as well as to both legislative chambers. Parliamentary democracy, then, means simplicity in accountability as well as in delegation.

The ideal-typical parliamentary democracy thus features an indirect chain of command, in which at each stage a single principal delegates to a single agent (or a set of several non-competing ones), and where each agent is accountable to one and only one principal. In brief, the indirectness and singularity of parliamentarism spell hierarchy and set this regime type apart from other constitutional designs, such as presidentialism. Figure 2.1 provides an illustration of the two ideal-typical regime types. Although we should not expect to find such clear-cut differentiation in the real world, this simple and powerful model helps us recognize that, as delegation devices, parliamentary regimes have properties that systematically set them apart from presidential ones.

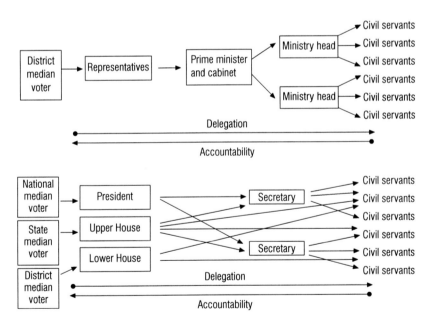

Figure 2.1 Delegation and accountability under parliamentary and presidential government (a) single-chain delegation model of a parliamentary system (source: Strøm *et al.* (2003: 65)).

Problems of democratic delegation

Delegation is inherently risky. You cannot always trust politicians, or, for that matter, anyone else to whom you delegate. Hence, the danger of any delegation is that it may turn into abdication, that the person who delegates may lose control rather than get help. Delegation in politics is no exception.

Such problems of delegation have not gone unnoticed among social scientists. Robert Michels, for example, was both aware of the need to delegate to party leaders and highly critical of its effects: 'democracy is inconceivable without organization', he wrote, yet organization 'gives birth to the domination of the elected over the electors, of the mandataries over the mandators, of the delegates over the delegators. Who says organization says oligarchy' (Michels, 1962: 61, 365). And there are numerous references to 'downstream' delegation problems between ministers and civil servants, from Max Weber (1972: 572–574), whose characterization of ministers as 'dilettantes' and civil servants as 'experts' clearly pointed to agency problems, all the way to the popular television comedy series *Yes, Minister* (Lynn and Jay, 1981).

Politicians may misbehave in one of two ways: through policy drift (or policy shirking, in the words of Brehm and Gates, 1997) or rent-seeking activities. In the former case, 'Politicians may want to pursue their own ideas even if these differ from those of citizens' (Manin *et al.*, 1999: 40). In the latter case, they may use political power to chase personal advantage. The argument that politicians pursue their own gain comes in many well-known forms. It is widely recognized that 'governments transfer wealth not just among subgroups of citizens but also directly to themselves' (McChesney, 1997: 35). And the 'grabbing hand' perspective in economics argues that politicians act not to maximize social welfare but instead to further their own selfish objectives (Shleifer and Vishny, 1998: 4). According to influential theories of bureaucracy, non-elected public officials are also likely to behave in ways that defy the voters' preferences (Downs, 1967; Niskanen, 1971).

Problems of democratic delegation thus give rise to some of the most scathing criticisms of modern democracies. Let us now frame these problems in the language of agency theory. The difference between what the principal wants and what the agent delivers is known as agency loss. Agency loss should not be a problem when the principal and agent have identical preferences, or when the principal is fully informed about the agent and his actions. It may occur, however, when the agent and the principal have different preferences and the principal suffers from incomplete information. Incomplete information may take the form of hidden information (principals do not fully know the competences or preferences of their agents or the exact demands of the task at hand) and/or hidden action (principals cannot fully observe the actions of their agents). The former condition can give rise to adverse selection, the latter to moral hazard. The former problem may lead principals to select the 'wrong' agents, who do not have the most appropriate skills or preferences. The problem of moral hazard, on the other hand, arises when agents, once selected, have opportunity and incentives to take unobservable action contrary to the principal's interests.

Adverse selection

Selecting agents that have the optimal combination of information, skills, and personal preferences is one generic challenge for democratic principals. Separating qualified candidates from unqualified ones is no great problem if political qualifications and predispositions are easily discernible and the tasks of the agent well defined. But the problem of many delegation relationships is precisely that the principal does not know very much either about the task at hand or about the pool of potential agents. Simply put, agents must be willing as well as able, and in order to attract such agents, principals must offer adequate incentives.

The trouble is that the incentive schemes that principals design sometimes systematically attract the least desirable agents. This is the core of the adverse selection problem, classically observed in markets such as those for insurance and used cars. Politically, the problem of adverse selection has been recognized at least since Plato, who famously observed that 'the city where those who rule are least eager to do so will be the best governed'. It also figured prominently in the political debate immediately following World War I. Among the principal protagonists in this debate was Gaetano Mosca. Although, of course, he never used this label, Mosca was centrally concerned with the problem of adverse selection, specifically with the dominance of parliament by societal elites. In his view, elections were controlled by organized minorities, leaving the great majority of citizens a choice among a very limited range of candidates that were not necessarily the most desirable of their kind (1950: 135–136). Consequently, parliaments would represent the interests of wealthy and powerful elites rather than the popular majority. Mosca saw this selection problem as a cause of patronage politics.

Many contemporary students of political representation similarly see the selection of 'good' agents as the primary democratic challenge. Brehm and Gates (1997: 202) find that in federal, state, and local bureaucracies in the United States, 'the problem of adverse selection trumps the problem of moral hazard'. Glenn R. Parker (1996) paints a disturbing picture of how adverse selection has contributed to the moral and political decline of the US Congress. Over time, he argues, the intrinsic rewards from congressional service, such as the value of producing public goods, have declined relative to the opportunities for rent extraction. The consequence, he argues, has been a decline in the quality of representation.

James Fearon (1999) similarly maintains that the most important task for voters is to select 'good types' for office: 'a candidate with similar policy preferences, who is relatively honest and principled (hard to buy off), and who is skilled' (Fearon, 1999: 68). It is not difficult to agree with Fearon's desiderata. Democracy is certainly jeopardized if it is precisely the most power-hungry or greedy, those least likely to succeed elsewhere, or perhaps those most likely to abuse authority, that are drawn to politics. Most people would surely prefer to be ruled by the likes of Cincinnatus rather than Macbeth, and there is a serious problem when the latter are in greater supply.

Moral hazard

Moral hazard is an equally basic problem in delegation. Whereas adverse selection stems from the agent's private information, moral hazard has to do with hidden action on his part. That is to say, moral hazard arises when the principal cannot, after entering a contract, fully observe the agent's performance of his tasks. Such information asymmetry may jeopardize successful delegation as much as adverse selection does. Once politicians have been elected, and especially after they have been elevated to executive office, they face a myriad of temptations to abuse their power to advance their personal policy agenda (rather than the platform on which they were elected or their constituents' preferences), to secure personal gain, or to trade illegitimate favours. The more difficult or costly it is for the principal to observe whether the agent engages in such behaviour, the greater the problem of moral hazard.

The problem of moral hazard is prominent in modern models of democratic agency. One example is John Ferejohn's (1986) model of electoral competition (see also Barro, 1973). Dominant models of electoral competition, Ferejohn notes, have a 'disturbing feature', namely the possibility that 'once in office, the politician's preferences may diverge from those of his constituents and that he may therefore choose policies at variance from his platform' (Ferejohn, 1986: 5). He assumes the politician to be 'an agent of the electorate whose behaviour is imperfectly monitored ... In other words, the voter's problem is to police moral hazard rather than to find and select the more capable of benevolent officeholders' (Ferejohn, 1986: 11–12). Ferejohn thus conceives of the basic problem in democratic representation as moral hazard rather than adverse selection, and his concern is whether electoral accountability can constrain such behaviour.

Moral hazard occurs when the temptation to abuse power is not checked through transparency, in other words when the principal cannot easily observe or ascertain the actions of the agent once the contract has been concluded. The greater the preference divergence between principal and agent, and the more costly it is for the principal to inform herself, the greater the risk. The magnitude of moral hazard is thus likely to be systematically related to certain parameters of delegation. First, the larger the potential political rents, the more serious the problem of moral hazard. That is to say, the more attractive the spoils of office are relative to alternative social rewards, the more we should worry about moral hazard. Second, the greater discretion politicians are granted, and the more generous the spoils under their control, the more severely their character will be tested. Recall Lord Acton's pithy observation that 'power corrupts, and absolute power tends to corrupt absolutely'. Third, the weaker the oversight mechanisms, the larger the threat of moral hazard. Finally, the longer incumbents stay in office, the more serious the moral hazard problem may become, especially with respect to corruption and other abuses of office. The problem of moral hazard can become particularly severe when in the competition for power politicians that abuse their power systematically 'crowd out' those that do not.

Delegating power to politicians is thus risky because the individuals most attracted to politics may not be the most desirable rulers and because the political game may favour those that pursue their own interests rather than those of the voters. Whether in the form of adverse selection or moral hazard, agency problems stemming from incomplete information can thus prevent citizens in contemporary democracies from getting satisfactory service from their political agents. Worse, there may be circumstances in which 'bad' agents systematically tend to crowd out 'good' ones.

Accountability

Agency problems are thus an inevitable concomitant of representative democracy. To counteract these dangers, the democratic chain of delegation needs to be coupled with political accountability mechanisms by which, if their behaviour or performance in office is unsatisfactory, politicians can be checked and if necessary removed. In the words of Manin *et al.*, 'Governments are accountable if citizens can discern representative from unrepresentative governments and can sanction them appropriately ... An "accountability mechanism" is thus a map from the outcomes of actions (including messages that explain these actions) of public officials to sanctions by citizens' (Manin *et al.*, 1999: 10).

Accountability implies that principals have two kinds of rights vis-à-vis agents: a right to demand information, and a capacity to impose sanctions. Three salient forms of sanction are the ability to (1) block or amend decisions made by the agent (veto power), (2) deauthorize the agent (remove him from office or curtail his authority), and (3) impose specific (monetary or other) penalties. Principals may have one of these rights (e.g. some form of veto power, or the right to obtain information) without the others. Accountability schemes vary in the comprehensiveness of the principal's right to information and sanctions, as well as in their exclusiveness. Governance structures in which the principal's rights are comprehensive and exclusive, that is to say, where for each agent there is only one principal, and where that principal has extensive information rights and sanctions, conform to the classic model of a hierarchy. As we have seen, hierarchy is one of the ideal-typical features of parliamentary democracies.

Accountability mechanisms thus need to convey information and permit sanctions to be imposed. Yet this can occur in different ways and at different stages of the delegation process. Principals can accomplish their objectives through such means as (1) contract design, (2) screening and selection mechanisms, (3) monitoring and reporting requirements, and (4) institutional checks (Lupia, 2003; also Aghion and Tirole, 1997; Kiewiet and McCubbins, 1991). The former two are mechanisms by which principals seek to contain agency losses *ex ante*, that is, before entering any agreement, whereas (3) and (4) operate after the fact of delegation (*ex post facto*).

Contract design typically seeks to establish shared interests, or incentive compatibility, between principals and agents, so that their preferences are aligned. Screening and selection represent efforts to sort out good agents from bad ones before a contract is made. In the case of screening, the principal does the sorting, whereas selection refers to costly action (for example, the acquisition of recognized credentials) by which the agent demonstrates his suitability. In politics, parties help voters screen candidates for public office, and parliament screens potential cabinet members. Selection occurs, for example, when aspiring politicians seek minor office, or stand for hopeless seats, to prove their worthiness for more attractive offices. Also, particular educational institutions, such as the ENA (in France) or Christ Church College, Oxford (in Britain), may offer valuable political credentials.

Ex post accountability mechanisms may rely on information produced by the principal (known as monitoring or police patrols), by the agent (reporting), or by some third party (institutional checks or fire alarms). In politics, legislators may monitor executive agencies through committee hearings in which ministers or civil servants have to appear and testify (see Mattson and Strøm, 1995). Alternatively (or additionally), executive agencies may regularly have to report to parliament. Moreover, the parliamentarians may rely on fire alarms, i.e. third parties that have their own interest in drawing attention to potential misbehaviour by the agent. Finally, parliaments employ institutional checks when they subject executive agencies to legal scrutiny or external audits, or in some other way submit them to the veto powers of a third party. As the concept implies, such practices are particularly common in checks-and-balances systems, but by no means confined to such.

Many important control mechanisms serve as vehicles of *ex ante* as well as *ex post* control. They can be used both to select agents in the first place and to subject them to sanctions and possible 'deselection' after the fact.

The most basic mechanism of representative democracy, elections, is clearly of this kind. Voters use elections both prospectively (to select office-holders) and retrospectively (to sanction incumbents).

All accountability mechanisms have their own costs, and none is universally effective (Lupia, 2003). The choice between them, then, depends on the agency problems at hand as well as on the resources of the principal. Briefly stated, however, *ex ante* mechanisms such as screening tend to be more effective against problems of adverse selection, whereas *ex post* oversight is more likely to be helpful in combating moral hazard. We should therefore expect to see greater unresolved problems of adverse selection in polities that rely heavily on *ex post* controls, and more severe issues of moral hazard where *ex ante* accountability devices predominate.

Party government and the Westminster model

Different democracies experience different agency problems, depending in part on their political institutions and in part on their political culture. The accountability mechanisms used to solve those problems will, we expect, reflect the dominant agency problems, so that societies plagued by problems of adverse selection will select accountability devices that are particularly suited to such issues. But the choice of accountability mechanisms also depends in large part on regime type.

In the democratic world, accountability mechanisms tend to cluster in two predominant patterns. One is a set of institutions in which the most important mechanisms of accountability operate *ex post*, in the form of various constraints on democratic agents. In their book on congressional delegation in the United States, Epstein and O'Halloran (1999: 99–101) identify fourteen different types of constraint, in their case 'procedural mechanisms that Congress writes into legislation to constrain the bureaucracy' (Epstein and O'Halloran, 1999: 100). Among these are contract design features (e.g. time limits, spending limits), veto provisions, reporting requirements, direct oversight, hearings, and appeal procedures. As the list suggests, many are primarily vehicles of *ex post* oversight. This whole plethora of constraints is in use in the checks-and-balances system of the US federal government.

The second pattern relies primarily on *ex ante* screening in the form of a strong civil society and particularly political parties. These are political organizations that align the preferences of the occupants of the most important political offices (parliament, the cabinet, and the heads of the different executive agencies). It is this second accountability device that typifies parliamentary democracies. Indeed, we shall refer to the ideal-typical parliamentary system, reinforced by cohesive and centralized political parties, as the Westminster model.

Party government

The secret of Westminster parliamentarism is thus centralized, cohesive, policy-oriented political parties. As Cox (1987) has demonstrated, party government and parliamentary government evolved simultaneously and symbiotically into the 'efficient secret' of British government (Bagehot, 1867): political organizations that align the preferences of the occupants of the most important political offices and subordinate them to central control.

Political parties are complex collaborative devices for mutual gain, formed because candidates for public office and voters find them useful for their respective purposes. To serve these purposes, political parties have to satisfy two incentive conditions. First, they have to provide sufficient inducement for political office-holders to submit to the discipline that they impose. Second, the policy cohesion that parties induce among office-holders must be sufficient that voters find the party label informative and useful. In addition, it is helpful (though not strictly necessary) for parties to attract activists that can help them in the recruitment, training, and selection of potential candidates for office, as well as provide inexpensive campaign labour.

The first condition means that party leaders must control the recruitment (election and appointment) of government personnel, as well as government policy making. For party government to be efficient, parties must be the preferred way in which legislators realize their main political goals: re-election, political power, and policy objectives. At the same time, parties must be sufficiently effective 'informational economizing devices' that voters and activists will sustain them. Voters can rely on party labels, or in other words delegate policy aggregation to party leaders, only if these are capable of enforcing policy agreement in government. If legislative politics is anarchic, then party labels can be of no use to the voters.

Furthermore, as Michael F. Thies points out, the policies underpinning the party label must resonate with voter preferences: 'Mixing apples and oranges is fine if you can sell yourselves as the fruit party, but if voters still like apples or oranges, but not both, they will no longer be able to learn much from the "Fruit Party" label that will help them with their voting decisions' (Thies, 2000: 249). The evolution of meaningful party labels in Europe was thus facilitated by the profound social cleavages generated by the industrial and national revolutions (Lipset and Rokkan, 1967). In Britain, due to the prior resolution of religious conflict and the temporary suppression of ethno-national ones, the predominance of the class cleavage helped foster two successive two-party systems with strong partisan attachments.

Finally, for voters to attach themselves to political parties, there must be electoral institutions that translate popular votes into partisan representation in a reasonably meaningful and transparent way. In the classical Westminster model, this is indeed the case. Under a competitive two-party system and plurality single-member districts, the electoral menu is simple and the process transparent.[11]

Under these conditions, party leaders can present to the democratic principals (the voters) a package of candidate agents whose policy preferences are fairly well understood, and whose behaviour will be strictly policed by this semi-public organization. Party control means extensive screening of prospective parliamentarians as well as potential cabinet members. Before candidates gain access to higher office, they must acquire the proper party credentials and prove themselves in lesser offices. Thus, even though the voter can only directly influence the selection of parliamentarians, the 'downstream' consequences of a victory for one team or another are straightforward and predictable. As Palmer puts it:

> The Westminster model of government similarly involves the holding of a competition (an election) between competing organizations (parties) for the virtually unconstrained right to exercise a monopoly power (by government, over legitimate coercion). The electorate seeks competing bids from parties in terms of promises to govern according to particular policy preferences and leadership characteristics. By appointing one disciplined party as its agent, the electorate accepts, by majority vote, what it judges to be the best bid.
>
> (Palmer, 1995: 168)

The institutional foundations of party government

Under parliamentary democracy, parties influence all stages of the chain of delegation. In particular, they generally control delegation from voters to representatives, as well as from representatives to the chief executive (Müller, 2000). Their effect attenuates, however, as we move 'downstream' the policy chain. As Müller puts it, 'Parties are least able to control the final stage in the delegation chain – the behaviour of civil servants. The fact that the role of political parties deteriorates the more the delegation chain develops, reflects increasing informational asymmetries and the relevance of normative constraints' (Müller, 2000: 330).

Through its reliance on party government, Westminster democracy relies heavily on prior scrutiny of candidates for political office. This *ex ante* screening is reinforced through internal selection of agents such as parliamentary candidates and cabinet members, particularly in socially cohesive parties. The stronger the 'partyness' of society (Sjöblom, 1987), and the more parties represent distinct social groups, the more they tend to rely on prior screening devices, such as strong extra-parliamentary membership organizations, to make sure that candidates represent 'their kind' and the best of their kind. Thus, candidates for office are recruited by and from the party organization. The second arena in which internal selection is used is parliament. In many parliamentary democracies, such as the United Kingdom, law or convention requires that cabinet members simultaneously hold parliamentary office. This is a common form of 'contract design' in Westminster systems, and some observers see it as the defining feature of parliamentary government (for example, Hernes and Nergaard, 1989; Lane and Narud, 1992).[12] Even in parliamentary systems without such requirements, cabinet members often have substantial parliamentary experience (see Andeweg and Nijzink, 1995; Saalfeld, 2000). Internal, partisan selection of agents has obvious informational advantages, which, as Juan Linz laments, may not be available in presidential systems: 'The presidential candidates do not need and often do not have any prior record as political leaders. They may not be identified with a party with an ideology or program and record, and there may be little information about the persons likely to serve in the cabinet' (Linz, 1994: 11).

Two common constitutional features of parliamentary democracy reinforce centralized party authority: the confidence vote and the dissolution power. We have already noted that it is the parliamentary majority's dismissal power, through a vote of no confidence, that defines parliamentary government. But paradoxically, the flip side of this procedure allows the cabinet and the party leadership to dominate the legislative branch. The confidence vote enables the prime minister to attach the cabinet's fate to some bill before parliament. This is indeed a 'doomsday device' (Lupia and Strøm, 1995), by which the entire cabinet can be removed in one fell swoop. Yet this ability to raise the stakes and redefine the parliamentary agenda often enables prime ministers to quell policy dissent within their respective parties or coalitions. It also allows them to manipulate the legislative policy process (Huber, 1996).

The dissolution power is another doomsday device that similarly allows the prime minister or cabinet to threaten the parliament with an immediate electoral verdict. Most parliamentary democracies feature some provision for early dissolution. In the Westminster model, within the limits of the maximum constitutional term, the election date is fully controlled by the prime minister and his party. Consequently, this dissolution power can be, and is, used strategically for partisan purposes (Strøm and Swindle, 2002).

Another consequence of Westminster parliamentarism is that the cabinet enjoys virtually monopolistic agenda control. The simple delegation scheme of parliamentary democracy implies a concentration of agenda control in the cabinet. Since voters delegate along a singular chain of delegation, the cabinet is the sole agent of the parliamentary majority. Thus, agenda control over the policy process is placed squarely, and indeed almost monopolistically, in the cabinet. The fact that civil servants generally are not partisan means that cabinet members will be more reluctant to delegate broadly to agents further 'downstream'. The cabinet's agenda control reinforces the hierarchical nature of parliamentary democracy. McKelvey's (1976) famous 'chaos' theorem shows that under some conditions an agenda setter can be a virtual policy dictator. Yet the power of agenda setters depends on the context and generally declines (or at least does not increase) with the number of veto players (Tsebelis, 2002). With comparatively few veto players, as is typical of parliamentarism, agenda setters 'rule'.

Parliamentary democracy and moral hazard

With their long, indirect, and singular chains of democratic delegation, parliamentary democracies face particular challenges. Such a chain has clear advantages in terms of simplicity and efficiency, but it offers ample opportunities for agency loss. With some caveats, the longer the chain of delegation, the greater the potential for agency loss (Lupia, 2003). Also, the singularity of agents means that principals cannot rely on agents to check one another, or to make competing bids from which the principal can choose.

Cohesive political parties help parliamentary democracies select and police their political agents. Yet political parties quite possibly exacerbate certain agency problems, as observers have long noted. Writing in a time when parties had already gained dominance, Ostrogorski (1907: II, 712–717) lamented that they had practically destroyed political accountability. Under party-based parliamentary government, he claimed, 'the responsibility which is supposed to govern parliamentary relations comes to nothing but general irresponsibility', because the MP's responsibility 'disappears in that of the party' … 'however incompetent or culpable' ministers may be, 'it is impossible to punish one of them without punishing all'. Given party cohesion, under party government, the fall of a cabinet could happen only by 'accident'. In between elections the government 'can do very much what it likes'. Parliamentary control 'is almost non-existent'.

Echoing the concerns of Ostrogorski, Carl Schmitt regretted the abandonment of the separation of powers between parliament and government. In his view, 'narrow and narrowest committees of parties and party coalitions make decisions behind closed doors' (1969 [1923]: 52). Moreover, Frederic Austin Ogg argued that executive agenda control in practice had eroded the cabinet's accountability to parliament: 'Armed with paramount rights of initiative, supported by procedural rules drawn in their favour, and holding the power of life and death over Parliament itself, the cabinet indicates what is to be done; and Parliament, on its part … dreading the consequences of refusal, complies' (Ogg, 1936: 461).

These criticisms alert us to the fact that Westminster parliamentary democracy may not safeguard equally effectively against all forms of agency problems. Strong political parties may help solve the democratic adverse selection problem by elevating to office well trained political agents with predictable policy preferences. On the other hand, they may create or exacerbate problems of moral hazard.

To combat moral hazard in democratic representation, it is difficult to do without effective mechanisms of *ex post* oversight. As Epstein and O'Halloran show, presidential systems such as the United States' make use of a wide range of *ex post* constraints. Parliamentary systems are less likely to have a such a plethora of effective constraints. In Dicey's (1959: 39 40) formulation, for example, parliamentary sovereignty means that Parliament 'has the right to make and unmake any law whatever; and, further, that no person or body is recognized by the law of England as having a right to override or set aside the legislation of Parliament'.[13]

Ex post accountability in parliamentary systems depends almost entirely on electoral competition. In between elections accountability is tenuous, for several reasons. First, parliamentary democracy lacks credible institutional sanctions. The hallmark of parliamentarism, the no confidence vote, is a blunt and unwieldy mechanism, whose use is rarely in the interest of the parliamentary majority. And this parliamentary majority has few alternative sanctions. The impeachment procedure has in most such polities fallen into disuse. Nor are other and less severe forms of censure or reprimand common. And recall provisions, which feature in some presidential constitutions, are unknown in all European parliamentary systems.

Second, parliamentary chambers lack the capacity to determine when sanctions are appropriate. Parliamentary systems generally do not have the necessary monitoring capacity. Presidential systems, and particularly the United States', tend to feature institutions that facilitate active oversight, of either the police patrol (committee hearings) or the fire alarm (audits, judicial institutions) variety (McCubbins and Schwartz, 1984). Such institutions are much less prominent, and have much less teeth, in the parliamentary system. Parliamentary committees, for example, have much lower oversight capacity, and in the countries that best approximate the Westminster model this capacity is almost entirely absent (see Mattson and Strøm, 1995).

Third, party government implies that the parliamentary majority typically lacks motivation to scrutinize its agents, except when their behaviour threatens to become an electoral liability. As parties gain importance as mechanisms of bonding (Palmer, 1995), they reduce incentives for *ex post* parliamentary oversight of the executive, as Ostrogorski already observed. Party government implies that the party, rather than parliament, will ensure that members of the executive branch toe the line in their policy decisions. And as to other forms of agency slippage, such as executive mismanagement or graft, it is hardly in the parliamentary majority's interest to expose it. Since party identification means that the ire of the voters would befall the members of the parliamentary majority as well as the incumbents of executive office, such matters are better hushed up than exposed. Hence, members of parliament, bound by party discipline and guided by their personal incentives, may not wish to 'rock the government's boat' (King, 1976).

Consequently, as Palmer observes:

> The characteristic that distinguishes franchise bidding from other regulatory solutions to natural monopoly also distinguishes the classic Westminster constitution from other systems: the absence of significant *ex post* behavioural regulation – binding checks and balances. . . . Once an election has been held, the successful party in a pure model of the Westminster system is effectively entitled to exercise power as it sees fit, subject only to the incentives provided by the prospect of another electoral competition.
>
> (Palmer, 1995: 168)

Thus, the dominant accountability mechanism in parliamentary democracy is electoral competition. There can be no doubt that electoral accountability is a powerful constraint on politicians (see, e.g. Mayhew, 1974). But it may not be equally effective against all forms of moral hazard. While the electoral connection may secure accountability on major issues, it is likely to be inadequate when issues fall short of catching the voters' attention or causing their alienation. In other words, accountability breaks down when the ultimate principals, the voters, have a severe information problem.

There are therefore two circumstances in parliamentary democracies that may exacerbate problems of moral hazard among elected public officials. One is that the institutions that convey public information about political decisions are comparatively weak. The other is that those politicians that are best placed to do so have little incentive to bring political misbehaviour to the attention of the public. In this respect, parliamentary government perverts the representatives' incentives: were government MPs to take seriously their duty to hold the executive accountable, they might bring the wrongdoings of their co-partisans in the executive branch to the voters' attention, with likely adverse electoral consequences. But since the parliamentary majority has no incentive to scrutinize the executive very closely, but instead to turn all government proposals into law, the fusion of legislative and executive powers may cause bad policies as well as agency loss. Thus, the greatest problem of parliamentarism may be that it fails to satisfy James Madison's concern that 'Ambition must be made to counteract ambition. The interest of the man must be connected with the constitutional rights of the place' (*Federalist*, 51).

Conclusion

Parliamentary democracy is a way to organize the delegation of authority from voters to public officials. Any delegation, and therefore any representative democracy, runs the risk of agency loss. But not all democracies are equally at risk for the same agency problems. Parliamentarism is a simple and elegant scheme of delegation, which benefits greatly from the role that political parties play as devices of preference alignment and screening (see Müller, 2000). Party cohesion under a Westminster system allows voters to make reasonably well informed choices and ensures a certain amount of responsiveness and accountability in government. Thus, as we have seen, parliamentary regimes may be better equipped than presidential ones to deal with problems of adverse selection. To the extent that the main problem in politics is to select the right 'type' of representative, the advantage should lie with regimes that devote more resources to the prior screening of candidates, as is the nature of parliamentarism. When governing parties are cohesive and reasonably large (as under single-party majority government), they are also more likely to pursue policies favouring encompassing rather than distributional interests (Olson, 1982).

But just as parliamentary democracy has identifiable advantages over its competition, so too does it have its weak points. The flip side of simplicity is that, compared to other regime types, parliamentary democracy exposes its agents to less constraint or competition from other agents. Hence, compared to more complex systems of delegation, parliamentarism suffers with respect to the accountability that such constraints may facilitate. Moreover, parliamentary systems are less likely than presidential ones to be transparent, because they contain fewer mechanisms by which agents are forced to share information and principals can learn. Just as important, political officials under parliamentary government lack the critical incentives to share information with the voters. Owing to its weaker capacity for the *ex post* oversight, moral hazard is therefore a peculiar problem under parliamentarism. Accountability in Westminster systems depends heavily on electoral competition, but such competition is not always sufficient to prevent democratic agency problems. Where electoral accountability is less effective, as in many parliamentary systems with proportional representation, this failure to police moral hazard may be even more acute.

Yet the contrast between parliamentary and presidential constitutions is not simply one between a regime designed to combat adverse selection and one focused on moral hazard. There are other values tied up in these institutional 'packages'. Thus, the ideal-typical parliamentary constitution is one that promotes efficiency by eliminating redundancies and taking incentives seriously. On the other hand, presidential constitutions promote credibility and transparency by protecting against hasty and potentially ill considered policy change and by forcing disclosure of the pull and tug of policy making in the public arena.

The broader lessons are that democratic agency problems are stubborn and that they come in different forms. Political delegation is necessary, consequential, and at the same time fraught with danger. Political parties and institutional constraints exist in large part for these reasons. In turn, and for better or worse, they affect the policy process in their own ways and sometimes in complex interaction. There is no simple institutional fix for all agency problems. Thus, neither parliamentary nor presidential constitutions can effectively safeguard against all disloyal, incompetent, or corrupt public servants. As long as principals and agents differ in their preferences and information, some agency losses must be expected. Yet, such agency losses come in different forms under different constitutions. The choices between them represent real trade-offs.

Notes

This chapter builds on our analysis in Strøm *et al.* (2003). We are grateful to all the contributors to that volume for their insights and analysis.

1. We define parliamentary government below. Note that the five countries mentioned all fail to qualify because the head of government is not accountable to the legislative majority through a no-confidence procedure.
2. In an ultimately less robust form, parliamentary government existed in Sweden between 1719 and 1772, the 'Age of Liberty' (Roberts, 1986).
3. For simplicity, we shall hereafter generally assume that both principals and agents are individuals, and that the principal is female and the agent male.
4. None the less, investiture requirements and especially dissolution powers can certainly enhance certain features of parliamentary system, as we shall discuss below.
5. For systems with bicameral legislatures, it suffices for the prime minister and cabinet to be accountable to the majority in one chamber. Empirically, this is typically the lower chamber. Constitutions under which the prime minister and cabinet are accountable to both chambers, such as Italy, are the exception.
6. While our approach has different ontological and epistemological underpinnings, we share Pitkin's concern for representation as the 'substantive acting for others' (Pitkin, 1967: 209).
7. For elections to be free and fair, they must be held under the rule of law and political competition (freedom to form and join organization, freedom of expression, alternative sources of information, freedom of candidacy), and there must be an independent and competent administration, as well as appropriate judicial bodies, to implement the election law (see Dahl, 1971: 3, 1989: 221–222).
8. In their study of role perceptions among Swedish members of parliament, for example, Esaiasson and Holmberg note that 'one alternative from the history of representational doctrine is missing, however – Burke's famous credo of "the nation as a whole". The reason for this is quite simply that Burke has been too successful; the norm that national interests come first is so well established in most European parliaments that scholars consider it meaningless to probe parliamentary representatives on this matter' (Esaiasson and Holmberg, 1996: 62).
9. Note that if we take the idea of singular agents to its logical extreme, the ideal-typical parliamentary democracy is also a unitary state (such as Britain, New Zealand, or Sweden, but not Austria or Canada), with a unicameral parliament (such as the Nordic countries or, again, New Zealand).
10. We recognize that even under an ideal-typical parliamentary democracy, principals sometimes delegate to multiple agents. Yet, under parliamentary democracy, these agents do not generally compete with one another.

11 Technically, the process is non-perverse in that voters can never hurt themselves (would never experience rational *ex post* regret) if they vote for their most preferred party.
12 Applied to the relationship between voters and parliamentarians, internal delegation implies a residence requirement for elected representatives. Although such rules, or at least norms, exist in some countries, they are not uniquely associated with parliamentarism.
13 As quoted in Norton (1994: 63).

References

Aghion, P. and Tirole, J. (1997) 'Formal and Real Authority in Organizations', *Journal of Political Economy*, 105: 1–29.
Andeweg, R. B. and Nijzink, L. (1995) 'Beyond the Two-body Image. Relations between Ministers and MPs', in H. Döring (ed.) *Parliaments and Majority Rule in Western Europe*, Frankfurt am Main: Campus and New York: St Martin's Press.
Bagehot, W. (1963 [1867]) *The English Constitution*, London: Fontana/Collins.
Barro, R. J. (1973) 'The Control of Politicians. An Economic Model', *Public Choice*, 14: 19–42.
Brehm, J. and Gates, S. (1997) *Working, Shirking and Sabotage*, Ann Arbor MI: University of Michigan Press.
Cox, G. W. (1987) *The Efficient Secret*, Cambridge: Cambridge University Press.
Crozier, M., Huntington, S. P. and Watanuki, J. (1975) *The Crisis of Democracy. Report on the Governability of Democracies to the Trilateral Commission*, New York: New York University Press.
Dahl, R. A. (1971) *Polyarchy*, New Haven CT: Yale University Press.
Dahl, R. A. (1989) *Democracy and its Critics*, New Haven CT: Yale University Press.
Dicey, A. V. (1959) *An Introduction to the Study of the Law of the Constitution*, 10th edn (1st edn 1885), London: Macmillan.
Downs, A. (1967) *Inside Bureaucracy*, Boston MA: Little Brown.
Epstein, D. and O'Halloran, S. (1999) *Delegating Powers*, Cambridge: Cambridge University Press.
Epstein, L. D. (1968) 'Parliamentary Government', in D. L. Sills (ed.) *International Encyclopedia of the Social Sciences*, New York: Macmillan and Free Press.
Esaiasson, P. and Holmberg, S. (1996) *Representation from Above. Members of Parliament and Representative Democracy in Sweden*, Aldershot: Dartmouth.
Fearon, J. D. (1999) 'Electoral Accountability and the Control of Politicians. Selecting Good Types versus Sanctioning Poor Performance', in A. Przeworski, S. C. Stokes and B. Manin (eds) *Democracy, Accountability, and Representation*, Cambridge: Cambridge University Press.
Ferejohn, J. (1986) 'Incumbent Performance and Electoral Control', *Public Choice*, 50: 5–25.
Furubotn, E. G. and Richter, R. (1997) *Institutions and Economic Theory. An Introduction to and Assessment of the New Institutional Economics*, Ann Arbor MI: University of Michigan Press.
Hernes, G. and Nergaard, K. (1989) *Oss imellom*, Oslo: FAFO.
Huber, J. D. (1996) *Rationalizing Parliament*, Cambridge: Cambridge University Press.

Kiewiet, D. R. and McCubbins, M. D. (1991), *The Logic of Delegation*, Chicago: University of Chicago Press.

King, A. (1976) 'Modes of Executive–Legislative Relations: Great Britain, France, and West Germany', *Legislative Studies Quarterly*, 1: 11–36.

Lane, J-E. and Narud, H. M. (1992) 'Regjering og nasjonalforsamling. Bemanning av de to statsorganene', *Norsk Statsvitenskapelig Tidsskrift*, 8: 303–316.

Lijphart, A. (1999) *Patterns of Democracy*, New Haven CT: Yale University Press.

Linz, J. J. (1994) 'Presidential or Parliamentary Democracy. Does It Make a Difference?' in J. J. Linz and A. Valenzuela (eds) *The Failure of Presidential Democracy* I, Baltimore MD: Johns Hopkins University Press.

Lipset, S. M. and Rokkan, S. (eds) (1967) *Party Systems and Voter Alignments*, New York: Free Press.

Lowell, A. L. (1896) *Governments and Parties in Continental Europe*, London: Longmans.

Lupia, A. (2003) 'Delegation and its Perils', in K. Strøm, W. C. Müller and T. Bergman (eds) *Delegation and Accountability in Parliamentary Democracies*, Oxford: Oxford University Press.

Lupia, A. and Strøm, K. (1995) 'Coalition Termination and the Strategic Timing of Parliamentary Elections', *American Political Science Review*, 89: 648–665.

Lynn, J. and Jay, A. (1981) *The Complete Yes, Minister. The Diaries of a Cabinet Minister*, London: BBC Books.

Mainwaring, S. and Shugart, M. S. (eds) (1997) *Presidentialism and Democracy in Latin America*, Cambridge: Cambridge University Press.

Manin, B., Przeworski, A. and Stokes, S. C. (1999) 'Elections and Representation', in A. Przeworski, S. C. Stokes and B. Manin (eds) *Democracy, Accountability, and Representation*, Cambridge: Cambridge University Press.

Mattson, I. and Strøm, K. (1995) 'Parliamentary Committees', in H. Döring (ed.) *Parliaments and Majority Rule in Western Europe*, New York: St Martin's Press.

Mayhew, D. R. (1974) *Congress. The Electoral Connection*, New Haven CT: Yale University Press.

McChesney, F. S. (1997) *Money for Nothing. Politicians, Rent Extraction, and Political Extortion*, Cambridge MA: Harvard University Press.

McCubbins, M. D. and Schwartz, T. (1984) 'Congressional Oversight Overlooked: Police Patrols versus Fire Alarms', *American Journal of Political Science*, 28: 165–179.

McKelvey, R. D. (1976) 'Intransitivities in Multidimensional Voting Models and some Implications for Agenda Control', *Journal of Economic Theory*, 12: 472–482.

Michels, R. (1962) *Political Parties*, New York: Free Press.

Mill, J. S. (1984 [1861]) 'Considerations on Representative Government', in J. S. Mill, *Utilitarianism. Liberty. Representative Government*, London: Dent.

Moe, T. M. (1984) 'The New Economics of Organization', *American Journal of Political Science*, 28: 739–777.

Mosca, G. (1950) *Die herrschende Klasse*, Munich: Leo Lehnen.

Müller, W. C. (2000) 'Political Parties in Parliamentary Democracies. Making Delegation and Accountability Work', *European Journal of Political Research*, 37: 309–333.

Müller, W. C. and Strøm, K. (2000) 'Conclusions: coalition governance in Western Europe', in W. C. Müller and K. Strøm (eds) *Coalition Governments in Western Europe*, Oxford: Oxford University Press.

Niskanen, W. A. (1971) *Bureaucracy and Representative Government*, Chicago: Aldine-Atherton.

Norton, P. (1981) *The Commons in Perspective*, Oxford: Blackwell.

Norton, P. (1994) *The British Polity*, 3rd edn, New York: Longman.

Ogg, F. A. (1936) *English Government and Politics*, 2nd edn, New York: Macmillan.

Olson, M. Jr (1982) *The Rise and Decline of Nations*, New Haven CT: Yale University Press.

Ostrogorski, M. (1907) *Democracy and the Organization of Political Parties*, London: Macmillan.

Palmer, M. S. R. (1995) 'Toward an Economics of Comparative Political Organization. Examining Ministerial Responsibility', *Journal of Law, Economics and Organization*, 11: 164–188.

Parker, G. R. (1996) *Congress and the Rent-seeking Society*, Ann Arbor MI: University of Michigan Press.

Pitkin, H. F. (1967) *The Concept of Representation*, Berkeley CA: University of California Press.

Plato, *The Republic*, Book VII (514a–541b).

Pratt, J. W. and Zeckhauser, R. J. (eds) (1985) *Principals and Agents. The Structure of Business*, Boston MA: Harvard Business School Press.

Przeworski, A., Alvarez, M. E., Cheibub, J. A. and Limongi, F. (2000) *Democracy and Development*, Cambridge: Cambridge University Press.

Roberts, M. (1986) *The Age of Liberty. Sweden 1719–1772*, Cambridge: Cambridge University Press.

Rose, R. (ed.) (1980) *Challenge to Governance. Studies in Overloaded Polities*, Beverly Hills CA: Sage.

Saalfeld, T. (2000) 'Members of Parliament and Governments in Western Europe. Agency Relations And Problems of Oversight', *European Journal of Political Research*, 37: 353–376.

Sartori, G. (1997) *Comparative Constitutional Engineering*, 2nd edn, Houndmills: Macmillan.

Schmitt, C. (1969 [1923]) *Die geistesgeschichtliche Lage des heutigen Parlamentarismus*, Berlin: Duncker & Humblot.

Shleifer, A. and Vishny, R. W. (1998) *The Grabbing Hand. Government Pathologies and their Cures*, Cambridge MA: Harvard University Press.

Shugart, M. S. and Carey, J. (1992) *Presidents and Assemblies*, Cambridge: Cambridge University Press.

Sjöblom, G. (1987) 'The Role of Political Parties in Denmark and Sweden, 1970–1984', in R. S. Katz (ed.) *Party Governments. European and American Experiences*, Berlin: de Gruyter.

Steffani, W. (1979) *Parlamentarische und präsidielle Demokratie*. Opladen: Westdeutscher Verlag.

Stepan, A. and Skach, C. (1993) 'Constitutional Frameworks and Democratic Consolidation. Parliamentarism versus Presidentialism', *World Politics*, 46: 1–22.

Strøm, K., Müller, W. C. and Bergman, T. (eds) (2003) *Delegation and Accountability in Parliamentary Democracies*, Oxford: Oxford University Press.

Strøm, K. and Swindle, S. M. (2002) 'Strategic Parliamentary Dissolution', *American Political Science Review*, 96: 575–591.

Strong, C. F. (1963) *A History of Modern Political Constitutions*, New York: Putnam.

Thies, M. F. (2000) 'On the Primacy of Party in Government. Why Legislative

Parties can survive Party Decline in the Electorate', in R. J. Dalton and M. P. Wattenberg (eds) *Parties without Partisans*, Oxford: Oxford University Press.

Tsebelis, G. (2002) *Veto Players: An Introduction to Institutional Analysis*, Princeton NJ: Princeton University Press and New York: Russell Sage Foundation.

Weber, M. (1972) *Wirtschaft und Gesellschaft*, Tübingen: Mohr.

Wessels, B. (1999) 'Whom to Represent? Role Orientations of Legislators in Europe', in H. Schmitt and J. Thomassen (eds) *Political Representation and Legitimacy in the European Union*, Oxford: Oxford University Press.

3 Delegation and accountability in parliamentary democracies

Smallness, proximity and short cuts

Patrick Dumont and Frédéric Varone

Introduction

The ideal type of parliamentary democracy is illustrated by a chain of delegation and accountability between principals and agents (Strøm, 2000). Agency theorists usually discuss two main types of agency loss: because of hidden information, principals may select agents who have preferences that are bound to conflict with theirs (adverse selection) and because their action may also be hidden whilst in office, they may not even be punished for acting detrimentally to the principal's welfare (moral hazard). However, a key assumption of the principal–agent approach is that political actors should be able to design specific institutional rules and arrangements guiding delegation and accountability in response to these agency problems. These devices include *ex ante* contract design, screening and selection on the one hand and *ex post* monitoring, reporting and institutional checks on the other hand.

We argue that, *ceteris paribus*, the size of a political system is a relevant variable in this context. *Small political systems* display various features such as information, uncertainty, expertise and sanctioning capacities, etc., that may affect the choices made in the design of specific institutional arrangements. Whilst it is clear that many other factors influence the design of such procedures, size-related variables may also have an independent effect on the outcome of this chain of delegation and accountability, namely the extent of agency loss. Strøm *et al.* indeed 'find it plausible for size to affect agency loss, not least through its effects on informational transparency' (2003: 711) and their empirical tests support the hypothesis that small countries display higher levels of voter satisfaction.[1] Hence, indicators about the size of, and the distance between, principals and agents should be included as independent variables in theoretical models that aim to explain variations in delegation and accountability procedures and outcomes across parliamentary democracies. More specifically, we focus on three independent variables (see Figure 3.1):

1   *Smallness* refers to the size of relevant (collective) actors and the number of institutional bodies in the political system in general and at each stage of the delegation and accountability chain in particular.

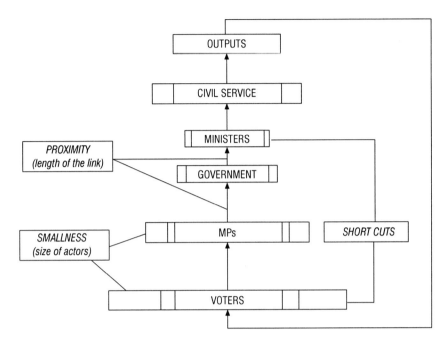

Figure 3.1 Smallness, proximity and short cuts in the chain of parliamentary democracy.

2   *Shortness* measures the *proximity* of actors according to the length of the link between principals and agents. It can mostly be understood as the level of incentive compatibility and is operationalized as overlaps in membership. It is an important feature of the chain, as Tirole, writing about organizations, points out that they are 'networks of overlapping or nested principal/agent relationships' (1986: 181).

3   *Directness* is related to the possibilities for bypassing certain links from principals to agents or, in other words, to *short cuts* in the ideal-typical delegation chain.

The notions of proximity (or shortness) and short cuts (or directness) refer explicitly to the design of the chain of delegation and are thus likely to vary according to the adaptations made by politicians in different political environments. Although the size of collective actors and the number of institutional bodies (or smallness) may also be adapted – for instance by lowering the age required for voting, allowing foreigners the right to vote, enlarging or lowering the number of MPs, ministers, and the size of the civil service – it is our ultimate explanatory variable of variations in delegation and accountability procedures and agency loss. More specifically, smallness, mainly because of its effects on information asymmetry, influences the design of delegation institutions and is *one of the* factors that (1) allow more proximity (short length of the links)[2] between principals and agents and (2) allow possible short cuts (bypassing of links). Shortness may also facilitate short cuts, regardless of smallness, for instance when an electoral system makes personal votes determinant not only in the choice of MPs but also in the choice of cabinet ministers. There may also be proximity between principals and agents in countries with a large population (of 'ultimate' principals), such as between MPs and government in the United Kingdom, and short cuts may also be present in large countries, for example referenda in Italy. We argue that the size of the principals along the chain of delegation is one of the factors, and certainly an understudied one, that is likely to affect both institutional arrangements (both the shortness and the directness of the links) and the eventual outcome (agency loss) of the delegation and accountability process in parliamentary democracies.

In the following sections, we will distinguish the hypothesized relations between smallness, proximity and short cuts, likely consequences on the design of delegation mechanisms and agency loss 'stage by stage', starting with the link from voters to MPs. At each stage, we illustrate the theoretical consideration with systematic examples from the case of Luxembourg, a small European parliamentary democracy with just over 450,000 inhabitants, before summing up the argument and looking at ways forward in the concluding section.

Smallness, proximity and short cuts in the chain of parliamentary democracy

Before deriving theoretical propositions and discussing potential indicators of these variables for each step of the delegation and accountability chain, we briefly present an overview of the political regime of Luxembourg.

If we describe how the Grand Duchy of Luxembourg fares with regard to the ideal type of parliamentary democracy, one observes a general picture of indirect chain of delegation with a reasonable adoption of the singularity principle. First, the country is a *unitary* parliamentary monarchy. Second, political parties are not legally recognized and thus they receive no governmental subsidies for central party offices, which are very poor both in infrastructure and personnel. Accordingly, the weight of extra-parliamentary party is much less important than in most West European countries and, as such, the deviation from the ideal-typical chain brought about by the actions of powerful parties is less pronounced than in many parliamentary democracies. Third, external constraints or actors which may influence policy outputs are related to the smallness of the country. Due to its size, Luxembourg has always been involved in organizations and arrangements that continuously reduce its sovereignty,[3] and has also developed neo-corporatist arrangements that are typical of small, open economies (Katzenstein, 1985; Allegrezza *et al.*, 2003). Altogether, we find constraints that reduce the role of actors of the ideal-typical chain and create deviations from the 'singularity principle' of delegation and accountability, and also features that closely conform to this principle.

From voters to MPs

The link from voters to MPs binds non-politicians to political professionals. It is also the link where the difference in number of principals (voters) and number of agents (MPs) is the most visible. This constellation is potentially fraught with the greatest dangers in terms of delegation and accountability, as it is here that the problems of *asymmetric information* between principals and agents and *coordination* between principals in order to delegate to the right persons are the greatest.

In terms of *screening and monitoring*, the size of the constituency, and of the country, as one MP candidate may switch constituencies from one election to another, is potentially an important factor. *Ceteris paribus*, the reputation of candidates before they enter politics is more likely to be known for all parties and voters in small countries and constituencies, and incumbents' behaviour will be more easily revealed in smaller countries, where information circulates more quickly. Hence, as *information asymmetry* is reduced, both adverse selection and moral hazards of agents are less likely. *Ceteris paribus*, as the number of actors gets smaller, preferences are also likely to be less spread out both in terms of demand (from voters) and offer (the number of political parties and candidates competing for votes).[4] 'Electoral *coordination*' (the ability of a group with enough votes to elect a candidate by concentrating their votes appropriately, see Cox, 1997) is likely to be less problematic. Indeed, it is not surprising that the question of size and democracy has been most developed in fields like electoral studies (turn-out, social and political trust, etc.) and by local government scholars stressing the virtues of smallness with regard to the relationship between voters and representatives. In terms of direct effects on democratic outcomes, smallness appears to have, *ceteris paribus*, a positive influence. Farrell and McAllister (2004) find that the closer the voter is to the MP (due to a certain degree of proportionality between assembly size and the size of voting population, such ratios are typically low in smaller countries), the higher the satisfaction with democracy is, *whatever the type of electoral system used*. This overall positive effect of smallness may be reinforced through its influence on other forms of proximity between voters and MPs induced by the adoption of specific electoral rules. Given the characteristics of small political settings, we hypothesize that, *ceteris paribus*, political actors who have the power to design and reform electoral systems will tend to grant their voters a more 'direct' say in the choice of their representatives.[5] Farrell and McAllister (2004) indicate that systems that allow a preferential vote lead (through a greater sense of fairness of electoral results in the voting population) to a higher level of democratic satisfaction. Thus, we may also find an indirect effect of smallness on democratic outcomes through the design of electoral systems. In the following paragraphs of this section we discuss such systems that enhance the *proximity* between principals and agents.[6]

Agency losses from voters to MPs are most likely when the latter's careers do not depend on the judgement of voters. Mitchell (2000) classifies electoral systems in three categories, ranging from those that provide opportunities for personal vote (candidate-based systems) which entails electoral accountability to voters rather than to parties, to those that prevent any personal vote (party-based systems). Single-member plurality and closed-list proportional representation systems are both considered as party-centred systems. Voters have no electoral choice of candidate except at the cost of voting for another party. At the other extreme, we find candidate-centred systems where preferential vote really makes a difference, either because the party list is not preordained or voters have other options, such as voting for candidates of different parties (which is allowed in *panachage* and *single transferable vote* systems) or expressing degrees of preferences within the votes made (by giving more than one vote to a candidate if it is permitted or by ranking them as in *single transferable vote* systems). In the systems which allow for votes between party lists, MPs are, *ceteris paribus*, less likely to act as agents of their party or of their party voters than as agents of the whole constituency. At the same time, once elected, MPs may well end up performing constituency service instead of devoting their time to legislating for the collective (all constituencies of the country) good in order to enhance their chances of re-election.

Mitchell also points out that 'there exists a trade-off between the directness of the link between voter and agent and the choice of agents that is crucial to voters' abilities to sanction agents' (2000: 346). Although single-member districts may create a 'direct' link (as the incumbent is the only representative of the constituency, he can more easily be held accountable), they offer the smallest range of alternatives for voters (only one candidate per party) and thus reduce the ability to directly sanction representatives. Multi-member districts in systems allowing real preferential or even *panachage* votes seem to combine the virtues of effective directness, as intra- and inter-party competition gives more opportunity for revelations about rivals' behaviour. These systems give the greatest possibilities to sanction incumbents if necessary, and thus the highest potential for legislative turnover, an important feature of democracy indeed.[7] Hence, the overall level of decisiveness of voters (a direct effect of their choice over a range of alternatives) in electing their representatives can be conceptualized as *proximity* because a higher level of decisiveness provides a shorter (least affected by dependence on party will) link between voters and MPs.

In summary, there is a potential effect of smallness on the proximity between the principals and agents through the design of electoral rules that *strengthen the relations from voters to MPs, and weaken the intermediary role of parties in delegation and accountability*, at least in comparison with the 'realistic view' of the chain of parliamentary democracy proposed by Müller (2000). Mitchell also stresses that parties exert the biggest influence at this stage. It would thus be interesting to see whether direct and indirect effects of size of a political system challenge this general pattern.

The case of Luxembourg provides initial answers to this question. Voting in Luxembourg is compulsory for all citizens aged eighteen or older. The country is divided into four electoral districts, and MPs are elected for a five-year term (the number of terms they can serve is not limited) in the unicameral parliament.[8] The constitution stipulates that there are sixty parliamentary seats (elected in four districts ranging from seven to twenty-three in magnitude)[9] which can be changed only through a constitutional amendment. In the 2004 elections, 200,092 people voted. The voting age population of Luxembourg citizens was 217,683. Thus, the ratio of voting-age population to MPs showed that each MP represented 3,628 voters. In comparative terms, this ratio is significantly higher than for the following respective recent elections, where in Germany or Italy there are 70,000 voters per MP (which decreases to 50,000 if both chambers are included), in a small country like Denmark the figure is around 20,000 and is slightly above 3,000 for Iceland, which is less populous than Luxembourg.

Luxembourg's electoral system is quite unique. Voters may cast a straight party vote list by ticking the appropriate cell, but then each candidate is awarded one vote, regardless of party rankings. Apart from the name on top of the list, all candidates are listed alphabetically. The voter can also choose specific candidates, either from the same party or from a variety of parties (*panachage*). Voters opt for preferential voting, whether intra-party or inter-party, and may even cast a maximum of two votes for each candidate (though the maximum number of preference votes equals the total number of constituency seats). Since the 1970s preferential voting has increased, from 31.3 per cent of the votes cast in 1979 to 47 per cent in 2004, with the proportion of inter-party *panachage* jumping from 18 per cent of the total vote in 1979 to 29 per cent in 1999 (CRISP, 1995; CRPGL, 2000).[10] Since preferential votes determine who gets elected, these voters decide which candidates become MPs. Hence, Luxembourg's electoral system is a candidate-centred one. Although these features facilitate MP turnover, the size of the Luxembourg population constrains the renewal of candidates' names, and from the 1840s to 1999 there were only 700 different MPs (only a few more than the current German or British main chambers).

On the other hand, as the electoral system reduces the importance of partisan candidate selection, it implies that, once elected, MPs are accountable to their constituency voters. This gives MPs an important incentive to pay attention to local interests (to 'bring home the bacon', to attend constituency social events, etc.). MPs who deviate from their party's national policy positions to protect their constituency do not usually have to worry about losing their seat in the next election. However, rebellion against the party as a whole would provoke harsh reactions in the powerful partisan press and rejection by the 'pillar'.[11] Hence, in practice, party splits in parliamentary voting are rare, not because powerful parties impose strict discipline, but rather because of political culture features.

From MPs to government

The delegation from MPs to government usually involves only professional politicians. Although information asymmetry has grown between the two sets of actors as parliaments have become less important in policy making, the information gap is not as big as between voters and MPs. Indeed, the latter are better able than voters to try to reduce this information deficit by investing their time in specializing in specific fields, sitting on instruments of control such as permanent specialized parliamentary committees, investigation committees, finance audit courts that help them dealing with their prerogative on national budget, etc.

However, MPs not only seek to control their agents, they also seek re-election, and thus invest time and effort in *constituency service* in order to please their voters. This is much less relevant when MPs are elected by a national or at least a very large constituency. Hence, the size of the constituency may well have an indirect effect on the *quality of ex post control* MPs exercise with regard to governments (the larger the constituency, the higher the possibility of MPs' influence on government, depending on whether they belong to the majority or opposition parties).

Moreover, the large number of MPs compared with a 'normal' number of specialized permanent committees or ministerial jurisdictions[12] makes *specialization* much more difficult if assembly size is restricted. Not only is it less probable to have an expert in, say energy questions, in each parliamentary group, but specialization 'on the road' is also less likely as these MPs have to attend *multiple parliamentary committees*. A smaller number of (minority) MPs (more) eager to control the cabinet would make this lack of expertise even more problematic. On the other hand, smaller parliaments usually imply smaller committees, which also means that proportional representation of all parliamentary groups in these committees is more difficult and often MPs are the sole representative of their party. They thus enjoy an informational advantage with regard to the other MPs of their parliamentary group in their fields of competence. They may more easily coordinate with their fellow members of committee in their control task as they are less likely to be sanctioned by their party (hidden action). These are important features of smallness, as the link between MPs and government is typically party-driven (Müller, 2000, Saalfeld, 2000): the behaviour of MPs is conditioned by their belonging to the majority or opposition parties.

In summary, it is difficult to assess the potential direct impact of *smallness* on the MP–government link, as it can have, in theory, *positive and negative* effects on this link (less time for controlling the activities of MPs, less capacity in terms of specialization and expertise, but potentially less dependence on the party). However, as Mattson and Strøm, (1995: 469) point out, it is reasonable to say that the size of the organization has an impact on individuals. MPs may behave quite differently in different settings (for instance, backbenchers should have a different status as they can have a more direct access to parliamentary chair, their decisiveness is also increased as the likelihood that each vote counts is increased in smaller settings, etc.).

Proximity is partly a question of *incentive compatibility* between principals and agents. Saalfeld (2000) advocates the share of cabinet ministers who were MPs before joining the cabinet as a proxy measure for the level of incentive compatibility. Smallness should enhance the advantages of such an internal selection. Turning the variable on its head, we could also verify the ratio of MPs who were once members of the cabinet. In smaller parliaments, these ratios are supposed to be higher for obvious reasons, as the ratio between the number of ministers and the number of MPs is typically higher than in larger settings.[13] Another variant of such measurement would be the proportion of MPs in a given legislature belonging to parties which were in cabinet in the last (say three or four) terms. As former members of the cabinet may now be in parliament or heading the party, experience gathered from office may still be relevant to the current parliamentary party group in understanding the behaviour of current agents. Saalfeld (2000) also proposes the number of years spent serving as an MP before becoming a minister as a variable reflecting the screening and selection mechanism driving the choice of ministers. However, we must remind ourselves that these choices are in fact made by parties (generally party chairmen). Nevertheless, even though MPs are not themselves choosing cabinet personnel, the measurement of these variables assumes that principals may have more or less familiarity in terms of background with their agents.[14]

Other formal and informal instruments regulating the relations between MPs and governments, both *ex ante* (investiture votes, coalition agreement) and *ex post* (committee oversight, confidence votes) are usually more controlled by party elites than by MPs themselves. Coalition agreements, for instance, are essentially negotiated by party elites, then approved by large party congress, before parliament is requested (in about half of Western European countries) to vote on this government plan of action. And this 'Bible of the government' largely determines the behaviour of MPs in parliament, as majority MPs are usually asked to abide by its commitments and thus observe party discipline with regard to government bills, etc. and opposition MPs are confronted by the government's control of the legislative agenda. In countries where investiture votes are required, MPs usually do not have many effective means of government oversight for the rest of the term, and even the confidence votes at their disposal are either not often used or not very effective.[15] Countries not requiring investiture votes are often governed by minority cabinets (Bergman, 1993). This feature strengthens parliament as a whole and especially opposition parties both in terms of policy-making influence and in their ability and incentives to effectively monitor the government, with even the possibility of unseating it quite easily existing. Hence, although the rules of the game are clearly part of a conception of proximity between principals and agents it is unclear whether we should consider these features regulating MPs–cabinet relations as allowing more effective delegation and accountability link, because they are all typically heavily constrained by parties.

Smallness has an impact on the *sanctioning* of misbehaving agents. Although it is easier to identify the stage at which a problem arises, people in charge of sanctioning are the same as those engaged in daily personal interactions with their agents and thus, may find it more difficult to apply sanctions. The proportion of MPs in the legislature (in which an investigation committee issues a report on a specific case) belonging to parties which were in cabinet in previous legislative terms may be an interesting proxy of proximity. The higher this proportion the smaller the chances of sanctions, as the costs of sanctioning members of an MP's own party would balance the gains from sanctioning members of other parties.

As there is an actor, parliament, between voters and government, *short cuts* are possible at this stage. Indeed, the composition of governments may be more *responsive to electoral* movements in small systems. This may render governments more inclined to take liberties with their obligations to parliament in order to follow or flatter public opinion. Strøm (2000) identifies it as one of the contemporary threats in the parliamentary democracy chain, under the label of *diverted accountabilities*. But the effect of this kind of short cut may not be so harmful if we consider potential agency losses along the whole chain of delegation in smaller countries. A more direct link between voters and governments may somewhat balance the excessive weakness of parliamentary *ex post* control of government in smaller systems, as voters would be given the possibility of sanctioning governments that were not controlled effectively by MPs because of their lack of capacity to do so.

Do we observe such phenomena in Luxembourg? First, let us mention that from 1945 onwards, all governments have been coalitions, and that centripetal competition has favoured the most centrist party the Christian democrats (CSV), which typically has governed in coalition with the Socialists (LSAP) or the Liberals (DP). However, the small ideological distance between relevant parties has also enabled all possible two-party coalitions (CSV–LSAP, CSV–DP, but also DP–LSAP from 1974 to 1979) to emerge. Furthermore, Luxembourg has displayed extraordinary cabinet and prime ministerial stability. There have been only nine Prime Ministers since 1919, a feature that is largely due to the quasi-permanence in power of the CSV (except 1974–1979) and to a lack of political personnel typical of small democracies (see below).

Since 1848 ministers may not simultaneously hold seats in parliament. The principle of internal selection of ministers is, however, widely respected, with 88 per cent of ministers, in the period 1970–1984, having been an MP before obtaining a ministerial appointment. This variable used as a proxy of 'incentive compatibility' or 'proximity' does not seem to be determined by the size of the parliament, but rather by this institutional feature of incompatibility or compulsory compatibility between the two roles. Hence, in the United Kingdom, 99 per cent of ministers were or are MPs because of this compulsory double belonging. Smaller countries like Austria, Finland, Norway, Sweden and the Netherlands have between 60 per cent and two-thirds of ministers with previous experience as a national MP (De Winter, 1995: 131). Nor does the average parliamentary seniority of cabinet ministers give a clear picture with regard to size concerns (De Winter, 1991: 48). An alternative measure consisting of calculating the proportion of MPs belonging to parties that were in power in the most recent legislatures is not much more promising.

The problem of lack of expertise shows a clearer relation: permanent specialized committees, with proportional representation of parties, date back to 1965. There are twenty-one such committees, each consisting of eleven MPs, so on average, each MP is part of *four* specialized committees. Some MPs also attend meetings of other bodies of the parliament such as the bureau or the conference of parliamentary party group chairs. When one compares this state of affairs with large countries where the average MP is part of one specialized committee, it appears clear that the opportunities for specialization are rare for MPs in small legislatures. When one adds to that the burden of constituency service for Luxembourg MPs who want to be re-elected, the time for such specialization simply does not exist.

In terms of short cuts, Luxembourg displays a large voter influence on the composition of governments. The Grand Duke usually asks the leader of the *largest party* to form a new government, but the *junior partner is almost always the party that made electoral gains* relative to the previous election. Moreover, coalition parties usually select ministers on the basis of their personal electoral success (see below). This direct link between electoral success and office, for parties as well as *ministrables*, rests on convention rather than law. Together with the growth of *panachage* voting, these conventions make cabinet ministers accountable not only to the parliamentary majority, but also to the voters. Accordingly, cabinet ministers try to promote their constituency interests, sometimes against the will of their formal principal, the parliamentary majority.

For the rest, the link between MPs and government in Luxembourg is heavily constrained by parties and thus by whether an MP belongs to the majority party. By drafting comprehensive *coalition agreements* (that until 1999 were secret, which meant that MPs could not screen the content before putting a vote of confidence to cabinet) before the cabinet takes office, parties strongly influence the policy link between parliament and government. This feature also has consequences for the link between cabinet and individual ministers, as the latter cannot become policy dictators under such coalition contracts. Although the coalition composition generally respects the will of the voting majority and the choice of ministers is constrained by their personal electoral results, government formation is controlled entirely by political parties. *Motions of confidence and of no confidence* are not institutionalized or regulated, and in practice, parliamentary action has brought down only two cabinets: one after a majority turned a vote on a specific motion into a question of confidence (1958), and the other when cabinet resigned to pre-empt such a vote (1966). The parliament's vote on the government's *annual budget* bill is considered to be a vote of confidence, but the problem of expertise is one reason that parliament cannot effectively use this *ex ante* control instrument.

Governments tend to dominate *general legislation* as well. bills proposed by the opposition can be stopped at different procedural stages and are unlikely to be put to a vote. Again, the parliament's lack of resources helps explain why very few private bills are even introduced. In addition, an MP's right to initiative is, to various degrees, subject to the approval of his parliamentary group (*Fraktion*). Majority MPs are further constrained by the coalition agreement and *inter-fractional* meetings (meetings of coalition parliamentary groups), while the actions of opposition MPs are influenced by their knowledge that any initiative will probably be blocked. In short, MPs generally do not invest much time in drafting bills because there is little prospect that they will be passed.

From government to ministers

Individual ministers are both principals, as they are members of the cabinet, and agents of the cabinet, as they are also heads of their department(s) (Andeweg, 2000; Blondel and Manning, 2002). If circular delegation occurs (because ministers manage to influence cabinet decisions in their own interests as head of a department, and naturally they have no incentive to control or sanction their own actions as agents) and ministers are autonomous from all actors preceding them in the chain of delegation, then agency loss is very likely and is almost impossible to retrieve later in the chain, as ministers are also principals of the last intervening actors, the civil service. In a way, although *proximity* between principals and agents is often desirable for the process and the outcomes of the democratic chain, an excess of proximity such as this dual role played by ministers may on the other hand be detrimental.

According to Laver and Shepsle (1996), ministers are mere agents of their party, as they are bound to pursue the party's policy preferences in their jurisdiction. As they cannot be agents of principals other than their party (either cabinet as a whole or other principals intervening at preceding links of the parliamentary chain) they are policy dictators in their jurisdiction. If this assumption were to be empirically verified, then according to the schizophrenic situation of cabinet ministers in the chain of delegation, the risk of agency loss would be at its highest as individual ministers' interests would dominate over government's interests with no possibility of control except from the party. Andeweg (2000) made an inventory of causes for a lower level of ministerial discretion than the one assumed by Laver and Shepsle: prime ministers (especially in single-party majority governments), coalition leadership (inner cabinets, coalition committees or party summits) and coalition agreements (especially if not all ministers have been involved in the negotiations and if the agreement is comprehensive and detailed) are according to this scholar sources of a hierarchical structure within the cabinet that constrains and controls the activities of individual ministers.

Collective decision making (through majority vote or consensus) creates a sense of collective responsibility, as even decisions that are not taken by an individual minister must be endorsed by all ministers. The *socio-psychological environment* that exists in *small bodies* like a cabinet exerts pressure on ministers to conform to cabinet decisions rather than act independently. Cabinets consisting of a compact group, where all major policy decisions have to be ratified by cabinet as a whole and which all members then have to publicly support and implement in their departments, are 'collective systems of government'. Under such a system, individual ministers are less likely to be autonomous with regard to their principal (government).[16] Andeweg (2000) argues that *overlapping jurisdictions* make potential conflicts more frequent and thus require more compliance with the full cabinet's interests. The coalition control technique of allocating junior ministers from a party different from that of the minister in charge is a specific type of this phenomenon, but the consequence in terms of the reduction of information asymmetry between the portfolio holder and the rest of the cabinet is similar. Ministerial discretion should then be lower in *small* cabinets than in larger ones, as members of the cabinets are forced to be in charge of *multiple portfolios*, which implies a higher probability of overlap with fellow ministers' jurisdictions and also reduces their capacity of specialization. The size of the cabinet is less proportionally related to the size of the population.

Nevertheless, we expect that small countries, not the least because they face problems of political personnel reservoir, will have on average smaller cabinets than in larger states. Hence, we expect that they will adopt, *ceteris paribus*, a more collective style of decision making than cabinets of larger states, as holding multiple portfolios increases the chances of overlapping jurisdictions and prevents ministers from deepening information asymmetry by specializing in their fields of competence. We also expect collective decision making to be more applicable in smaller cabinets.

In the case of minority government, *parliamentary committees* also constrain ministers a great deal. Ministers have to rely on a majority to pass legislation, and bills actively initiated or substantially amended by parliament may be written in such a way that they have almost no discretion (Huber and Shipan, 2002). This is a more desirable bypass (*short cut*) of a link and a greater source of limitation on ministerial autonomy than the one provided by parties in multi-party coalitions.[17] However, just as government formation can be more or less responsive to electoral results, the *selection of ministers* may well be influenced by *voters* in countries where the electoral system makes them more decisive: preferential votes help identify the candidates who are most supported by the population, and party leaders are thus constrained in their choice of ministerial personnel. Hence this type of *short cut* should be *ceteris paribus* more common (and potentially less dangerous, as the reputation of candidates is more likely to be well known by voters) in smaller political systems.

With respect to screening and selections mechanisms, Andeweg (2000) points out that individual ministers may, however, be tempted to follow preferences they did not have when they were selected, and thus may ruin the efforts put into these mechanisms. Indeed, the origins of preferences may well be endogenous, as ministers can 'go native' and defend their department's interests or their party's more fiercely than the cabinet as a whole, once they get into office. This risk may well be higher in small cabinets where ministers have to head multiple departments and have no incentive to specialize. A minister who is not an expert in the department's field is in a bad position in terms of information asymmetry with regard to his civil service. Thus, he is more likely to be 'captured' and to relay exaggerated demands from his department. He is also less likely to act autonomously from cabinet because he is not in an advantageous position in terms of information asymmetry with regard to the rest of the cabinet. Both the weight of cabinet's collective decision making and the influence of the civil service are thus likely to exert strong limitations on the autonomy of ministers' actions in small political settings.

How does the case of Luxembourg fare with regard to this link? First, the Grand Ducal Decree of 1857 concerning the organization of the government stipulates that all decisions that need the consent of the Grand Duke are to be discussed and decided *collectively* by the cabinet (Majerus, 1990: 174). Second, the PM chairs the Council of Ministers (cabinet meeting), sets the agenda, and coordinates ministerial departments. Yet the PM is *not legally a hierarchical chief* over the other ministers. Although it is not a formal rule, either the PM or the vice-PM acting on the PM's behalf, may nevertheless call for a cabinet discussion of any departmental issue. Hence, a minister's individual discretion is residual in the sense that the management of his department's competences is subject to collective deliberation.[18] Since the cabinet is *small* (currently thirteen ministers, one minister-delegate and one Secretary of State, and at the beginning of the 1970s the whole cabinet still consisted of only seven ministers), there is no institutionalized inner cabinet and all issues are discussed and decided in the full cabinet meeting. Because multiple portfolios are in the hands of a small number of ministers, overlaps are frequent and make this collective decision-making process necessary. As the number of actors is rather small, such a mode is not inefficient and reinforces cabinet solidarity. Finally, the *coalition agreement* and instruments of coalition maintenance (see Dumont and De Winter, 2003) further limit the discretion of individual ministers with regard to the whole cabinet. Thus, a series of institutional arrangements have been designed (where their efficient working is probably facilitated by the size of the government) to prevent excessive proximity between cabinet and individual ministers.

Ministerial portfolios have remained concentrated in few hands, despite the fact that the number of ministers has more than doubled in the post-war period. In 2004, Prime Minister Juncker is also the Minister of State (head of all the administration) and the Minister of Finance. Former prime ministers held up to four additional concurrent responsibilities, including Agriculture, Labour, Social affairs and Defence (as PM Dupong did immediately following World War II). In these circumstances, specialization is not possible and arguably ministers have to rely on their civil servants to provide them with expertise. Other examples from the 2004 cabinet include: one minister for the separate departments of Justice, Defence and the Budget and another has responsibility for Labour, Employment, Culture, Higher Education, Research and Cults. In the past, there were combinations that were even less homogeneous, and overlaps often involve concurrent ministers.

From ministers to civil service

At this stage, a single minister (individual actor) delegates and controls implementation to a large collective agent consisting of many bureaucrats.

Smallness again has an important effect, as the level of *expertise* of implementers is likely to be lower than in countries where the civil service is a very large body. In smaller systems, either civil servants will be asked to *specialize* so that policies are efficiently implemented, but then there will often be only one civil servant in charge (where there will be dozens in larger countries), raising problems of *accessibility and availability*, or the civil service will be organized so that the process of implementation of a specific policy does not rely on a single person, but this at the expense of technical expertise. Huber and McCarty (2004: 490) state that 'in any polity governed by the rule of law, bureaucratic behaviour during policy implementation is conditioned by the bureaucrats' fear that they could be punished if caught taking actions that the law forbids (or not taking actions that the law requires)' but reveal that, if bureaucratic *capacity* is low, then bureaucrats will be harder to control because their inability diminishes their incentive to do their best to implement the policies decided by their principal. In turn, politicians may refrain from framing precise legislation such as ministerial decrees or circulars issued to limit the discretion of their civil servants, as drafting them is costly and bureaucrats are not likely to abide by them anyway. The threat of cuts in budgets that could encourage ministers and their civil servants to work hand in hand (if reallocations of budgets within ministries are left to the discretion of the minister) in a highly capable bureaucracy is not likely to have such a positive effect either, as the implementation of such a sanction would render the civil service even less capable. This problem of capacity is distinct from that of information asymmetry, which has been proved to affect delegating procedures and outcomes. We believe that both may have an impact, either separately or through interaction, and we believe that the size of the civil service is a factor among others.[19]

As for problems of *information asymmetry*, one notices that *ex ante* mechanisms are harder to implement at this stage, as the typical recruitment of the agents is not internal to the pool of principals. The bulk of civil servants are normally recruited through exams on their knowledge and expertise, and their preferences are generally unknown. Depending on systems, ministers may be allowed to adapt to this agency loss potential by hiring a personal staff (ministerial cabinet) that will do most of the elaboration of policies, take important implementation decisions, and control the behaviour of civil servants. They may also name or promote high civil servants who they know are close to their ideal preference points, and may even be able to *politicize* the ministry through a number of instruments in order to have 'cosy relations' with chosen civil servants, and thus enhance *proximity*.[20] Ministerial volatility could be an indicator of *proximity* between ministers and civil servants, as long-term ministers are more likely to have a cosy relationship (or at least a relationship based on trust and mutual knowledge of preferences) with their department and to have developed a level of expertise allowing them to control their agents more effectively. Given the scarcity of political personnel who can be seen as experts in a field, the level of ministerial volatility should be lower, *ceteris paribus*, in smaller political systems.[21] Anyway the instruments mentioned here as potential facilitators of proximity are controlled by political parties and, thus, the problem of diverted accountability makes this type of solution undesirable with regard to the ideal-typical chain.

We argue that smallness increases problems of information availability and acquisition, as ministers who handle multiple portfolios have less opportunity to specialize and control each department. Moreover, with multiple portfolios owners in coalition governments, risks of department overlaps are greater, which means that civil servants may have multiple principals and can play them off against each other. Thus, both in terms of hidden information and risks of hidden action, smallness is at this level of the chain dangerous.

The assessment of the quality of this link is more problematic than others: only the delegation and accountability processes can be analysed, as the performance in terms of policy outputs and outcomes is typically influenced by a large number of other external factors. Hence it is very difficult to attribute responsibility of misbehaviour to civil servants as many other factors may have contributed to (the absence of) a specific policy outcome. We argue that smallness and its effect on proximity make it more difficult for principals to *sanction* their agents, either positively (reward) or negatively. Although identifying the administrative actors responsible for policy outputs is easier than in larger systems, the close ties existing between ministers and highly placed civil servants enhance trust and reduce the incentives to sanction, all the more so if the latter are politicized. The political costs of clear responsibility may in effect be too high in small webs of personal, intertwined relationships among politicians and between them and bureaucrats. Proximity between principals and agents may become excessive in small systems, as the risk of sanctions' spill-over (resulting in principals being hurt themselves when they sanction their agents) becomes correspondingly higher, because these actors are perceived by voters and MPs as people working in close contact and the strong ties between bureaucrats are likely to affect their relationship with their principal if one of them is being punished. Hence politicians are prevented from sanctioning their bureaucrats for misbehaviour. All this should make for blurred accountability, especially at this last stage, in smaller systems.

According to OECD sources on Luxembourg, the number of civil servants working in ministries is roughly 1,000 full-time equivalents in 2001, with an additional 4,000 full-time equivalents working in agencies of the central administration (e.g. direct taxation administration). Although figures may differ according to various definitions, the share of the public employment over the labour force as a whole (in 2003 the state employed approximately 20,000 people in the central administration, note that this figure includes teachers and people working in other public administration services, STATEC, 2004) is one of the lowest in OECD countries. This means that – although our argument is about the absolute number of bureaucrats – their relative share is also small as compared to the whole labour force.[22] This lack of resources in personnel raises the question of capacity. Although interpersonal knowledge increases trust between principals and agents, and informal, flexible working rules may emerge to compensate for this lack of resources, limited capacity is clearly an important constraint for a smooth delivery of desired policy outputs.

In Luxembourg, civil service positions are awarded on the basis of competitive exams. Although politicization in the lower and middle ranks is very low, top civil service appointments and promotions are highly politicized. Co-operation between government and the civil service is assured via the appointment of about fifty government advisers, organized in a four-level hierarchy, who become the ministers' personal staff. Most are drawn from the top civil service to ensure that they have the requisite experience. A General Secretary of the Council of Ministers is chosen from among the more than 400 civil servants in the Cabinet Office. Because most of these 'promotions' are made along party lines, those who are assigned to a department other than the one in which they were previously working are likely to be reassigned to much less attractive positions if their party is not part of the subsequent government. Thus, screening and selection (*ex ante*) procedures also intervene in the relationship between ministers and civil servants to assure the former that their agents will not betray their preferences.

The Minister of State heads the entire government administration. The accountability of civil servants working in ministries is thus doubly indirect, as they are accountable for their doings neither directly nor via their departmental minister. Instead citizens with complaints address them to the Minister of State, not to the relevant departmental minister. Reforms in 2003 have introduced new instruments aimed at giving citizens a greater say through the creation of an ombudsman, and greater transparency in disciplinary decisions against civil servants is expected with the creation of an adviser to government for instructing disciplinary cases. Thus, the problem that size causes, in terms of excessive proximity between ministers and civil servants for issuing sanctions against agents, seems to be taken care of. Individual ministers are politically accountable to the parliament for the actions of their civil servants, and they may be asked to respond to parliamentary inquiries. On the other hand, MPs are provided with information from the civil service only through the government as intermediary. The problem of hidden information, specifically the problem of obtaining information for the purpose of holding the government accountable, is thus a constant concern of parliamentary committee members. Orders to withhold (or delay) information may come from cabinet ministers, and the politicization of the top civil service means that ministers are obeyed, despite the fact that hearings and the consultative advice of professional chambers (third-party testimonies) are designed to mitigate this potential information problem.

Finally, in terms of ministerial volatility, one has to take into account that one party, the CSV, was almost always in power and that pillars in the society have made portfolio allocation more constrained by party lines than guided by personnel expertise: for instance, the CSV has always held the posts of Prime Minister, Minister of Finance, Minister of Agriculture and Minister of Education (the latter two portfolios are very salient for their 'pillar') whilst the departments of Social Affairs and Public Works were always headed by Socialist ministers and Middle Classes by Liberals (Dumont and De Winter, 2000). Moreover, as the number of specialists or heavyweights expecting to head one of the small number of competences available to their party is very small, ministerial volatility is low in Luxembourg. Ministers tend to stay for long periods in cabinet with the same competences (three times lower than the average ministerial turnover calculated by Huber and Shipan in their 2002 research on nineteen countries). The average ministerial tenure is quite high at 6.8 years in the 1945–1984 period, according to Bakema (1991),[23] but this seems to be due to the permanence of the CSV in power. On the basis of Bakema's data, Bergman *et al.* (2003: 204) calculated the proportion of ministers that had a minimum duration in office of four years, and from among the Western European countries Luxembourg had the lowest rate (46 per cent).[24] Thus, because there were ten changes in the party composition of government (partial alternations) in the thirteen elections fought in the post-war period, the average experience of junior party ministers is naturally lower than that of the CSV's ministers. Thus, these ministers are usually in a worse position in terms of information asymmetry with regard to their department and thus more likely to rely on their agents.

Conclusion

We aimed at exploring the relations between three size-related concepts regarding the shape of, and the actors involved in, delegation and accountability processes in parliamentary democracies. We argue that measurement is feasible (see indicators proposed in Table 3.1) and that there seems to be evidence of *systematic relations* between smallness, proximity and short cuts; although a number of theoretically relevant control variables should also be included. Nevertheless, we argue that smallness (the size of actors, number of bodies) is one of a limited number of variables of the political environment that has *potential effects on each link of the parliamentary democracy chain, particularly on the proximity between actors and on possibilities of short cuts along this chain.* This is an important quality for a variable if we advocate for empirically studying the whole chain. The main reason we believe that considering the full chain is necessary is that significant relationships at one link may be hidden because of the impact of a short cut (bypass of links) in the chain, or perhaps more likely, short cuts may turn significant results into insignificant ones, and thus may completely alter the conclusions and ruin careful efforts at analysing a single link.

We have seen that Luxembourg seems to fit in neatly with the simple and indirect chain of delegation and accountability of parliamentary

Table 3.1 Some indicators of size-related variables on the delegation and accountability chain

Delegation and accountability chain	Smallness	Proximity	Short cuts
Voters – MPs	Number of voters Size of electoral constituencies	Number of MPs/voters Decisiveness of voters' choice (electoral system rules and behavioural consequences) Effective turnover of MPs in Parliament	
MPs – cabinet	Number of chambers controlling government Number of MPs (absolute, per parliamentary group, per permanent specialist committee, per minister)	Number of ministers drawn from the parliament (former MPs) Duration of individual career in Parliament and/or in a specific committee before becoming minister	Electoral responsiveness in composition of government
Cabinet – ministers	Size (number of ministers) Number and duration of governments	Internal mode of decision-making (collegiality versus majority rule)	Electoral responsiveness in the choice of ministers
Ministers – civil service	Number of ministerial portfolios/ministers Size of the civil service	Ministerial cabinets Ministerial volatility Partisan nomination of high civil servant (spoil or merit system) Proportion of tenured civil servants/contracts	

democracies. Strøm's proposition (2000) that this chain might be most applicable to small, homogeneous and stable societies in which principals have greater faith in their screening procedures is thus confirmed in this case. Altogether, we have been able to illuminate some of the relations between smallness, proximity and short cuts, although certain links and operationalizations were more or less successful with this regard.

We believe that the way forward is to formalize a fully specified model suitable for empirical testing on *comparative* data. So far, we have been unable to answer the questions 'When is small really small?' and 'Where is the cut-off point?' We agree with Collier and Adcock (1999) that in any case the decision to use dichotomous or graded measures of a concept depends in part on the goals of the research. Moreover, we do not yet know at what stage of the chain smallness has the greatest effect on the proximity between principals and agents and on the possibility of short cuts or whether this is different from one country to another (there may be quite different shapes of 'funnels', with more or less drastic reductions of the number of actors at each link, in comparative terms), even leaving aside the degree of linearity of these effects. An initial empirical comparative test should be performed with countries quite extreme in terms of size but as comparable as possible on other variables of political environment (e.g. federalism, party system, etc.) that are likely to have an effect on this democratic chain.

Finally, we suggest the following: assuming the *principal–agent framework*, politicians adapt to their changing environment by designing *ex ante* or *ex post* control mechanisms that limit possibilities of agency loss. Given their informational advantages which are likely to prevent adverse selection, their relative lack of expertise and the costs of sanctioning, politicians in smaller systems are *ceteris paribus* less likely to put effort into designing specific accountability mechanisms than politicians in larger systems. Both because they need less and because they are less capable of imposing control and sanctions/rewards on their agents; hence, *the smaller the political system, the smaller the degree of adaptation* (through the design of institutional reforms aimed at improving smooth delegation with less agency loss).

As assessing the *quality* of delegation procedures is a difficult enterprise (in terms of decision-making process and policy outputs), we propose a focus on the *quantity and direction (that is, towards more or less discretion for agents)* of such institutional provisions regarding the relations between actors of the ideal-typical chain.[25] Thus, they should be, *ceteris paribus, less numerous* in smaller countries than in larger ones. If we set up a model explaining the quantity of institutional adaptations in parliamentary democracies then we should control for a number of other theoretically relevant factors.

If we find no systematic pattern distinguishing delegation and accountability *processes* in smaller and larger countries, another type of analysis would be to test whether we observe systematic differences in the policy *outcome* of the full delegation chain. The evaluation of the outcome of the general process by voters, who are the ultimate principals, would then be an appropriate dependent variable. A proxy suitable for comparative analysis may be the level of citizen satisfaction with the process ('how well democracy works') expressed in surveys. As trust in agents is likely to be affected by variables like the size of the system, we expect that size will have an impact on the evaluation of the working of democracy whether or not institutional differences between smaller and larger systems are observed. Initial empirical results (Strøm *et al.*, 2003) indeed suggest that smaller political settings display more voter satisfaction.

Hence, the aim of future research on the effects of smallness is not trivial, as the rejection of our broad hypothesis would run counter to one of the most important aspects of the principal–agent framework. This would lead us to a second stage, the assessment of the effect of smallness on delegation outcomes, and would also be a way of considering the trade-off between input and output legitimization of political systems described by Scharpf (1997). In case of substantial findings in this second stage, we could eventually tackle the normative question of the optimal size for political systems.

Notes

1 Although this empirical evidence is limited, the effect of the size of population is significant even when controlled for five other variables, including measures of competitiveness of the party system, partisan cohesion, external constraints on the chain of parliamentary democracy and level of economic development.

2 For example, activities like screening, selection and monitoring are easier to install.

3 From the German Confederation (1815–1866) and Zollverein (1842–1918), through the Union économique belgo-luxembourgeoise (1921), the 1944 Benelux Treaty on the Customs Union, founding member of the European Communities, and now the centre of regional integration experiments, including parts of France, Belgium and Germany (*La Grande Région – Die Grossregion, EuRegio SaarLorLuxRhin*).

4 In terms of political offer, the number of competing parties is of course affected by the electoral system chosen, as pointed out by Duverger's law (1951), but as Colomer (2003: 1) argues, 'it's parties that choose electoral systems', and the features of the political setting they are evolving in certainly figure among the data they use to come up to a choice. See below.

5 Although a proper empirical study is still to be conducted, it seems that the use of systems allowing real preferential votes is more (and increasingly more, as recent reforms in Scotland and New Zealand can attest) widespread for local elections, that are by essence small political settings. One nevertheless finds such preferential vote systems for national elections of large countries (see Australia's alternative vote, for instance).

6 As this is the first link of the chain, the possibility of short cuts involve voters and the government and/or ministers rather than MPs. We treat this question in the following section of the chapter.

7 The legislative turnover variable should account for the process of selection made by parties first: when an incumbent is simply withdrawn from the party list by his party, legislative turnover is not an indicator of the quality of control by voters any more, but by parties (that may or may not use the anticipation of voters' reaction as a criterion for withdrawal).

8 Aside from the Chamber of Deputies, the Council of State, designed in 1856 as the legal adviser to the government, has an important role in the legislative process, as no vote can be taken on a bill proposal or amendment until the Council of State issues its advice on this piece of legislation. Although it also has some kind of suspensive veto rights, it nevertheless cannot be considered as a second chamber, as in any case its members are not elected by voters (see Dumont and De Winter, 2003).

9 The largest district, that is, not a national constituency, in terms of magnitude is to be found in Germany, with seventy-seven MPs to be elected. Depending on the electoral formula, district magnitude has, however, no relationship with the size of the population of the country: hence the United Kingdom elects MPs on single-member constituencies whilst a much smaller country like the Netherlands has a national constituency that elects all 150 MPs.

10 The current estimation of the level of inter-party *panachage* for the 2004 elections (on the basis of post-electoral opinion polls) is higher than 35 per cent of the total votes cast.

11 Even though the most widely read newspapers appear nowadays more critical of the traditional parties they used to have links with, the written press is still politicized. For instance, *Le Journal* is the official newspaper of the Liberal Party (DP); the two largest newspapers are the *Wort*, with connections to the Christian Democrats (CSV), and the *Tageblatt*, which is the official newspaper of the Socialist trade union (OGBL) and is also the newspaper that the Socialist Party (LSAP) still recommends to its members in the official statutes of the party. The latter two newspapers are nevertheless becoming increasingly critical of these parties.

12 Most parliaments in Western Europe rely on ten to twenty permanent specialized committees, according to Mattson and Strøm (1995: 260).

13 Even though there is some degree of proportionality between the size of the assembly (highly correlated to the size of the population, see above) and the size of government, the latter cannot consist of a couple of ministers only even for very small countries, owing to the variety of public services to be performed by any sovereign state.

14 De Winter (1991) has collected data on these variables for Western European countries (1945–1984).

15 Cabinet defeats in parliament account only for 11 per cent of government terminations whilst conflict about policy between coalition parties accounts for 24 per cent. These figures taken from Müller and Strøm (2000) show that governments' fate depends more on government parties' will than on the effectiveness of control activities by the parliament.

16 Blondel and Manning (2002) refer to the 'reliability' of individual ministers.

17 Party executives are usually involved in the resolution of important conflicts; they also monitor their ministers in weekly meetings with party leaders and play the most important role in ministerial personnel selection (see Müller and Strøm, 2000).

18 Even if consensus is always sought in the Council of Ministers, it is not required. Decisions can be made by *majority rule*. Ministers who do not vote in favour of a particular decision *can excuse themselves from collective responsibility* by recording their opposition in the written report of the cabinet meeting (see Dumont and De Winter, 2003).

19 Some scholars have nevertheless shown that, in their relations with the EU institutions, for instance, small member states manage to compensate for their very limited staff resources by establishing clear priorities in the broad range of issues to be dealt with, greater informality and greater flexibility in working procedures, and greater autonomy for civil servants in issues that are not regarded as one of the few national interests smaller states typically have (Thorhallsson, 2000; Lacgrcid *et al.*, 2004).

20 We see that problems of information and capacity may interact. Huber and McCarty (2004) observe that politicians also have the greatest incentives to politicize the civil service when the latter has a low capacity.

21 Laver and Shepsle (2000) have developed the same kind of argument for small parties, as the latter cannot be expected to have a reservoir of talent that enables them to fill all ministerial positions in a single-party minority cabinet.

22 However, as Luxembourg nationals represent less than 35 per cent of the total interior labour force (people living in France, Belgium and Germany but working in Luxembourg account for 38 per cent and foreigners residing in Luxembourg about 27 per cent), and as 90 per cent of civil servants are nationals, the rate of Luxembourgers working in the public sector is quite high (around one-third).

23 This is the highest average ministerial duration of the fourteen countries reported in Bergman *et al.* (2003: 204).

24 In the first ten years of the post-war period, partial elections (roughly half the MPs were renewed) were held every three years, and there were usually reshuffles on these occasions. Also, the only two cabinet resignations of Luxembourg's post-war governmental history occurred in the period analysed by Bakema. This also partially explains why the percentage of ministers with more than four years in office is so low. As since 1954 the parliamentary term lasts five years and the cabinets are stable, the proportion should now be higher, despite some rare individual resignations.)

25 For instance, using the richness of information gathered in Strøm *et al.* (2003).

References

Allegrezza, S., Hirsch, M. and von Kunitzki, N. (eds) (2003) *L'Histoire, le présent et l'avenir du modèle luxembourgeois*, Luxembourg: Institut d'études européennes et internationales du Luxembourg.

Andeweg, R. B. (2000) 'Ministers as Double Agents? The Delegation Process between Cabinet and Ministers', *European Journal of Political Research*, 37: 377–395.

Andeweg, R. B. and Nijzink, L. (1995) 'Beyond the Two-body Image: Relations between Ministers and MPs', in H. Döring (ed.) *Parliaments and Majority Rule in Western Europe*, Frankfurt am Main: Campus and New York: St. Martin's Press.

Bakema, W. E. (1991) 'The Ministerial Career', In J. Blondel and J.-L. Thiébault (eds) *The Profession of Government Minister in Western Europe*, Basingstoke: Macmillan.

Bergman, T. (1993) 'Formation Rules and Minority Governments', *European Journal of Political Research*, 23: 55–66.

Bergman, T., Müller, W. C., Strøm, K. and Blomgren, M. (2003) 'Democratic Delegation and Accountability: Cross-national Patterns', in K. Strøm, W. C. Müller and T. Bergman (eds) *Delegation and Accountability in Parliamentary Democracies*, Oxford: Oxford University Press.

Blondel, J. and Manning, N. (2002) 'Do Ministers do What they Say? Ministerial Unreliability, Collegial and Hierarchical Governments', *Political Studies*, 50: 455–476.

Centre de recherche et d'information socio-politiques (CRISP) (1995) *Les Élections au Grand-Duché de Luxembourg. Données sur les scrutins de 1974, 1979,1984,1989 et 1994. Résultats et comportements*, Etude réalisée pour la Chambre des Députés du Grand-Duché de Luxembourg, Brussels: CRISP.

Centre de recherche public Gabriel Lippmann (CRPGL) (2000) *Les Élections au Grand-Duché de Luxembourg. Rapport sur les élections législatives du 13 juin 1999*, Etude réalisée pour la Chambre des Députés, ed. F. Fehlen and Ph. Poirier, Luxembourg: CRPGL.

Collier, D. and Adcock, R. (1999) 'Democracy and Dichotomies. A Pragmatic

Approach to Choices about Concepts', *Annual Review of Political Science*, 2: 537–568.

Colomer, J. M. (2003) 'It's Parties that choose Electoral Systems (or Duverger's Laws Upside Down)', paper presented at the American Political Association annual meeting, Philadelphia, 28–31 September.

Cox, G. (1997) *Making Votes Count: Strategic Coordination in the World's Electoral Systems*, Cambridge: Cambridge University Press.

De Winter, L. (1991) 'Parliamentary and Party Pathways to Cabinet', in J. Blondel and F. Müller-Rommel (eds) *Governing Together. The Extent and Limits of Joint Decision-making in Western European Cabinets*, London: Macmillan.

De Winter, L. (1995) 'The Role of Parliament in Government Formation and Resignation', in H. Döring (ed.) *Parliaments and Majority Rule in Western Europe*, New York: St Martin's Press.

Dumont, P. and De Winter, L. (2000) 'Luxembourg: Stable Coalitions in a Pivotal Party System', in W. C. Müller and K. Strøm (eds) *Government Coalitions in Western Europe*, Oxford: Oxford University Press.

Dumont, P. and De Winter, L. (2003) 'Luxembourg: A Case of More "Direct" Delegation and Accountability', in K. Strøm, W. C. Müller and T. Bergman (eds) *Delegation and Accountability in Parliamentary Democracies*, Oxford: Oxford University Press.

Duverger, M. (1951) *Les partis politiques*, Paris: Armand Colin.

Farrell, D. M. and McAllister, I. (2004) 'Voter Satisfaction and Electoral Systems. Does Preferential Voting in Candidate-centered Systems make a Difference?' Working paper, Irvine CA: Center for the Study of Democracy, University of California.

Huber, J. D. (2000) 'Delegation to Civil Servants in Parliamentary Democracies', *European Journal of Political Research*, 37: 397–413.

Huber, J. D. and McCarty, N. (2004) 'Bureaucratic Capacity, Delegation and Political Reform', *American Political Science Review*, 98: 481–494.

Huber, J. D. and Shipan, C. (2002) *Deliberate Discretion? The Institutional Foundations of Bureaucratic Autonomy*, New York: Cambridge University Press.

Katzenstein, P. (1985) *Small States in World Markets. Industrial Policy in Europe*, Ithaca NY: Cornell University Press.

Kiewiet, D. R. and McCubbins, M. D. (1991) *The Logic of Delegation*, Chicago: University of Chicago Press.

Laegreid, P., Steinthorsson, R. S. and Thorhallsson, B. (2004) 'Europeanization of Central Government Administration in the Nordic States', *Journal of Common Market Studies*, 42: 347–369.

Laver, M. and Shepsle, K. A. (1996) *Making and Breaking Governments*, Cambridge: Cambridge University Press.

Laver, M. and Shepsle, K. A. (2000) 'Ministrables and Government Formation: Munchkins, Players and Big Beasts of the Jungle', *Journal of Theoretical Politics*, 12 (1): 113–124.

Majerus, P. (1990) *L'Etat Luxembourgeois. Manuel de droit constitutionnel et de droit administratif*, Luxembourg: Imprimerie Saint-Paul.

Mattson, I. and Strøm, K. (1995) 'Parliamentary Committees', in H. Döring (ed.) *Parliaments and Majority Rule in Western Europe*, New York: St Martin's Press.

Mitchell, P. L. (2000) 'Voters and their Representatives. Electoral Institutions and Delegation in Parliamentary Democracies', *European Journal of Political Research*, 37: 335–351.

Müller, W. C. (2000) 'Political Parties in Parliamentary Democracies: Making Delegation and Accountability Work', *European Journal of Political Research*, 37: 309–333.

Müller, W. C. and Strøm, K. (eds) (2000) *Coalition Governments in Western Europe*, Oxford: Oxford University Press.

OECD, Human Resources Management (HRM) (2002) *Highlights of the Public Sector Pay and Employment Trends. A 2002 Update*, Document PUMA/HRM (2002)7, Available at: http://www.olis.oecd.org/olis/2002doc.nsf/43bb6130e5e86e5fc 12569fa005d004c/2bb07a980c0242ecc1256c480027f34b/$FILE/JT00132606.PDF (accessed 10 August 2004).

Saalfeld, T. (2000) 'Members of parliament and governments in Western Europe. Agency Relations and Problems of Oversight', *European Journal of Political Research*, 37: 353–376.

Scharpf, F. W. (1997) *Games Real Actors Play. Actor-centered Institutionalism in Policy Research*, Boulder CO: Westview Press.

STATEC (2004) *Le Luxembourg en chiffres*, Luxembourg: Statec. Available HTTP: http://www.statec.lu/html_fr/publications/luxenchiffres2004FR.pdf   (accessed 10 September 2004).

Strøm, K. (2000) 'Delegation and Accountability in Parliamentary Democracies', *European Journal of Political Research*, 37: 260–290.

Strøm, K., Müller, W. C. and Bergman, T. (2003) 'Challenges to Parliamentary Democracy', in K. Strøm, W. C. Müller and T. Bergman (eds) *Delegation and Accountability in Parliamentary Democracies*, Oxford: Oxford University Press.

Thorhallsson, B. (2000) 'The Administrative Working Procedures of Smaller States in the Decision-making Process of the EU', paper presented at the fiftieth annual conference of the Political Studies Association UK, London, 10–13 April.

Tirole, J. (1986) 'Hierarchies and Bureaucracies. On the Role of Collusion in Organizations', *Journal of Law, Economics, and Organization*, 2: 181–214.

4   A theory of efficient delegation

David Epstein and Sharyn O'Halloran

Most of the other chapters in this volume address the ubiquitous nature of delegated authority within any governmental system. Be it a presidential or a classic Westminster model, inherent in representative democracy (we would venture to say even in non-democratic systems, but less clearly so) is a hierarchical relation between an electorate and those empowered with the rights and responsibilities to enact public laws. Whether this chain of delegation be long and detached from direct elections, or short, with many points of accountability (see Strøm *et al.*), all must resolve to make public policy that fundamentally impacts the well-being and prosperity of its citizens. From our vantage point, the question is not whether delegation occurs, for surely it does, or if different forms of government allow more or less accountability, for surely they do. Rather, given a particular system of government, a chain of delegated relations, how will elected officials choose to design the public laws that they are empowered to enact?

Let us begin from the ground up. Associated with every piece of public policy are a number of key decisions – all the details of standards, rates, procedures, personnel, winners, losers, and so on. In making these decisions the legislative body can set up its own internal institutions (we usually think in terms of standing committees) to evaluate policy choices, give power to external actors (here we think in terms of an executive, bureaucracy or quasi-governmental organization), or employ some combination of the two. If the legislative body decides to delegate authority to an external body, it can either provide detailed instructions in the implementing legislation or give wide latitude in interpreting the law.

For example, when the British Parliament or US Congress passes a health care law, it can specify the details concerning eligibility, benefits, coverage, cost containment, and scope of services themselves, or leave these details for bureaucrats to fill in. When the European Union enacts directives, it can make the requirements for compliance quite explicit, or leave more room for individual member states to interpret the statute according to local laws and political exigencies. When the United Nations passes a peacekeeping resolution, it can include a variety of checks on the use of force by troops, or leave these decisions to commanders 'on the ground' The fundamental question of delegation is: where does legislating end and implementation begin, and what impact does this choice have on policy outcomes?

Our answer to these questions begins with the observation that the amount of discretionary authority, latitude in policy making, delegated is a decision made by political actors trying to further their own political ends. When deciding where policy will be made, these actors therefore trade off the internal costs of policy production against the external costs of delegation. Thus, to borrow the language of industrial organization, the decision to delegate is similar to a firm's make-or-buy decision.

Like owners of a firm, we assert that politicians will choose the mode of policy production that most directly benefits their own bottom line, be it through direct action, through delegation to outside agencies, or some measure of each. In the end, legislators will choose to arrange the specifics of policy making in the most politically efficient way possible.

Note well the term 'politically efficient'. Policy making may well not be technically efficient, allocating resources according to their greatest marginal value; indeed, it may be quite inefficient according to a strict economic benchmark.[1] Rather, we claim that policy will be made in such a way as to maximize politicians' own goals, bringing policy outcomes as close to their own preferred policies as possible. Politicians will prefer to do things themselves as long as the benefits they derive from doing so outweigh the costs; otherwise, they will delegate to others.[2]

In the political sphere, what do these costs comprise? Here we bring together two literatures well known in the American context and juxtapose them as competing models of policy production. The internal costs of delegation stem from lack of expertise and the uncertainty that arises from committee-floor competition over policy content. The external costs of delegation stem from the standard principal–agent costs of moral hazard and adverse selection. The extent that a political system or organizational structure mitigates these costs is the extent to which one form of policy production will be deemed superior to the other.

In this chapter, we first motivate our theory with reference to the previous US literature on delegation, which we summarize and put into a comparative context. We then present our view of efficient delegation and analyse a formal model of politicians' make-or-buy decision. The last section concludes and applies our approach to a number of specific delegation settings.

Delegation, American style

To European eyes, the traditional US literature on delegating authority must look rather strange, centring as it did on the normative question of whether such arrangements were legitimate or not in a democratic society. Is delegation, to put it simply, an abdication of Congress's duty to make law, passing to executive branch actors state authority that should rightfully be exercised only by those directly responsible to the public via regular elections?

Some scholars took exactly this view, arguing that the lack of active congressional participation was a sure sign of failure in US democratic institutions. Lowi (1969) was one of the most strident members of this camp, accusing legislators of abandoning their duties by delegating power to unelected bureaucrats and omnipotent congressional committees. He believed that the original delegations of power in the late nineteenth century, were well conceived and structured so as to make agencies hew to congressional intent. But, over time, delegation became less and less tied to specific mandates and more open-ended, allowing agencies an illegitimate amount of discretion. Legislators had abdicated responsibility for the execution of public policy, he argued, to be replaced by 'interest-group liberalism', meaning that agencies reacted to the wishes of those organized groups which pressured them for favourable policy decisions. This, in turn, was wont to devolve into agency 'capture' – public power exercised for the benefit of a few private interests, against the public good and unsupervised by democratically elected legislators.

Scholars of the public administration school, on the other hand, argued that bureaucrats were by and large dedicated public servants who could do their jobs well if they could be assured that political meddling would be kept to a minimum. Indeed, Huntington (1971) claimed that Congress does best by restricting its role to constituency service, leaving detailed regulation to policy experts in the bureaucracy. This view harks back to the turn-of-the-century Progressive civil service revolution, where agencies were first established to 'take the politics out of policy'.[3] Accordingly, mechanisms that insulated agencies from political control were seen as beneficial to the smooth functioning of government.

Why all this fuss over delegation? After all, everyone does it; indeed, it is ludicrous to think that the entire public business of the United States can be efficiently run by its 536 directly elected members of government (435 members of the House, 100 senators, and one president). Why this peculiarly American obsession with the notion that administrative policy making through regulations is illegitimate?

One might argue that it derives from the historical equation in the American mind that 'legislatures = legitimate policy making', since power is most directly exercised by the people when legislatures make the law. Indeed the schism over the proper balance between executive and legislative power dates back to the 1787 Constitutional Convention. For many delegates, Congress was supposed to be the leading branch of government, the guardian of popular liberty that would prevent the restoration of British tyranny. Indeed Chief Justice John Marshall traced the genesis of American political parties to the rancorous dispute over the federal government's exercise of delegated authority.[4] From this perspective, perhaps European commentators are simply cosier with the notion of tyranny, willing to subject their populace to the arbitrary whims of bureaucrats.

We think a more realistic account would take two essential facts as its starting point. First, and in contrast with most European countries, the US constitution was drafted before the modern administrative state emerged, and so the mechanisms for controlling executive action are scarcely mentioned in the document at all. The one exception lies in Article 1, Section 8, of the constitution, which provides a catch-all clause giving Congress the right to pass any legislation deemed 'necessary and proper' to exercise its listed powers. *Federalist* 44 further articulated this premise, stating, 'No axiom is more clearly established in law or in reason than wherever the end is required, the means are authorized, wherever a general power to do a thing is given, every particular power for doing it is included.' Beyond this dictum, however, administrative procedures were added in an *ad hoc* fashion in the first half of the twentieth century, mainly through judicial interpretations of old statutes.[5]

Second, heads of administrative agencies are private citizens in the United States, as opposed to the elected legislators who run cabinet departments in most parliamentary systems. Thus one of the basic mechanisms of accountability is absent from the US system altogether.

Be that as it may, the US literature ended up focusing on the act of democratic controls over bureaucratic actions. The study of bureaucratic control through the courts, for example, enumerated the methods by which bureaucrats could be made to follow Congress's statutory intent and serve the public interest. Through their interpretations of the 1946 Administrative Procedure Act (APA), the courts tried to make agencies look as much like (idealized) legislatures as possible. Agencies were to give advance notice of rules and regulations under consideration and afford all parties with even a tangential interest in the outcome a chance to speak their mind (that is, they were to engage in 'notice and comment' rule making). Furthermore, agencies should respond to all suggestions, and their eventual decision must be supported by a lengthy, specific record of their deliberations (which, ironically, was incorporated into the 'concise and general statement' that the APA required all rules to include). Interest groups and courts were seen as key checks on bureaucratic power, ensuring that agencies would act, in the words of Stewart (1975: 1675), 'as a mere transmission belt for implementing legislative directives in particular cases'.

This literature saw Congress as less important in the ongoing control of agencies. Much of the support for this viewpoint came from the observation that Congress rarely exercised its most obvious levers of control: agency budgets were seldom cut, Congress did not spend much time revising its original mandates, and presidential nominees were hardly ever rejected. (A commonly cited example was the fact that the average Senate confirmation hearing lasted seventeen minutes.)

But congressional scholars counter-attacked in the early 1980s with a series of essays promoting the principal–agent view of legislative oversight. Following Fiorina (1977), the battle lines were drawn clearly in Weingast and Moran (1983), who distinguished the 'bureaucratic' approach (bureaucrats are not influenced by Congress) from the 'congressional dominance' approach (Congress does exert significant influence). Weingast and Moran made the important point that the behavioural patterns emphasized by advocates of the bureaucratic approach – the scarcity of conspicuous oversight activities – were indeed consistent with a world in which Congress has little influence over bureaucrats. However, they are also consistent with a world where Congress perfectly controls the bureaucracy. If the mere threat of congressional retaliation is enough to cow executive branch agents into submission, then these agents will never step out of line and legislators need never impose any overt sanctions. Thus it is possible that the traditional tools of congressional control are so effective that they are never actually used – this is the problem of 'observational equivalence'. Weingast and Moran went on to examine Federal Trade Commission (FTC) decisions in the late 1970s and concluded that changes in enforcement patterns corresponded to changes in the preferences of the relevant congressional oversight committees, interpreting their findings as support for the congressional dominance viewpoint.

This theme of congressional oversight-at-a-distance was also the subject of McCubbins and Schwartz (1984), who examined the question of how a relatively uninformed Congress could possibly control bureaucrats who were much more knowledgeable about their particular policy area. True, they could go out and gather their own information or force the agent to disclose information at oversight hearings ('police patrol' oversight), but this would quickly become prohibitively costly, consuming legislators' scarce time and energy. On the other hand, legislators have access to a cheap source of information: namely, those interest groups affected by the agency's decisions. These groups are generally well informed about the relevant issue area and are more than willing to let their representatives know when an agency is acting contrary to their interests. Thus legislators can control agencies simply by sitting back and waiting to see if any groups come to their doors with complaints ('fire alarm' oversight). As in Weingast and Moran, if the fire-alarm system works perfectly, then bureaucrats will never step out of line and no fire alarms will actually be sounded.[6]

Our approach, in contrast with this normative line of argumentation, is positive: we ask when delegation *will* occur, rather than when it *should* occur. After all, policy makers in all political systems have a choice every time they write a new law: they can spell out all relevant policy details themselves, or they can couch the statute in general terms, leaving more substantive issues for bureaucrats to work out themselves. And some laws are written one way, while others are written the other: tax codes (in just about every country), for instance, leave little discretion in setting rates, while monetary policy is regularly delegated to central banks with almost no checks on their actions.

When, then, will legislatures choose one method of policy making over the other? Or, since this is really just a matter of degree, we can ask more precisely: how much discretion will be delegated to executive actors on a bill-by-bill basis? This is the problem to which we now turn.

Information and efficient delegation

Our objective is to construct a generalized positive theory of political dele-gation. Our theory encompasses any situation characterized by a separa-tion of expertise and control. One set of actors, that is, has the right to make policy in a certain area, reserving some decisions for itself and handing others off to another set of actors, who have relatively more expertise about the policy area in question. If we, somewhat infelicitously, call the former actor the *delegator* and the latter the *delegate*, then possible delegator–delegate pairs are: parliaments and cabinets, party members and party leaders, the federal government and state governments, legis-latures and courts, and so on.

Our approach complements that of Strøm *et al.*, elsewhere in this volume, who explore principal–agent problems in delegation. Although both their chapter and ours emphasize the importance of institutions in policy making, there are several important differences as well. First, under a principal–agent approach, broadly speaking, the problem with delega-tion is that the recipient of delegated authority might shirk her responsibilities, in such a way that it is difficult to contract around. We analyse the informational dimensions of delegation instead: expertise is necessary to construct well formed policy, but politicians are wary of dele-gating to experts who do not necessarily share their policy goals.

In addition, the principal–agent approaches assume that authority will be delegated to the agent, and then ask what arrangements will govern the relations between the principal and agent in the policy process. Our point is to not assume delegation, but rather to derive it, asking when political actors choose to do things themselves, when they delegate, and the constraints placed on delegated authority when it is used. Even in parliamentary systems, the cabinet must choose how specific to make laws and regulations; how much detail to spell out initially, and what to leave to the professional civil servants who implement the policy. The same goes for EU directives; how much leeway member state governments will have in their implementation of the directives is a choice made by EU govern-ing bodies, and it varies from case to case.

Our approach also complements another important line of delegation research: delegating to overcome a time consistency problem. The classic case is central banks: governments know that in the long run they are better off not meddling with monetary policy, but they also know that, if an election is coming up and the economy is doing badly, they will be unable to resist the temptation to interfere. Markets know this, of course, and demand higher interest rates for their investments in government bonds. The solution to this problem is for the government to tie its own hands by establishing an independent, conservative central bank with unilateral control over monetary policy.[7]

To better understand the informational issues involved in delegation, we build our model in three stages: (1) internal delegation only; (2) external delegation only; and (3) a combination of internal and external delegation. The argument is presented informally in the text; readers interested in the technical details are invited to peruse Appendix 4.1.

Internal delegation

One option is to give power completely to internal sources; to use in-house expertise to make policy. All organizations have some form of internal expertise: legislatures have committees, Presidents have their staff, the European Union has the Commission, and so on.

If internal resources can provide sufficient expertise to handle the task at hand, and if there are no conflicts of interest, then one need never delegate to outside sources. However, a number of factors usually militate against relying solely on internal experts.

First of all, it is difficult to match the amount of information available to external bureaucrats. Legislative committees, for instance, have dedicated staffs that help put together policy proposals, but they cannot compete with agencies in either the number of people dedicated to a particular task, or the sheer degree of expertise needed to make policy.

Second, internal experts often have multiple tasks that they are working on at any given time, and they may rationally allocate resources away from certain tasks and towards others. As shown in Holmstrom and Milgrom (1991), when faced with multiple tasks, agencies will tend to work on those where their efforts are more easily observable. Thus busy staff might spend more time on flashier projects like public relations releases, and less time on boring environmental regulations or health-care plan alternatives.

Third, and more subtly, internal experts need to be motivated to collect and accurately convey information. But their incentives to do so are blunted by the fact that *they will not be the ultimate decision makers.* Thus they might not spend the resources necessary to become informed about a given topic. Or, if they have the information, they might convey it in such a way as to further their own agenda, rather than that of the decision maker. It now seems, for instance, that intelligence agencies consistently overestimated the Soviet Union's industrial output during the Cold War. The more formidable an opponent the Soviet Union was, of course, the more funding these agencies needed to combat it, so their own budgetary incentives gave them reason to mis-estimate the Russia's capacity. In general, these problems of *strategic information transmission* mean that information flows within organizations can never be perfect.[8]

External delegation

An alternative is to give power over to an external decision maker; this is a real delegation of authority, since the delegator no longer controls the final outcome. If one could delegate to an external agent with all the information needed to make good choices, and no conflict of interest, then the problem would be solved. Again, though, such a situation is unlikely to occur.

On the positive side, external agencies do have the authority to make final policy, so they have greater incentives than internal agents to gather information relevant to the problem at hand. Add to this the possibility of making such agencies as large as one likes, and it is clear that one advantage of external delegation is enhanced expertise in policy making.

Even more than internal agents, though, external agents are unlikely to share the preferences of the political decision maker with the authority to delegate. Whether it is executive agencies versus the legislature, member governments versus the European Union, or career civil servants versus the cabinet, one can never be sure that the recipients of delegated power will use this authority in just the same way as would the delegator.

Thus delegated authority is almost always constrained in some way; for instance, through time limits, spending limits, appointment power limits, legislative vetoes, rule-making requirements, and so on. Some commentators, such as McCubbins *et al.* (1987, 1989) argue that the careful use of administrative procedures can put agencies on 'auto-pilot' and give politicians the best of both worlds: access to bureaucratic expertise, exercised on behalf of the aims of the enacting coalition.

Why, then, do politicians not always control their external agents by reducing their discretion to a minimum? The answer, of course, is that there are costs to limiting discretion in this way. One of the reasons that bureaucracies are created in the first place is to implement policies in areas where politicians have neither the time nor the expertise to micro-manage policy decisions, and by restricting flexibility, politicians limit the agency's ability to adjust to changing circumstances. This trade-off is captured well by Terry Moe (1990: 228) in his discussion of regulatory structure:

> The most direct way [to control agencies] is for today's authorities to specify, in excruciating detail, precisely what the agency is to do and how it is to do it, leaving as little as possible to the discretionary judgment of bureaucrats – and thus as little as possible for future authorities to exercise control over, short of passing new legislation.... Obviously, this is not a formula for creating effective organizations. In

the interests of public protection, agencies are knowingly burdened with cumbersome, complicated, technically inappropriate structures that undermine their capacity to perform their jobs well.

Administrative procedures, then, play an important role in limiting delegated authority. But there is also a need to strike a balance between granting agencies too much leeway and constraining them so tightly that there is no room to incorporate bureaucratic expertise into policy outcomes. The closer are the preferences of the delegator and the external agent, the more authority will be ceded, but rarely will agencies have either unfettered control over their policy area, or have their hands tied so completely that they have little say over the content of policy outcomes.[9]

Whether through internal or external delegation, then, there is no easy answer to the problem of separate expertise and control as long as those with expertise have different policy goals than the politicians doing the delegating. Little wonder, then, that politicians spend considerable resources trying to align the incentives of their agents, or scouring the available job candidates for those who will pursue the delegator's policy agenda rather than their own.[10]

In some policy areas, this may not be so hard: consider for instance the issue of airline safety, which is characterized on the one hand by the need for technical expertise, and on the other by an almost complete absence of potential political benefits. That is, policy makers will get little credit if things go well and no airline disasters occur, but they will have to withstand intense scrutiny when things go wrong: airline regulation is an issue with only a political down side, and failures tend to be spectacular and well publicized. Furthermore, legislative and executive preferences on this issue will tend to be almost perfectly aligned: have fewer accidents rather than more as long as the costs to airlines are not prohibitive. The set of individuals receiving benefits, the flying public, is diffuse and ill organized, while those paying the costs of regulation, the airline companies, are well organized and politically active. And, keeping in mind the easy observation of deficiencies in the system, delegated power is relatively simple to monitor. For all these reasons, even if legislators had unlimited time and resources of their own (which they do not), delegation to the executive would be the preferred mode of policy making.

But such situations are rare; in important areas such as the environment (public tastes for less pollution versus corporate desires to expand markets), health (health consumers versus medical professionals versus insurance companies versus pharmaceutical manufacturers), social security (current versus future recipients), trade policy (importers versus exporters versus resellers versus consumers), multiple groups are organized on all sides of the issues, and those sitting in different places within the government will probably weigh differently the competing demands being placed on policy.

Combined delegation

We now come to the more general case, where politicians make use of both internal *and* external sources of expertise, possibly alone or in combination with the other. A simple version of the sequence of events is illustrated in the 'game tree' in Figure 4.1.[11] There are three actors in this game: a politician (P) empowered to make some choice (this can be an individual, like a President, or a body such as a cabinet, legislature, or Security Council), an internal expert (I), and an external agent (E) who could receive delegated authority. As the game is played, the internal expert (I) first gathers information about the issue at hand, and makes a report to the politician (P). Based on the report, the politician can choose the policy outcome herself in an unrestricted manner (p^P), or choose to delegate authority to E. If she delegates, P sets two parameters: the *status quo* (SQ) and some amount of policy discretion d, so that the agency can deviate from SQ by no more than d. Clearly, the larger d is the more latitude the agency will have. On the other hand, if d = 0, then the agency has no discretion at all, and the game becomes identical to the one where the politician sets policy herself. If the agency does get some (non-trivial) discretion, it can set policy p^E in the range [SQ − d, SQ + d].

We would like to know a number of things about the outcome of this game. First and foremost, where is policy made? Will the politician make policy herself, based on her internal expertise, or delegate power to the external agent? If we let d stand for the delegation decision, then the question is whether P chooses to delegate ($d = 1$) or not ($d = 0$). Second, if P delegates, how much discretionary authority will the agent have? That is, how large is the value of d? And third, how helpful is the internal expert in this process? For the present model, there are just two possibilities for the internal expert: the equilibrium can be 'separating', in which case the expert does convey useful information to P and thus affects the policy

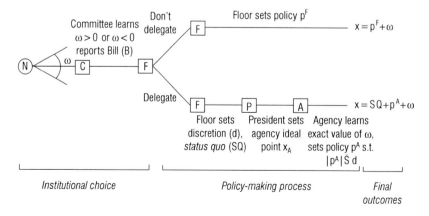

Figure 4.1 Game tree.

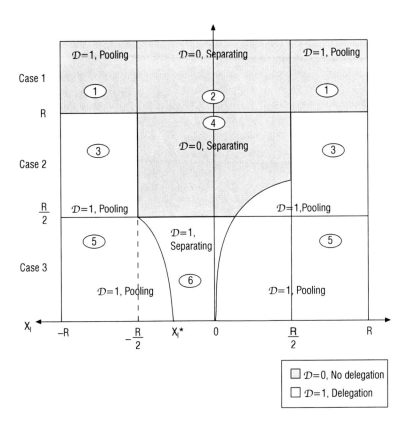

Figure 4.2 Equilibrium outcomes illustrating ranges of delegation.

process, or the equilibrium can be 'pooling', in which case the internal expert plays no role, and the report made to P is simply ignored.[12] Three variables will affect these outcomes: x_I, the difference between the policy preferences of the politician and the internal expert; x_E, the degree of policy conflict between the politician and the agency; and R, the degree of uncertainty in the environment.

The answers to the questions posed above are contained in Figure 4.2. The horizontal axis shows x_I, while the vertical axis shows x_E; the larger are either of these values the more tension there is between the internal expert and the external agency, respectively, and the politician. The shaded areas represent those cases for which $d = 0$; that is, the politician does not delegate at all; the unshaded areas represent values for which substantive authority is delegated. For easier explanation, the diagram has been broken down into a number of regions, each with a distinct pattern of behaviour.

In Region 1, denoted by the encircled number 1 and which appears in both the top left and top right sections of the diagram, both the internal

and external experts have ideal points relatively far away from the politician. In this case, we call both I and E 'preference outliers'; that is, their
ideal points are too extreme relative to the politician's to play a significant
role in the policy-making process.

The analysis of Region 2 is the same from the agency's perspective; it is
too much of an outlier to receive discretionary authority. But now the
internal expert can credibly convey information in its message. Whereas
the signalling equilibrium in Region 1 was pooling, it is separating here.
In both Regions 1 and 2 the agency's preferences are too extreme relative
to the politician, so that the game will be played as if the possibility of delegation did not exist. In other words, these cases are identical to the baseline game, discussed above, with no agency at all.

Consider next Regions 5 and 6 at the bottom of the figure. Here, the
agency and politician are relatively close in policy terms, so no matter
what information the internal player I conveys to P, the agency will receive
some delegated authority; $d = 1$ for both regions. As in the previous two
cases, we have pooling for extreme values of x_I and separation for moderate values, but compared to Regions 1 and 2 the range of separation has
shrunk considerably. Note that in these regions the presence of an agency
has a significant effect on the internal expert's prior actions and the politician's interpretation of them.

The middle two regions, Nos 3 and 4, present an intermediary case.
Here, x_E falls into a moderate range, and the informational content of it's
report will determine whether or not the agency receives delegated
powers. If I and P play a pooling equilibrium, then the politician prefers
to delegate authority; if the signalling equilibrium is of the separating
variety, then the agency will receive no discretion.

Discussion

What can we take away from the results illustrated in Figure 4.2? First, we
can make predictions about which policy areas will be delegated, and how
discretion will change as a function of actors' preferences and the amount
of uncertainty in the policy area. Note two features of the figure: first, for
any fixed value of x_E, as x_I draws nearer the politician's ideal point x_P, the
equilibrium delegation decision either remains unchanged (for high and
low values of x_E), or it switches from agency policy making to no delegation. Therefore, on average, the more cohesive is the politicians' own
internal decision-making process, the more likely it is that policy will be
made by specific, detailed legislation rather than by delegation to administrative agencies.

Second, given any fixed value of x_I, for smaller and smaller values of x_E,
the equilibrium eventually flips to $d = 1$, that is, to one of delegation. So,
on average, the closer the agency's preferences to those of the politician,
the more likely it is that policy will be made through delegation. So dele-

gation increases the more the politician can rely on the agency to have policy goals similar to her own.

Third, utility in our model is measured in a policy space relative to the value of R, the degree of uncertainty in the policy environment. In other words, the value of R measures the importance of informational concerns; when R is large, politicians will care more about making well formed policy, and when it is small they will care more about getting the right benefits to the right constituents. One natural question to ask, then, is what happens to the equilibria in Figure 4.2 as the value of R increases?

The answer is shown in Figure 4.3, which illustrates how the equilibrium ranges in Figure 4.2 change as R gets larger and larger. As the plots show, Regions 5 and 6 in Figure 4.2 (for which $d = 1$) expand with R, until they take over almost the entire graph. Thus, as the world becomes more and more complex, delegation becomes more attractive.

These predictions have been tested in Epstein and O'Halloran (1999) in the context of US law making over the 1947–1992 period, and by

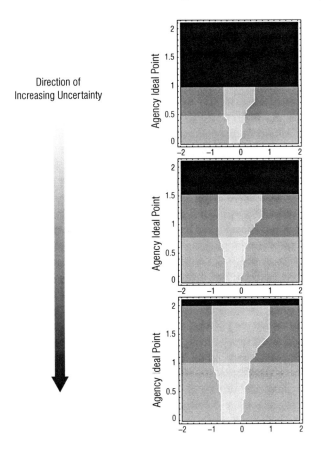

Figure 4.3 Changes in equilibrium as uncertainty increases.

Huber and Shipan (2002) for health care in a comparative context, both with respect to different countries and across the fifty US state governments. So far, they have held up well.

But our basic arguments have consequence for the previous literature on the control of delegated authority, reviewed above. One implication of our model is that political control over executive agencies will necessarily be imperfect; there may still be outcomes *ex post*, that is, that all actors would have preferred to avoid *ex ante*. This view contrasts with some previous discussions, such as McCubbins and Schwartz (1984: 174–175), who imply that oversight and administrative procedures force agencies to enact politicians' preferred policies, with no room for regrets:

> It is convenient for Congress to adopt broad legislative mandates and give substantial rulemaking authority to the bureaucracy. The problem with doing so, of course, is that the bureaucracy might not pursue Congress's goals. But citizens and interest groups can be counted on to sound an alarm in most cases in which the bureaucracy has arguably violated Congress's goals. Then Congress can intervene to rectify the violation. Congress has not necessarily relinquished legislative responsibility to anyone else. It has just found a more efficient way to legislate.

Similar arguments are found in the works of other congressional dominance theorists, such as Fiorina (1982) and Weingast and Moran (1983). To suppose that politicians can costlessly delegate to agencies, though, is to assume away the principal–agent problem altogether: it arises, but is then solved through the design of incentives and governance structures.

If this were the case, politicians could blithely delegate all policy areas to experts, secure in the knowledge that they could dictate policy outcomes through the use of complicated procedural requirements as well as if they had made policy themselves. The fact that politicians do not do so is one indication that control over agencies is imperfect. We therefore part company somewhat with the strong versions of the 'congressional dominance' thesis; we believe that administrative procedures matter, but that political actors cannot perfectly align the incentives of bureaucrats with their own interests, given the disparity of information between the two. Furthermore, in so far as politicians value agency expertise, it is not clear that they should even want to try. After all, if final outcomes will be brought back to the politicians' ideal points no matter what, this might dampen the incentives that agencies have to gather specialized information. In short, politicians may not be able to distinguish 'fire alarms' from 'false alarms' without investing so much energy in expertise that they defeat the original purpose of delegation.

Our approach implies that we should expect to see delegation in those areas where internal policy making is least attractive relative to policy making via agencies. Therefore, agency losses will be inevitable. This argument highlights the dangers of formulating a theory of oversight divorced from a theory of delegation. If policies that are decided in agencies are not chosen at random, if they represent areas in which internal policy making is most prone to failure, and if contracts between political actors are necessarily incomplete, then it would be contradictory to assume that oversight and control will be perfect.

Conclusion

This chapter offered a view of policy making that centres on a simple question: where are key policy decisions made? Policy made by ill informed legislators may end up going disastrously awry, but delegating everything to expert bureaucrats empowers unelected functionaries to make important decisions. In theory, basic political choices should be made by those actors closest to the public, while the technical details are left to bureaucrats. But political incentives may intervene – politicians may keep for themselves difficult areas with rich pay-offs (tax policy), and delegate political losers (like airline safety) with little in the way of guidance for executive agents.

Our theory applies equally to both separate-powers and parliamentary forms of government. In the pure 'Westminster model' (Lijphart 1984), a majority party in parliament elects a cabinet, essentially delegating to that body all policy-making responsibilities. The cabinet then formulates and implements policy until the next set of elections, with any formal ratification by elected legislators being perfunctory. Other than the initial manoeuvring to form a government and instilling it with the power to make policy, members of parliament serve a less active role in the details of policy formation than their US counterparts. In these circumstances, no bill-by-bill strategic calculations need be performed on how much authority to cede executive actors; rather, the question is the degree to which members of the cabinet spell out policy details in the implementing legislation, and how much they trust their civil servants to fill in the details.

Furthermore, it is becoming generally accepted in the comparative institutions literature that the Westminster model is at the far end of a spectrum that includes a variety of forms of parliamentary government, and that substantive policy decisions can be made at multiple points along the way. First, if a coalition government is to be formed, then the coalitional contract will often be explicit about certain policy decisions to be undertaken. Second, there is the normal ministerial policy-making stage that takes place at the cabinet level, possibly constrained by policy bargains made in phase one.[13] Third, members of parliament, sometimes acting through legislative committees, may have input into the content of public policy. And fourth, civil service bureaucrats will make important decisions when implementing policy directives.

At each of these stages, institutional variables will determine the nature and scope of policy input. Coalition governments will form only if there is no majority party and if a minority government is not feasible. Therefore, plurality winner electoral systems, which tend to produce a majority party, will often eliminate the need for intra-coalitional bargaining, while proportional representation systems encourage multi-party coalitions. Ministerial policy making may be constrained by the degree of control that the parliament has over the government in general and individual ministers in particular, as when the assembly can pass a censure vote on a particular minister. The strength of parliamentary committees varies greatly from one country to another; in some instances they are non-existent, whereas other countries have well developed and influential committee systems, including Japan, Germany, Sweden, and Italy.[14] And finally, political control over bureaucrats varies according to the civil service laws of different countries. In some instances, control is well defined and strict, while in others, like France, ministries have a reputation for independent policy making.[15]

The general point, then, is that within parliamentary systems a range of institutions exists, some exhibiting a complete fusion of legislative and executive powers and others possessing independent centres of decision making within the legislature. Note that our theory would predict that, as policy conflict increases between parliaments and the government, assemblies will have incentives to cultivate their own policy-making prerogatives.[16] This is the paradox of separate powers in reverse: in the United States, the presence of separate powers gives legislators incentives to delegate and thereby blur the distinctions between legislation and implementation, while in parliamentary systems the domination of policy making by the cabinet gives backbenchers incentives to create their own independent sources of expertise and policy influence.

To the extent that a given parliamentary system exhibits multiple points where policy details can be amended, the division of labour should follow our general theory. Fractured legislatures with little policy-making expertise should be willing to let cabinets and technocrats handle the intricate details of complex policy. Legislatures with policy goals distinct from the cabinet or ruling coalition (as in the case of minority governments) may find it in their interest to establish competing centres of legislative power and oversight.[17] And technical issues may be safely delegated to professional civil servants with minimal political interference, since policy expertise is at a premium.

These predictions await testing against systematic data, both across countries and within countries over time. But they do illustrate the power of our general approach to policy making, which consists of three steps. First, identify the various centres of decision making in a given governmental system; this includes all areas in which the details of policy are specified. Second, from the institutions governing policy choice, determine which actors have the power to choose one of these alternatives on a case-by-case basis. Third, identify the political interests of these actors, as generated by the electoral and constitutional structures in place. This three-step process should yield predictions on the circumstances under which policy will be made in one way or another.

Again, this division of labour may or may not coincide with technical efficiency. Sometimes rational political actors will find it to their advantage to ensure that policy incorporates the greatest technical expertise available, they may delegate to escape their own internal collective action problems, or they may insulate policy making from political control to ensure the durability of political bargains. But this need not be the case; unequal political pressures, political information, and political power – via the ballot box or otherwise – create the possibility that policy will reflect more parochial concerns rather than doing the greatest good for the greatest number. Yet our approach also emphasizes that, in any political system, the advantages or disadvantages of a particular mode of policy making must always be judged relative to the next best feasible alternative. As neither mode of policy production is perfect, the final outcomes may indeed be relatively efficient, $1,000 hammers and all.

Appendix

We now present our formal model of legislators' decision to delegate.[18] We assume four players: the median voter in the Legislature (L), a legislative Committee (C), the Executive (E), and an Agency (A), all of whom have single-peaked preferences that can be summarized by ideal points x_i, $i = L, C, E, A$ in a unidimensional policy space $x = \mathfrak{R}^1$; for convenience we set $x_L = 0$ and $x_E = 0$. All players have quadratic preferences over outcomes: $U_i(x) = -(x - x_i)^2$ for $i = L, C, E, A$. Outcomes x in turn depend on both the policy passed and an exogenous parameter ω, according to the formula $x = p + \omega$. Legislators treat ω as unknown when deciding where policy will be made; all other parameters are common knowledge. The *ex ante* prior probability distribution over ω is $f(\omega)$ uniform in the interval $[-R, R]$.

The first move of the game is made by nature, which randomly selects the value of (ω) from the distribution $f(\omega)$. Then the Committee observes only the sign of ω, so it receives the signal ω^- if $\omega < 0$ and ω^+ if $\omega \geq 0$. The committee then reports a bill $b(\omega; x_E)$ to the floor, where $b \in \{\omega^-, \omega^+, \varnothing\}$, standing for a report that ω is negative, positive, and no report, respectively. The legislature then chooses the value of a variable $d \in \{0, 1\}$, where $d = 0[1]$ indicates that it chooses to play the Legislative Policy-making [Agency Delegation] game.

In the Legislative Policy-making game, the median legislator observes the committee bill, updates her beliefs over ω to $g(\omega)$, and then passes policy $p^L(b) \in \mathfrak{R}^1$, giving a final policy outcome of $x = p^L + \omega$. In the

Agency Delegation game, the legislature sets two parameters, the *status quo* $SQ(b, x_E) \in \mathfrak{R}^1$ and agency discretion $d(b, x_E) \in \mathfrak{R}^1$. The Executive then sets the ideal point of the Agency, $x_A(SQ, d) \in \mathfrak{R}^1$, after which the Agency observes the exact value of ω and sets policy $p^A(SQ, d, \omega)$ such that $|p^A| - d$, giving a final outcome of $x - SQ + p^A + \omega$. After final policy is set, all players receive their utility pay-offs and the game ends.

A strategy for the Legislature is a vector (d, p^L, SQ, d), consisting of a choice of where to make policy, how to respond to all committee bills, and the *status quo* and discretion given to the agency. The Committee chooses a bill $b(\omega; x_E)$ depending on its information about the random variable and the Executive's ideal point. The Executive chooses an agency ideal point $x_A(SQ, d)$, and the Agency chooses a policy $p^A(SQ, d, \omega)$. We solve for the set of Bayesian Nash equilibria.

Proposition 1

The equilibrium to the Agency Delegation game consists of the status quo SQ, agency discretion d, and agency ideal point $x_A(SQ, d)$ given by:

1 $SQ = 0$
2 $d = R - x_p$ if $x_p \leq R$, $d = 0$ otherwise
3 $x_A = x_F, \forall SQ, d$

This proposition gives the equilibrium strategies for all players in the Agency Delegation game. To start our analysis of its implications, notice that the Executive always prefers more discretion to less:

$$EU_E = \frac{R(d - R)[(d - R)^2 + 3(x_E - 2SQ)^2]}{3}$$

$$\frac{\partial EU_E}{\partial d} = R[(d - R)^2 + (x_E - 2SQ)^2] > 0$$

On the other hand, the committee will want the agency to have more discretion if it is on the same side of the floor as the agency:

$$EU_C = \frac{R\{-3x_E^2 d + 6x_E x_C d - 3x_C^2 R + (d - R)[(d - R)^2 + 12SQ(SQ - X_C)]\}}{3}$$

$$\frac{\partial EU_C}{\partial d} = R[-x_E^2 + 2x_E x_C + (d - R)^2]$$

Substituting in the equilibrium condition that $d = R - x_E$, this becomes $2x_E x_C R$, which is positive if and only if $x_C > 0$, given the assumptions that x_E and R are both non-negative. Thus committees that share an agency's policy views, compared to the legislature, prefer agencies to have more latitude when setting policy than they actually do in equilibrium.

We now solve for the legislature's equilibrium choice of institutions, setting d equal to 0 or 1. Assume that $d = 0$ unless the legislature strictly prefers to delegate, and note that in equilibrium, the bill from the committee will either be separating, in which case legislative beliefs will be $g[b(\omega^-)] = \omega^-$ and $g[b(\omega^+)] = \omega^+$, or it will be pooling, in which case $g[b(\omega)] = [-R, R]$ for all ω; it is impossible for the Committee to reveal information for one value of ω without revealing the complementary set of information for the other value of ω. For convenience, denote the Committee's strategy as $b(\omega = \omega^-, \omega = \omega^+)$, so that the separating equilibrium is characterized as $b^* = (\omega^-, \omega^+)$ and in the pooling equilibrium $b^* \in \{\omega^-, \omega^+, \varnothing\}$.

Proposition 2

$d = 0$ *if* $x_E > R$, *or if* $b^* = (\omega^-, \omega^+)$ *and* $R \leq 2x_E \leq 2R$, $d = 1$ *otherwise*

We now calculate the circumstances under which the message from the committee will be separating, and when it will be pooling.

Proposition 3

Define condition α to hold if:

$$x_E > R \text{ and } |x_C| \leq \frac{R}{2}, \text{ or}$$

$$\frac{R}{2} < x_E \leq R \text{ and } x_C \in \left[-\frac{R}{2}, \min(x_C^{Sep_2}, R)\right], \text{ or}$$

$$x_E \leq \frac{R}{2} \text{ and } x_C \in \left[-\frac{R}{2}, \min(x_C^-, x_C^{Sep_1}, R)\right]$$

where

$$x_C^{Sep_2} = \frac{8x_E^3 - 12Rx_E^2 + R^3}{24x_E^2 - 24x_E R}$$

$$x_C^{Sep_1} = \frac{x_E}{3}$$

$$x_C^- = \frac{4x_E^3 + 3R^2 x_E + R^3}{3(4x_E^2 - 4Rx_E - R^2)}$$

Equilibrium proposals $b^*(\omega)$, policies $p^{l*}(b)$, and legislative beliefs $g^*(b)$ are given by:

$$b^* = (\omega^-, \omega^+) \text{ if condition } \alpha \text{ holds}$$

$b^* \in \{\omega^-, \omega^+, \varnothing\}$ otherwise

$$
p^*(b) = \begin{cases} \dfrac{R}{2} & \text{if } \alpha \text{ holds and } b = \omega^- \\[2mm] -\dfrac{R}{2} & \text{if } \alpha \text{ holds and } b = \omega^+ \\[2mm] 0 & \text{otherwise} \end{cases}
$$

$$
g^*(b) = \begin{cases} \omega \in [-R, 0] & \text{if } \alpha \text{ holds and } b = \omega^- \\[1mm] \omega \in [0, R] & \text{if } \alpha \text{ holds and } b = \omega^+ \\[1mm] \omega \in [-R, R] & \text{otherwise} \end{cases}
$$

Notes

The authors would like to thank Susanne Lohmann, Avinash Dixit, Sean Gailmard, and seminar participants at the ECPR joint sessions, Edinburgh, 29 March–2 April 2003, and at the University of California Los Angeles for helpful comments. The National Science Foundation provided generous support under grant SBR-95-11628.

 1 Think of the legendary (some say apocryphal) $1,000 hammers procured by the US Defense Department.
 2 Thus the actual distribution of authority may be 'truly' inefficient, by which we mean that it is not even defensible as a second-best efficient solution, given incentive constraints. Contrast this view with, for instance, the theory that defence procurement may be subject to expensive and time-wasting bureaucratic red tape, but that these costs are necessary to avoid the even larger costs associated with corruption and industry overcharges.
 3 The Progressives' battle cry was 'There's no Democratic or Republican way to pave a street, only a right and wrong way.'
 4 See the discussion in Chernow (2004: 351) for more on this issue.
 5 This story is well told in the indispensable Shapiro (1988).
 6 Of course, in the presence of competing interest groups, one might worry that some groups might pull their fire alarms even when the agencies in question are not stepping out of line. See Epstein and O'Halloran (1995) for a strategic analysis of oversight that includes the possibility of such 'false alarms'.
 7 See Rogoff (1985) for the classic statement of this view, and McCubbins *et al.* (1987) for a view of administrative procedures as devices to 'lock in' the preferences of the enacting coalition. In a way, time consistency problems are principal–agent games too, being played between current and future versions of the same actor.
 8 See Crawford and Sobel (1982) for the original analysis of this 'cheap talk' game.
 9 See Epstein and O'Halloran (1994) for a fuller discussion of these topics.
10 Or, to use Moe's less gracious terminology, politicians always prefer to hire 'loyal idiots'.
11 The model that goes with this tree is presented in all its technical glory in Epstein and O'Halloran (1999).
12 The terminology of separating and pooling equilibria comes from the theory

of signalling games. See Gibbons (1992) for a comprehensive, comprehensible discussion of the issues.

13 The essays in Laver and Shepsle (1994) explore issues of cabinet policy making across modern European democracies.

14 In the Italian case, there are even some instances in which committees can write and pass legislation on their own.

15 See Huber (1996) on the policy-making process in France. The Japanese bureaucracy has traditionally been regarded as an independent policy-making force as well (Johnson 1982), but see McCall-Ramseyer and Rosenbluth (1993) for an argument that political control is greater than previously supposed. See also Horn (1995), who argues that independent bureaucracies help governments commit to a set of future policies, thereby alleviating the time consistency problem legislators face when enacting policy.

16 In fact, Peters (1997: 68) argues that just such a transformation is now taking place. For instance, British legislators established a system of select committees to serve as a counterweight to Prime Minister Thatcher's attempts to dominate all cabinet policy making.

17 See Strøm (1990) for a discussion of parliamentary policy committees under minority governments.

18 Proofs of the propositions below are given in Epstein and O'Halloran (1999).

References

Chernow, R. (2004) *Alexander Hamilton.* New York: Penguin.

Crawford, V. and Sobel, J. (1982) 'Strategic Information Transmission', *Econometrica* 50: 1431–1451.

Epstein, D. and O'Halloran, S. (1994) 'Administrative Procedures, Information, and Agency Discretion', *American Journal of Political Science*, 38: 697–722.

Epstein, D. and O'Halloran, S. (1995) 'A Theory of Strategic Oversight. Congress, Lobbyists, and the Bureaucracy', *Journal of Law, Economics and Organization*, 11: 227–255.

Epstein, D. and O'Halloran, S. (1999) *Delegating Powers*, New York: Cambridge University Press.

Fiorina, M. (1977) *Congress: Keystone of the Washington Establishment*, New Haven CT: Yale University Press.

Fiorina, M. (1982) 'Legislative Choice of Regulatory Forms: Legal Process or Administrative Process?' *Public Choice*, 39: 33–71.

Gibbons, R. (1992) *Game Theory for Applied Economists*, Princeton NJ: Princeton University Press.

Holmstrom, B. and Milgrom, P. (1991) 'Multitask Principal–Agent Analyses: Incentive Contracts, Asset Ownership, and Job Design', *Journal of Law, Economics, and Organization*, 7: 24–52.

Horn, M. J. (1995) *The Political Economy of Public Administration*, Cambridge: Cambridge University Press.

Huber, J. (1996) *Rationalizing Parliament*, New York: Cambridge University Press.

Huber, J. and Shipan, C. (2002) *Deliberate Discretion? The Institutional Foundations of Bureaucratic Autonomy*, New York: Cambridge University Press.

Huntington, S. (1971) 'Congressional Responses to the Twentieth Century', in R. Moe (ed.) *Congress and the President: Allies and Adversaries*, Pacific Palisades HI: Goodyear.

Johnson, C. (1982) *MITI and the Japanese Miracle*, Stanford CA: Stanford University Press.

Laver, M. and Shepsle, K. (eds) (1994) *Cabinet Ministers and Parliamentary Government*, New York: Cambridge University Press.

Lijphart, A. (1984) *Democracies*, New Haven CT: Yale University Press.

Lowi, T. (1969) *The End of Liberalism: The Second Republic of the United States*, New York: Norton.

McCubbins, M. and Schwartz, T. (1984) 'Congressional Oversight Overlooked: Police Patrols versus Fire Alarms', *American Journal of Political Science*, 2: 165–179.

McCubbins, M., Noll, R. and Weingast, B. (1987) 'Administrative Procedures as Instruments of Political Control', *Journal of Law, Economics, and Organization*, 3: 243–277.

McCubbins, M., Noll, R. and Weingast, B. (1989) 'Structure and Process, Politics and Policy: Administrative Arrangements and the Political Control of Agencies', *Virginia Law Review*, 75: 431–482.

Moe, T. (1990) 'Political Institutions: The Neglected Side of the Story', *Journal of Law, Economics, and Organization*, 6: 213–253.

Peters, B. G. (1997) 'The Separation of Powers in Parliamentary Systems', in K. von Mettenheim (ed.) *Presidential Institutions and Democratic Politics*, Baltimore MD: Johns Hopkins University Press.

Ramseyer, M. and McCall-Rosenbluth, Frances (eds) (1993) *Japan's Political Marketplace*, Cambridge MA: Harvard University Press.

Rogoff, K. (1985) 'The Optimal Degree of Commitment to an Intermediate Monetary Target', *Quarterly Journal of Economics*, 100: 1169–1990.

Shapiro, M. (1988) *Who Guards the Guardians?* Athens GA: University of Georgia Press.

Stewart, R. B. (1975) 'The Reformation of American Administrative Law', *Harvard Law Review*, 88: 1669–1813.

Strøm, K. (1990) *Minority Government and Majority Rule*, New York: Cambridge University Press.

Weingast, B. and Moran, M. (1983) 'Bureaucratic Discretion or Congressional Control? Regulatory Policymaking by the Federal Trade Commission', *Journal of Political Economy*, 91: 775–800.

5 A delegation theory for explaining the bureaucratization of public administrations

Víctor Lapuente Giné

Bureaucracy is one of the most characteristic features of modern governments. However, within the framework of Delegation Theory, there are few comparative studies on the origins of bureaucracies. Using a New Political Economy (NPE) approach, the aim of this chapter is to explain cross-national differences in the levels of bureaucratization of public administration. The explanation I offer in this chapter provides the microfoundations to the rulers' decisions, in both autocratic and democratic regimes, that lead to the adoption of bureaucratic arrangements.

In the second section I provide a working definition of bureaucratization. I consider the key features of public bureaucracies that differentiate them from private organizations; why politicians (the chief executives in the public sector) do not possess the level of discretion in managing employees that chief executives (CEOs) in the private sector possess. In contrast to private organizations, where CEOs have the last word in personnel management, many politicians delegate the management of public employees to independent institutions such as Civil Service Commissions or Corps. I classify contracts between rulers and public employees as a function of the level of delegation of staff policy that politicians give to autonomous public employees' institutions. The degree of delegation from politicians to independent institutions of the powers to hire, fire, and promote public employees indicates the level of bureaucratization of a public administration. Contracts with low levels of bureaucratization will be those in which politicians retain a high degree of discretion or where there is no delegation to autonomous corps. Contracts with high levels of bureaucratization will be those in which politicians' discretion is very low because most important decisions about hiring, firing and promoting public employees are taken by independent institutions.

In the third section I present a game-theoretic model to explain the bureaucratization of public administrations. The driving force behind the model is a double problem of trust between politicians and public employees. First, rulers face a basic problem of credibility in their relationships with public employees because rulers cannot credibly commit themselves to reward employees properly. Public employees do not trust politicians when the latter are sufficiently powerful to renege on their promises (about higher salaries, future promotions, or permanence of the office in the short to medium term). There are two solutions to the politicians' credibility problem: a political system of separation of powers that imposes costs on rulers that renege on their promises and bureaucratizes public offices or a delegation of personnel management to autonomous institutions. However, there is a second problem of trust, the standard problem of moral hazard in principal–agent relationships. For example, public employees may be disloyal to their superiors, the politicians, and may collude with politicians' challengers. Politicians do not trust public employees when they have opportunities to support their challengers. The theoretical model predicts the circumstances under which self-interested politicians will bureaucratize their public administrations by delegating personnel management to autonomous institutions. The main theoretical finding is that, in order to increase their credibility for more efficient policy implementation, politicians will delegate to autonomous bureaucratic institutions when there is no separation of powers within the polity and politicians do not face problems with disloyal servants. In the presence of disloyal servants, the costs of bureaucratization for rulers in systems with a concentration of powers exceed the benefits. In these contexts, rulers retain responsibility for staff policy.

In the fourth section I offer a quantitative empirical analysis of the hypotheses developed in the previous section for two groups of countries: seventeen OECD members and thirty-five developing countries. The empirical analysis confirms the predictions of the model. There seems to be a relation of substitution between the separation of powers within a polity and the level of bureaucratization of the public administration. Rulers interested in efficient policy implementation have to increase the level of bureaucratization of their administrations the more concentrated the powers are within the polity. We observe that the more veto players there are in a polity the lower the level of bureaucratization of the administration. This relation disappears in those countries that have suffered recent civil wars and consequently have more exposure to disloyal behaviour by civil servants.

A working definition of bureaucratization

The word 'bureaucratization' carries a plurality of connotations, and after reviewing literature from economics, political science and sociology, it is difficult to find clear and measurable criteria to classify organizations with respect to their level of bureaucratization. To build a working definition of bureaucratization a good starting point is to consider the differences between private and public hierarchies. There are common sets of rules in public administrations that appear to have no equivalent in the private sector, such as competitive bidding statutes, internal accounting and control systems, 'and perhaps most strikingly, civil service personnel systems, meaning personnel systems in which some important decisions about hiring, firing, and promotion are routinely made by an external commission that is not under the control of the chief executive' (Frant, 1993: 990). Many private organizations may have extensive internal rules constraining employers and employees, 'but they give ultimate discretion to the chief executive. Not so in many public organizations' (Frant, 1993: 990). Chief executives in public organizations, the politicians that are running the public administration, frequently delegate the management of public employees to autonomous bodies.

I classify contracts between rulers and public employees as a function of the discretion rulers have to hire, fire, and promote public employees. *The degree of delegation from politicians to independent institutions of the powers to hire, fire, and promote public employees indicates the level of bureaucratization of a public administration.* Contracts with low levels of bureaucratization will be those in which delegation from politicians to autonomous institutions is low. This is the type of situation we observe in private sector firms when there is no severance pay.[1] Contracts with high levels of bureaucratization will be those in which the delegation to autonomous institutions is high. This is the type of situation we observe in many public administrations, where the minister often has to deal with subordinates they have not chosen and can neither fire them nor move them to another department.[2] However, this is not the case in all public administrations. If we compare public administrations across countries (see the fourth section), then we find a continuum of levels of discretion for politicians.

The credible commitment game

A theoretical model for both democracies and autocracies

The model developed in this section can be applied to processes of bureaucratization in democratic and authoritarian regimes. I assume that in both cases rulers desire what Moe (1984: 761) calls 'political efficiency'; they want to remain in power. I follow Fisher and Lundgreen (1975), who consider that, in order to remain in power, all kinds of rulers need to create loyal and efficient personnel who faithfully execute their orders. Authors within traditional comparative public administration tend to explain bureaucratization mainly as a consequence of rulers' concern about employees' loyalty. Silberman contends in *Cages of Reason* (1993) that with bureaucratization, public servants lose the incentives they could have to engage government's enemies. The costs of rebelling against an incumbent within a bureaucratized system (i.e. losing a secure tenure) are higher than in the absence of such bureaucratization. The problem with this explanation is that it overshadows the predominant function public workers are supposed to deliver in all type of regimes: implementing rulers' desires. Some rulers can certainly be overthrown by disloyal servants, but most politicians, especially in democratic regimes, cannot survive in office without an efficient delivery of public policies.[3]

In contrast, authors within NPE are biased towards efficiency arguments and neglect the role played by loyalty in bureaucratization processes. More specifically, for NPE scholars, politicians care more about future states of efficiency of public administration than about real current efficiency. For Moe (1990: 135–137), political uncertainty (created by legislative instability) is always behind the preferences of interest groups and legislators over the ideal type of bureaucracy. The main purpose of politicians is to protect the laws they enact from future modifications. An objection to these explanations is that, in the moment of choosing the structure of their public administrations, politicians, paradoxically always accused of being shortsighted by NPE scholars, appear to prefer future considerations over today's implementation of their policies. If NPE explanations have difficulties in explaining bureaucratization in democratic regimes, they seem even less adequate for authoritarian systems. By the very nature of the regime, autocrats' main aim is not to preserve legislation from future governments. Nevertheless, some bureaucratization processes have been developed under authoritarian rule (i.e. Japan, Spain). The aim of my model is to explain bureaucratization in both democratic and authoritarian settings and I assume rulers in both regimes have identical preferences for their respective public administrations; politicians desire to remain in power and, for that purpose, they need loyal and efficient public employees.

Credible commitment in organizations

In contrast to the economic principal–agent theory that assumes adversarial relations between subordinates and superiors, other scholars underline the conception of mutual gain within organizations. These authors stress the fact that relationships within a firm are governed by non-contractual exchanges, and these exchanges are made possible by the accumulation of trust between employers and employees. The theoretical model outlined in this chapter uses insights from those scholars, particularly from the work of Gary Miller (1992, 2001, 2002), to understand the relationship between rulers and public employees.

Gary Miller's *Managerial Dilemmas* (1992) analyses the relation between employers and employees in private sector companies. He uses the example of a 'piece rate' system, but the underlying problem of credibility he identifies can be extended to any kind of relation between a boss and their subordinate (e.g. asset specific investments, information flows, promotion or wage increase promises). In a piece-rate contract the employer pays the employee an amount based on the number of units, or pieces, the employee produces. In principle, this system of incentives is an ideal way to solve the principal–agent problem in production, because it aligns the self-interest of employers with organizational goals. However, as Miller recalls, most research on the piece-rate contract has revealed that in practice the system is fraught with problems.

Miller explores a theoretical explanation for this empirical failure. A game is played between the employer and the employee over the issue of information asymmetry. Managers can never be sure what the employee's marginal cost of effort functions are, and employees are systematically trying to protect that information asymmetry. With a price for each piece produced of p, if the employee discovers a more efficient production technique or if they decide to work hard, they may start to earn more money than the employer expected, and the employer has an incentive to adjust piece rates downward, to $p - x$, in response to higher salaries. Then, the employee has incentives to strategically misrepresent their situation and not implement new techniques or work hard. The result is inefficiency as the employer fixes a lower piece rate and the employee makes a lower effort than is socially desirable. It is a stable outcome, but it is not efficient, because there is range of outcomes in which both the employee and the employer can be better off.

From the theoretical point of view, the basic problem with piece rates is that employees believe that employers will inevitably adjust piece rates downward in response to high salaries. Employers acknowledge this problem, and know that the solution is to make a credible commitment not to lower the piece rates. Therefore, Miller considers, the relation between employer and employee is similar to the 'commitment problem' game developed by Kreps (1990). In Miller's adaptation of the commitment problem game (Figure 5.1), the employee moves first and has a choice between trusting the superior (working hard) or not trusting the superior (making minimum effort). If the employee trusts the superior, the superior then has a choice between honouring trust (providing proper reward) and violating trust (cutting piece rates to a minimum or laying off excess employees). In making this move the superior has an incentive to violate trust, because they obtain benefits from adjusting piece rates down, but this leaves the subordinate worse off than if they failed to trust the superior. Anticipating this violation of trust, the employer refuses to trust the employee, which results in an outcome of minimum effort, a Pareto-suboptimal Nash equilibrium.

This basic problem of credibility can be observed in other aspects of the employer–employee relationship (Gibbons, 2001: 334). For example, when a new project has been given to a subordinate within a firm, they can explain the new project to someone with the necessary expertise (or authority) to develop it. However, the superior could steal the subordinate's project, presenting it as their own. Another example is the employee's decision to make a specific investment in training that will improve their productivity. The employee does not know whether the

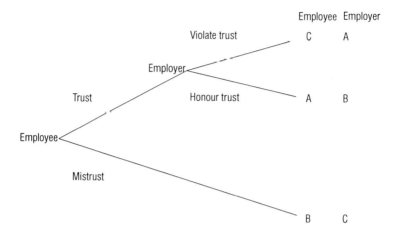

Figure 5.1 Miller's adaptation of the commitment problem game. Employer's
outcome ranking A>B>C. Employee's outcome ranking
A>B>C. Mistrust (pay-offs: B, C) represents a Pareto-suboptimal
Nash equilibrium (source: Adapted from Miller, 1992).

owner will reward them properly once the additional earnings of the
investment are generated (Miller, 2000; 317).

How can this basic problem of credibility of the principal be solved? In
fact, there is no definite solution as there is never a probability equal to 1
that the principal is not going to renege on their promises. But there are
ways to reduce the negative consequences in terms of low efficiency. An
obvious solution would be transforming the one-shot game into a
repeated one. When there are expectations of frequent future interactions, actors must trade off the short-term temptation to defect in the first
round against the long-term cost if the other player decides to punish
them later for their defection in the first round. However, repeated interaction is not a general solution, since the Folk Theorem shows that there
are no clear predictions as to the outcome of repeated games. On the contrary, there are infinite possible equilibriums. Therefore, I am going to
focus on one-shot games. Although there is no systematic account of the
solutions that can mitigate the credibility problem in the literature,[4] the
works of Gary Miller (1992, with Falaschetti, 2001, with Whitford, 2002),
point to two possible solutions: a 'separation of powers' within companies,
and the development of a stricter corporate law.

A first solution to the problem of the principal's credibility is the introduction of some kind of system of 'separation of powers' within organizational structures, similar to that between political branches in
democratic political systems. The economic approaches to organizations
normally consider aspects of law, economics, and organization theory

(Williamson, 1984), but lack insights from politics, and it is this task that Miller addresses.[5] Miller tries to dismantle the orthodox principal–agent theory's myth that anything that helps to reassert the owner's control of the managers' activities must be applauded. He offers evidence from the private sector, where he shows that the entire firm, including owners, may be worse off when principal–agent 'problems' are 'solved' by reining in managerial independence (Miller and Whitford, 2002: 239–246). Miller and Falaschetti (2001: 400–401) consider that 'in a Madisonian way', managers and owners must act as mutual constraints. They propose a separation of powers between the owners and managers that is similar to the solution that Holmstrom (1982: 324–340) provides to the 'team production' problem. According to the latter, in the case of 'team production', the owner of a company must act as a 'passive owner' and rely on a manager, whose preferences must be different from the owner's. If the owner (who obtains the benefits) is at the same time the manager (who fixes the price for each piece rate), workers have incentives to shirk because the owner has opportunities for opportunistic defections (adjusting piece rates downward). There are reasons for firms to rely on independent and separated powers; the managers should not act as perfect agents of the owners.

A second solution to the credibility problem, the development of corporate law, has been less analysed. Miller and Falaschetti (1999: 37) argue that a corporate law that forces owners to be relatively passive in the management of the firm may have positive consequences for efficiency. They also emphasize the importance of possessing internal constitutional provisions within companies that give some sense of predictability to decisions of promotion and wage increases. Their proposal is very similar to my definition of bureaucratization; introducing limits to politicians' discretion in personal management issues.

In conclusion, there is a growing literature that underlines the importance of an accumulation of trust between employers and employees in order to improve organizational performance. However, we lack a model that predicts the circumstances under which principals or superiors within organizations will choose either a separation-of-powers system or bureaucratization to solve their problem of credible commitment. The purpose of the next section is to develop such a model.

The credible commitment game between a politician and a public employee

The interaction between politicians (rulers) and public employees can be modelled by a two-person game such as the one shown in Figure 5.2. The game is similar to Miller's trust game between an employer and an employee depicted above, in Figure 5.1, but now the politician (the employer) has the choice of playing the trust game and retaining their

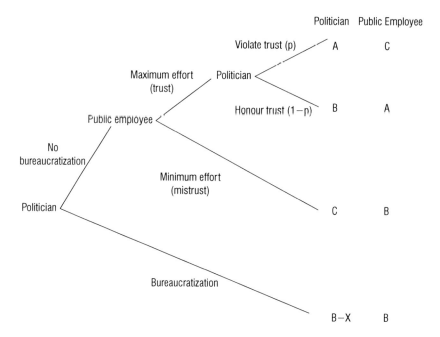

Figure 5.2 The credible commitment game. Public employees' outcome ranking A > B > C. Politicians' outcome ranking A > B ≫ C.

power of hiring, firing, and promoting public employees or not playing it and delegating the management of public employees to an *independent institution* which I defined above as bureaucratization.[6]

That *independent institution* may be a politically autonomous institution such as the Civil Service Commissions that we observe at different levels of the US public administration or the Corps existing in the French and the Spanish administrations. Although politicians may retain some extra-ordinary mechanisms in staff policy under certain circumstances, these institutions have autonomy to manage the hiring, firing and promotion of public employees under normal circumstances. In the concept of *independent institution* I also include those laws and statutes through which politicians 'tie their hands' in their relationship with public employees. For example, when politicians enact rules that guarantee secure tenure or automatic promotion as a function of seniority, politicians are reducing their discretion in personnel management. Therefore, we can define that situation as a delegation of powers from the politicians to the public employees or as a bureaucratization of the public administration of a given country.

Bureaucratization provides predictability to the actors' pay-offs. The assumption behind the model is that, rather than confronting political superiors, public employees will deal with their own peers for establishing rewards and punishments. Instead of the high-powered (although non-credible) incentives coming from politicians, public employees will have low-powered incentives (although more credible because they are made by peers) coming from statutes or peers. For example, with bureaucratization, public employees will not obtain the maximum pay-off (A) because politicians will not be able to offer them fast promotions to the top levels of administration as a reward for maximum effort. Instead, civil servants will have lower incentives such as a slower perspective for promotion. But, at the same time, bureaucratization also prevents the worst outcome for public employees (C), because there is no option for being betrayed by politicians when choosing maximum effort. Similarly, politicians do not enjoy the benefits of a high-powered system of incentives when they decide to bureaucratize, but they also avoid the worst pay-off (C). However, in contrast to public employees, politicians face a cost ($-X$) for using bureaucratization; they are committed to paying some employees for life and they lose flexibility to respond to external shocks which may demand changes in the size and composition of civil service.[7] However, in general, bureaucratization prevents the best and the worst outcomes for both players and it can be seen as the second-best option that is to be preferred only when the best solution involves too many risks for the actors.

Before analysing politicians' decision about bureaucratization, we should consider the similarities and differences between Miller's trust game described above and my trust game (the decision of the public employee whether to trust the politician or not and the corresponding decision of the politician whether to honour that trust or not). To implement a public policy, the public employee can make a maximum effort (trust) or a minimum effort (mistrust). This effort may be working very hard or making a specific investment for a concrete policy implementation. In general, I am referring to all those efforts that without being written down in a labour contract are made by employees: 'every firm requires its employees to take actions that cannot be coerced quality-improving suggestions, transaction cost-decreasing cooperation with other employees, customer-pleasing friendliness. These actions, by their very nature, cannot be induced by any formal incentive system' (Miller and Falaschetti, 1999: 27). A minimum effort would be working to rule and fulfilling only those tasks specified in the labour contract. As in Miller's game, if the public employee chooses minimum effort, the result is an inefficient outcome and both actors would be better off with the other result (maximum effort/honour trust).

In contrast, if the public employee makes a maximum effort, the politician can honour trust, which in this case means rewarding the public employee. However, the politician has an incentive to violate trust, as in Kreps's or Miller's games. For example, at period t (i.e. the beginning of a term) a politician can promise several subordinates that he will promote them if they make an asset specific investment. But at $t + 1$, once the specific investment has been made, the politician may have incentives for promoting only one or two employees or stopping the implementation of the policy and shifting the budget to another agency. This problem is worse, especially in democratic settings with four-year terms for politicians, when employees start an asset-specific investment and they do not know whether the politician that promised some type of reward will remain in office. If a politician from another party takes over the position, the chances of not being rewarded rise for civil servants. In Figure 5.2 we see how opting for 'Honour trust' gives the Politician a lower pay-off (B) than choosing the option 'Violate trust' (A). Anticipating this, the public employee refuses to make a maximum effort.

Up to this point the game is identical to the one used by Kreps or Miller shown in Figure 5.1. However, the decisiveness or capacity for taking a decision that changes the *status quo*, such as reneging on a promise, is limited in some political settings. If the politician is the only relevant political actor, then they are entirely free to violate trust. However, the politician may be only one of several relevant political actors in a polity. In this case, the politician will need an agreement with the other *veto players* (using the terminology of Tsebelis, 1995, 2002) in order to break a promise given to an employee. Veto players are the political actors whose agreement is necessary to introduce a change in the *status quo* of a political system. This concept is introduced in the model through the probability p in the politician's decision. A politician plays his most preferred option 'Violate trust' with a probability p and his second-best option 'Honour trust' with a probability $1 - p$ where p is a function of the concentration of powers existing in a polity. When we are in a situation that Tsebelis would define as a one veto player setting (one political actor makes all the decisions), p would be equal to 1. The value of the probability p decreases when there is an increase in the number of veto players and there are more political actors whose agreement is necessary to introduce a change in the *status quo*, such as reneging on a promise given to public employees. An example of p near to 1 would be an autocratic regime where the dictator or his party does not need the agreement of any other actor to hire, fire or promote employees.

There are two mechanisms, one direct and one indirect, through which a high level of separation of powers (or low p) precludes executives from violating employees' trust. In a direct way, as happens in the United States, the hiring and firing decisions for some top offices are not made unilaterally by the President; rather he needs the support of both legislative chambers. Therefore, a cross-party agreement is necessary and it seems unlikely that, for instance, a Democrat-controlled Senate would support a Republican President's decision to renege on a promise given to public employees. In an indirect way, the existence of separation of powers gives more stability to policy decisions (Tsebelis, 1995, 2002). If an executive, for whatever political reason, decides to cancel the implementation of a policy, violating the trust of all public employees devoted to that implementation process, then they will have greater problems taking that decision, the more veto players (high separation of powers) exist within the polity. In a context with greater concentration of powers there is no such restriction on the party in government to change the legislative *status quo* and, eventually, to violate the trust of those who implement current policies.

The existence of an executive with *limited* capacity to make decisions (because of a high number of veto players) can paradoxically solve the problem of trust behind the model. The choice for the public employee in the previous move has changed in relation to Miller's trust game. Now the options are choosing minimum effort, which gives the public employee a pay-off of B, and choosing the lottery of maximum effort, which depends on the level of concentration of powers (p):

Expected utility (maximum efficiency) $= pC + (1 - p)A$

Expected utility (minimum efficiency) $= B$

Assuming risk-neutrality, the public employee will choose maximum effort, if $[pC + (1 - p)A > B]$. This happens when the concentration of powers in the polity (p) is lower than the critical value: $(A - B/A - C)$. If $[p < (A - B/A - C)]$ the public employee will make a maximum effort. On the contrary, if the politician's capacity to make decisions is higher than that critical value $[p > (A - B/A - C)]$, such as happens in contexts of high concentration of powers (p near 1), the public employee will prefer minimum effort.

Therefore, if we look at the politician's initial decision over whether to bureaucratize or not, we observe that when $[p < (A - B/A - C)]$ (low concentration of powers), the public employee will make a maximum effort and the politician always obtains a higher pay-off by choosing 'No bureaucratization' over 'Bureaucratization'. The pay-off for the politician in the case of 'No bureaucratization' will lie between A and B, depending on the concrete value of p. In contrast, in the case of 'Bureaucratization', the politician will obtain $(B - X)$, which is always a lower pay-off. Thus, when there is a low concentration of powers, the politician does not need to bureaucratize the public administration. When $[p > (A - B/A - C)]$ (high concentration of powers) the public employee will make a minimum effort and the politician must balance the pay-off C of 'No bureaucratization' against the pay-off $B - X$ of 'Bureaucratization'. If $[(X < (B - C)]$ (if the costs of bureaucratization are not very high) the politician will prefer 'Bureaucratization'. To summarize, *there is a substitution effect between the separation of powers and the bureaucratization of a public administration.* In order to be trustworthy in the eyes of their employees, politicians must either possess a system of separation of powers or delegate staff policy to autonomous institutions. Another theoretical finding is that considering the importance of the costs of bureaucratization helps explain why, when there are similar problems of credible commitment, we observe much more bureaucratization in the public sector than in the private sector. Public administrations are not subject to market pressure and they can assume the high costs linked to bureaucratization. Few firms could afford the costs of some bureaucratization processes. For example, an early movement towards the bureaucratization of Western public administrations according to Finer (1997: 963) was in 1445 when Charles VII decided to put the mercenary bands used in the Hundred Years War on what could be called 'unemployment dole'. It was the first step towards the adoption of secure tenure in the French army. The cost of this proto-bureaucratization was prodigious, because it implied the permanent installation of the *taille* tax. Contrary to monarchs, firms cannot raise taxes to finance expensive bureaucratization processes.

The credible commitment problem and the loyalty problem

As I argued above, politicians desire not only efficient personnel, but also loyal ones. The problem of loyalty may be important in the private sector, but it is probably even more important in public settings. In the public sector it is not a matter of losing benefits, sometimes it may be a matter of losing one's head if public employees are not loyal. Loyalty concerns are introduced in the game depicted in Figure 5.3. The only difference between this game and the previous one is here politicians are not sure about the nature of the public employees. In the game described before, we assumed that employees were loyal. In this game, I consider they are loyal with a probability q and disloyal with a probability $1 - q$.

For the sake of simplicity, loyalty affects politician's pay-offs only in two outcomes: 'Minimum effort' and 'Bureaucratization'. In both cases, the politician's pay-offs become a lottery between the same pay-offs as in Figure 5.2 (if they face a loyal servant) and the worst pay-off D (in the case of facing a disloyal servant). I assume that loyalty has no effect on the other two outcomes of the game, because a public employee who exerts 'Maximum effort' in the implementation of incumbent's policies will be hardly recruited by any challenger and, more important, it is difficult to conceive a disloyal employee exerting a 'Maximum effort'.[8] In the case of 'Minimum effort', with a probability q, the politician will obtain the same result as in the previous game (C), and with a probability $1 - q$ the politician will obtain the worst possible outcome (D), which can be seen as the outcome when public employees, in both democratic and authoritarian regimes, use their privileged position to support the government's main challenger.

In the case of 'Bureaucratization', although the proportion of disloyal servants remains the same $(1 - q)$, there is an increase in the number of

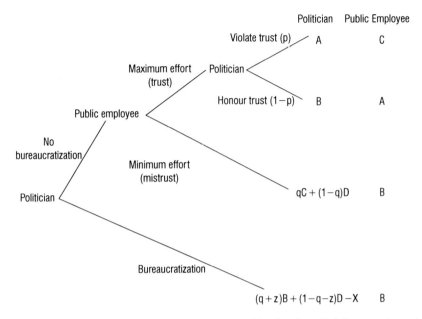

Figure 5.3 The credible commitment game with loyalty. Public employees' outcome ranking $A > B > C$. Politicians' outcome ranking $A > B > C > D$.

public employees who behave loyally. This increase is captured in the model by the letter z. The reason for an increase in loyal (and a decrease in disloyal) behaviour is that certain public employees who were prepared to support challengers in the absence of bureaucratization could be reluctant to do so when they face the risk of losing a *bureaucratized* office with secure tenure. The opportunity cost of defection rises in the presence of bureaucratization for public employees. For example, in Japan during the Meiji Restoration, the new leaders who took power in 1868 belonged to the lower aristocracy and were worried about civil servants' loyalty. The opposing and powerful higher aristocracy could buy public employees' loyalty. In response, the new incumbents created a systematic structure of incentives with secure tenure, that can be seen as a bureaucratization of Japanese public administration, with the main aim of deterring disloyal behaviour (Silberman, 1993; 10, 43).

The insights from this game mimic the predictions of the previous model in the case that all public employees are loyal ($q = 1$): when there is a high separation of powers ($p < A - B/A - C$), there is no need for 'Bureaucratization'; and when there is a low separation of powers ($p > A - B/A - C$), politicians will delegate to an independent bureaucratic institution if the costs of bureaucratization are not very high ($X < B - C$). However, when there is a potential pool of disloyal servants

$(q<1)$, politicians' decision whether to bureaucratize or not changes. If there is a high separation of powers $(p<A-B/A-C)$, the politician will continue to prefer 'No bureaucratization'. But in the case of low separation of powers $(p>A-B/A-C)$, the politician will compare between two expected utilities:

Expected utility (No bureaucratization) $= qC + (1-q)D$

Expected utility (Bureaucratization) $= (q+z)B + (1-q-z)D - X$

Similar to our discussion about loyal employees, the decision whether to bureaucratize or not depends on the cost of that process. In this case, the costs of 'Bureaucratization' must be lower than $[q(B-C)+z(B-D)]$. Moreover, when we assume potential disloyal employees, two more conditions must be fulfilled before taking the decision to 'Bureaucratize'. First, the increase in the probability of loyal behaviour that 'Bureaucratization' induces in public employees (z) must be higher than $[X-q(B-C)/B-D]$. If the process of bureaucratization does not preclude disloyal behaviour, then 'Bureaucratization' is not a rational option for politicians to take. And, second, the level of loyal public employees (q) must be higher than a certain probability $[X-q(B-D)/B-D]$. Therefore, bureaucratizing in the case of high concentration of powers depends on three conditions: that the costs of bureaucratization are not very high, that there exists a certain deterrence effect on disloyal behaviour produced by the bureaucratization, and the pre-existence of a high level of loyal employees.

   To sum up, the following hypotheses on the delegation from politicians to autonomous bureaucracies can be drawn from the theoretical model developed in this section:

1   If there is separation of powers within the polity $[p<(A-B/A-C)]$, there will be no bureaucratization of the public administration.
2   If there is concentration of powers within the polity $[p>(A-B/A-C)]$, there will be bureaucratization of the public administration if the costs of bureaucratization are not very high, if bureaucratization prevents disloyal behaviour, and if there is a certain number of loyal servants.

Empirical test

In this section I offer a quantitative empirical analysis of the hypotheses developed in the previous section for two groups of countries: seventeen OECD members and thirty-five developing countries. In general, there is a lack of reliable data on characteristics of public bureaucracies. However there are a number of indicators, mainly addressed to business groups, which collect data on the performance or the quality of bureaucracies. Those indices try to ascertain the degree to which public administrations are burdened by red tape or are able to deal efficiently with business requests. However, there are few studies that attempt to measure cross-national differences in the structure of bureaucracies, using a definition of bureaucratization such as the one I developed above: the degree of delegation from politicians to autonomous institutions, of the powers to hire, fire, and promote public employees. The two data sets that may be the best proxy to my definition of bureaucratization come from Evans and Rauch (1999) for developing countries and from Kai-Uwe Schnapp (2001) for OECD countries. Due to the fact that the number of observations is low in both data sets (thirty-five and seventeen respectively), I have not included control variables such as the GDP *per capita* or the type of political regime (democracy/dictatorship) in the analysis below as after testing they have no significant influence over the level of bureaucratization.

Bureaucratization in developing countries

Evans and Rauch's 'Weberianness Scale' is an indicator built on comparable expert evaluations gathered over the period 1993–1996. The index was created from ten items that originated from experts' answers to several questions related to employees in public administrations. The individual responses to the ten questions were aggregated to create a country-level data set, in which each country's score is the average of the responses of all experts answering each question for that country. The Weberianness Scale does not aim to measure the autonomy of the public administration in staff policy, rather it seeks to collect data on some of the characteristics that Weber considered as defining features of bureaucracies. Nevertheless, many of the items included in the Weberianness Scale can be proxies of the degree of autonomy that civil servants enjoy from politicians. The reason is that one key feature of Weber's bureaucracy is its autonomy from political interference. The political leader must keep the bureaucracy in place and the bureaucracy counterbalances political power (Weber, 1978). For example, some items in Evans and Rauch's Weberianness Scale measure the importance of exams (instead of political appointments) in recruiting civil servants or whether civil servants are likely to stay in the civil service (instead of being dismissed by politicians). The data cover thirty-five countries: thirty 'semi-industrialized' countries as identified by Chenery (1980) and five poorer countries selected to increase representation of the Caribbean, South Asia and sub-Saharan Africa. For both Evans and Rauch's data (developing countries) and Kai-Uwe Schnapp's data (OECD), I have created dummy variables of bureaucratization, with value 1 if the country's public administration scores above the average and with value 0 if the country possesses low bureaucratization and its value is below the average.

The variable that I use as the best proxy to my definition of 'separation of powers' is the variable *veto players*. The key empirical question is who are the 'politicians' analysed in the theoretical model as the equivalents of the 'employers' used in Miller's trust game. According to most American political economy studies, the legislature should be the public sector equivalent to private sector shareholders. Nevertheless, in a European parliamentary context it is difficult to see the legislature as the only owner/shareholder, because most laws are enacted by governments which frequently control both the elaboration and the implementation of budget. For parliamentary regimes we should focus on parties in cabinet. In fact, using political parties as shareholders is what Tirole (1994) recommends. However, it means leaving aside the role of legislatures, which are also important 'residual claimants' in the public sector, because they benefit from the existence of surplus budgets in a similar way to how shareholders obtain benefits from the reneging of managers' promises to employees (i.e. adjusting piece rates downward).

The best way to take into account both legislatures and political parties is by using Tsebelis's veto players concept. In order to change the *status quo* of the relationship between politicians and public servants, such as the approval of a law or the introduction of a system of incentives, a certain number of political actors have to agree to the proposed change (Tsebelis 1995, 2002). These actors are called veto players, and are specified by the constitution (if there is a formal separation of powers between the executive and the legislature) or by the political system (if there are different parties that are members of a government coalition). According to hypothesis 1, the more veto players within a polity (or the more separation of powers) the less probable will be the bureaucratization of public administration. The variable veto players concept was developed by Beck *et al.* in *Database of Political Institutions* (2001) and it measures the number of veto players existing within each country. To give a broader view for each country, the observation is the mean of the number of veto players in 1970 and 1990.

Following hypothesis 2, the existence of bureaucratization depends on other factors: the costs of bureaucratization, the politicians' beliefs in the loyalty of public employees, and the capacity that bureaucratization has to deter disloyal behaviour. We do not have data on the costs of bureaucratization, but it is plausible to assume that, in contrast to private sector firms that face market pressures and cannot normally commit themselves to guarantee a secure life payment for their employees, public administrations do not face the same kind of cost restrictions.

More relevant are politicians' concerns over employees' loyalty, because loyalty arguments have been acknowledged as key factors for explaining bureaucratization (Silberman 1993; Finer 1997). There are no cross-national indicators of the level of loyalty of public employees, but there are proxies to the circumstances where there is more potential for disloyal behaviour and where the harm caused by disloyal servants to the ruling politician is higher. An obvious case where employees' engagement with challengers may be more likely and more damaging for rulers is civil war[9] (Silberman 1993). Therefore, in order to control for problems of disloyalty, I have created a dummy variable 'civil war since 1960' with value 1 for those countries which suffered from civil war between 1960 to 1995 and with value 0 for those countries who have not experienced civil war in the same period. Data on civil wars was obtained from Alvarez *et al.*'s (1997) ACLP World Political/Economic Database. According to hypothesis 2, when bureaucratization does not prevent disloyal behaviour, and when there are many potentially disloyal employees, it is less likely that politicians will decide to bureaucratize their administrations. Both features – the ability of bureaucratization to prevent disloyal behaviour and a high number of loyal servants – clearly decrease during civil wars. In civil wars bureaucratization does not preclude disloyal behaviour because bureaucratic promises of secure tenure are less credible. Employees do not know whether the bureaucracy will be dismantled if the challenger wins the civil war. It is also easier to find disloyal servants in times of civil war, because civil servants possess valuable information about the regime and the government's enemy may try to buy this information. Therefore, the main theoretical finding of the model, the substitution between separation of powers and the level of bureaucratization within a polity, should not be observed in those countries with civil wars. In polities divided by civil wars, irrespective of the number of veto players or the credibility politicians have, rulers are not going to pay the costs of 'Bureaucratization' when the benefits are so low, since 'Bureaucratization' will not prevent disloyal behaviour nor are there enough loyal servants.

Table 5.1 shows the results of a logit regression with the dummy variable bureaucratization as the dependent variable, created from Evans and Rauch's Weberianness Scale. First, we observe how the *number of veto*

Table 5.1 Determinants of bureaucratization in developing countries

Independent variable	Logit regression
Number of veto players (separation of powers)	−1.903**
	(0.975)
Civil war since 1960	−4.123**
	(2.133)
Interaction between number of veto players and civil war since 1960	2.809**
	(1.416)
Constant	2.912*
	(1.519)

Notes
Logit regression. Dependent variable: Bureaucratization (**5% significance, *10% significance). $n = 35$. Pseudo $R - 2 = 0.13$.

players exerts a significant influence on the level of bureaucratization in the direction predicted by the theory: the more veto players exist in a polity the lower the probability that a country has a high level of bureaucratization. As predicted by hypothesis 1, a decrease in the number of veto players within a given country produces an increase in the probability that the level of bureaucratization of the public administration is high.

Second, one can see how civil wars have a significant negative impact on bureaucratization. The existence of civil wars produces loyalty concerns among rulers and they prefer not to incur the cost of bureaucratization. Hypothesis 2 predicts that the high concentration of powers, which under normal conditions leads to bureaucratization, is not conducive to bureaucratization when there are extreme problems of loyalty, such as the ones generated during a civil war. In polities with a high concentration of powers, it is not rational for politicians to bureaucratize in a time of civil war because in civil wars bureaucratization does not prevent disloyal behaviour, and there are a greater number of potentially disloyal servants than in peacetime. For these reasons, I introduce an interaction between the separation of powers and civil wars in order to see if, in countries experiencing civil war, the variable of separation of powers has a negative impact on the level of bureaucratization similar to that which we observe in countries without civil wars. The empirical test shows that the existence of civil wars completely changes the direction of the influence of the separation of powers. Not only does the number of veto players not decrease the level of bureaucratization (as predicted by the theory), but it also has a significant positive impact on bureaucratization (an extreme result that is not predicted by the theory). The greater the separation of powers within a country experiencing civil war the greater the level of bureaucratization in its public administration. This positive effect of the number of veto players on the level of bureaucratization is outside the predictions of the theoretical model developed here. Further research is needed to find the theoretical link between separation of powers in contexts of civil war and bureaucratization.

Bureaucratization in OECD countries

Kai-Uwe Schnapp (2001) builds his data from Auer *et al.* (1996) and offers values for seventeen OECD countries. He creates a 0–6 scale for the level of 'closed-ness of civil service career systems', that measures the degree of bureaucratic autonomy and closedness to external entries. The more 'closed' civil service career systems, such as those of Greece, Belgium or France, are those in which politicians have very limited discretion to affect the civil service's firing, hiring and promotions. At the other end of the continuum we observe the more 'open' civil service career systems of Sweden, Netherlands or Finland, where bureaucracies are less independent from politicians.

Table 5.2 Determinants of bureaucratization in OECD countries

Independent variable	Logit regression
Number of veto players (separation of powers)	−0.968*
	(0.584)
Constant	2.507*
	(1.421)

Notes
Logit regression. Dependent variable: Bureaucratization (*10% significance). $n = 17$. Pseudo $R − 2 = 0.141$.

Table 5.2 shows the results of a logit regression with the dummy variable bureaucratization for those seventeen OECD countries. As predicted by hypothesis 1, the variable number of veto players exerts a significant negative effect on the probability that the level of bureaucratization is high. Due to the absence of extreme problems of loyalty in OECD, since none of the seventeen countries included has experienced war since World War II, hypothesis 2 cannot be tested with this sample of countries.

Neither this negative relation between the separation of powers and the level of bureaucratization for the seventeen OECD countries nor the similar correlation observed in the regression analysis for the thirty-five developing countries fully verifies the causal relationship between the separation of powers of a political system and the bureaucratization of its public administration predicted in the theoretical model of this chapter. A more exhaustive empirical analysis is needed to further corroborate it. However, both the theoretical model and the preliminary empirical test shown in this chapter point out that there seems to be a relationship between the differences in administrative structures and the incentives that politicians face in different political systems. In light of the limited empirical analysis shown here, one cannot reject the validity of competing theories over the importance of the level of development of a country. However, it can be argued that the theoretical model developed in this chapter seems to perform better than a theory focused on the role of economic level or on the type of political regime, because neither the level of economic development, measured through the GDP *per capita*, nor the political regime, captured by the dichotomy democracy versus dictatorship, present any significant effect on the level of bureaucratization (analysis not shown here).

Conclusion

In contrast to private sector organizations, in many public sector ones some important decisions about hiring, firing and promotion are routinely made by external commissions that are not under the control of the chief executive/ruler. Not all public organizations have the same limits on the discretion of politicians in personnel management. There is variation in what I define in this chapter as the degree of bureaucratization of public administrations.

In neither economics nor political science are there convincing explanations for this variation in the level of bureaucratization. Economists find rational choice-based theories do not explain why the principals of an organization (politicians) renounce the use of instruments such as firing, hiring and promoting that are extremely important in solving the problems of adverse selection and moral hazard caused by the agents (public employees). From political science several explanations have been put forward, but they mainly rely on non-rational motivations such as cultural and historical differences and do not provide testable propositions.

The purpose of this chapter is to provide a theoretical model that explains the rationality behind the decisions of some rulers who reduce their level of discretion over the management of public employees and decide to delegate personnel management to independent institutions. Following the insights of several organizational economists, I consider that relations within a firm are governed by non-contractual exchanges and those exchanges are made possible by the accumulation of trust between employers and employees. For the public sector I develop a game similar to the trust games proposed by Kreps (1984) and Miller (1992). The public employee moves first and has to choose between trusting the politician (maximum effort) or not (minimum effort). Once the employee has placed their trust in the politician, the politician then has to choose between giving the employee a proper reward or not. Politician's commitment to honouring the employee's trust is not credible, since it would not be in the politicians' own interest to keep the commitment once the public employee had chosen to give the politicians the opportunity to live up to the commitment. The problem is how to produce a credible commitment.

The added value of this chapter is that it includes within the same framework the two main solutions to the credible commitment problem that are suggested in the literature: a system of separation of powers and bureaucratization of public offices. The model predicts that when there is a separation of powers within the polity, there will be no bureaucratization or delegation of staff policy to an independent institution. On the contrary, when there is a concentration of powers within the polity, there will be delegation to an independent institution if the costs of bureaucratization are not very high and if politicians do not face problems of disloyal behaviour from public employees. The main theoretical finding can be summarized as follows: in the absence of important concerns about civil servants' loyalty, politicians will delegate personnel management to independent institutions when there is concentration of powers within the polity.

It is common in the literature to argue that the aim of a separation-of-powers system is to protect people from government, and there is a trade-off, because the more you protect the people (through a separation of powers) the more you disable the government to act (Przeworski, 1996; Tsebelis, 2002). However, if we illuminate political systems with theoretical developments from organizational economics, the trade-off disappears, and we may arrive at opposite predictions: *the more you protect people from government* (through a separation-of-powers system) *the more you enable the government to act*, because the government makes a credible commitment respect to public employees and the costly bureaucratization is not needed.

Notes

I am grateful for comments and suggestions to Dietmar Braun, Carles Boix, Jari Eloranta, Jose Fernandez-Albertos, Fabrizio Gilardi, Jane Green, Avner Greif, John Huber, Ignacio Lago, Margaret Levi, Martin Lodge, Jose Maria Maravall, Iain McLean, Gary Miller, John Nye, Adam Przeworski, Berthold Rittberger, Leire Salazar, Ignacio Sanchez-Cuenca, Michael Wallerstein, and the attendants of the workshop 'Delegation in Contemporary Democracies', ECPR, 2003.

1 Abraham and Prosch (2000) analyse the rationality behind the severance pay found in some private sector companies. Their study of severance pay as a 'hostage' that employers use to create a credible commitment in their relations with employees is very similar to my approach to bureaucracy.

2 The ruler has two faces: one as employer and other as legislator. Therefore, they can always change the laws that protect civil servants and remove them even in the case of the highest possible bureaucratization. Nevertheless, we do not normally observe these changes, as legislating always involves costs of negotiation and implementation, even in autocracies.

3 By efficient delivery I do not mean social efficiency, but an efficient delivery of the policy that the ruler chooses for their survival: it can be the provision of a public good, the implementation of rent-seeking activities or a generalized system of corruption.

4 In the literature on central banks and independent regulatory agencies there is much discussion. See the contribution of Fabrizio Gilardi in this volume for a good summary of the arguments.

5 An author who also has tried to import insights from politics to the study of private organizations is Alfred D. Chandler. In *Scale and Scope: the Dynamics of Industrial Capitalism* (1990) he compares the federation of some tobacco companies with that of the Thirteen States of America, because in both cases there was a tension between an increasingly powerful central government and older local authorities.

6 I use a game-theoretic model to show the micro-foundations behind politicians' decisions on bureaucracies. An adequate explanation of bureaucratization must entail causal relations but must also specify the micro-foundations or the mechanisms that describe the process by which one variable influences the other (Kiser and Hechter, 1998). Structuralist explanations of the origins of bureaucracies, such as Tilly's (1990) or Ertman's (1997), point out macro variables, such as an increase in the war effort or the type of local government, that have an impact on bureaucratization processes. Nevertheless, as Kiser and Baer (2001) remark, structuralists pay little attention to the micro level or mechanisms of the human decision-making processes that link those macro-structures with bureaucratization processes. The purpose of the game developed here is making those mechanisms explicit.

7 It can be argued that politicians' bureaucratization is non-credible and politicians can repeal the bureaucratization when they desire. This would distort the incentives that Corps design for public employees because there is no guarantee that politicians will not subvert the delegation of staff policy and thus cancel the bureaucratic system of incentives. I am not contending that the delegation of staff policy is exempt from problems of credibility. Delegation is, by definition, subject to revocation by politicians. However, if politicians want to recover their initial powers in personnel issues, they must pay costs: the costs that are involved in a process of changing laws and the costs of losing credibility in the eyes of social actors that are interacting with the government in other dimensions. Those costs are included within the letter X in the model.
8 Anyway, the inclusion of loyalty in all politicians' pay-offs – and in public employees' – does not alter the substantive results of the model.
9 There are many more instances, apart from civil wars, where servants' loyalty can be a great concern for rulers. The impossibility of obtaining data for those circumstances limits the scope of this empirical analysis, and the possible inferences must be done only for the concrete loyalty problems caused by civil wars.

References

Abraham, M. and Prosch, B. (2000) 'Long-term Employment Relationships by Credible Commitments. The Carl Zeiss Foundation', *Rationality and Society*, 12: 283–306.

Albrow, M. (1970) *Bureaucracy*, London: Macmillan.

Alvarez, M., Cheibub, J. A., Limongi, F. and Przeworski, A. (1997) *ACLP World Political/Economic Database*.

Auer, A., Demmke, Ch. and Poltet, R. (1996) *Civil Services in the Europe of Fifteen. Current Situation and Prospects*, Maastricht: European Institute of Public Administration.

Beck, T., Clarke, G., Groff, A., Keefer, P. and Walsh, P. (2001) 'New Tools in Comparative Political Economy. The Database of Political Institutions', *World Bank Economic Review*, 15 (1): 165–176.

Bekke, H. A. G. M. and van der Meer, F. (2000) *Civil Service Systems in Western Europe*, Bodmin: MPG.

Chandler, A. D. (1990) *Scale and Scope: the Dynamics of Industrial Capitalism*, Cambridge MA: Belknap Press of Harvard University Press.

Chenery, H. B. (1980) 'The Semi-industrialized Countries', unpublished manuscript, Washington DC: World Bank.

Ertman, T. (1997) *Birth of the Leviathan: Building States and Regimes in Medieval and Early Modern Europe*, Cambridge and New York: Cambridge University Press.

Evans, P. B. and Rauch, J. (1999) 'Bureaucracy and Growth: A Cross-national Analysis of the Effects of "Weberian" State Structures on Economic Growth', *American Sociological Review*, 64 (5): 748–765.

Finer, S. (1997) *The History of Government from the Earliest Times*, 3 vols, Oxford: Oxford University Press.

Fischer, W. and Lundgreen, P. (1975) 'The Recruitment of Administrative Personnel', in C. Tilly (ed.) *The Formation of National States in Western Europe*, Princeton NJ: Princeton University Press.

Frant, H. (1993) 'Rules and Governance in the Public Sector: The Case of the Civil Service', *American Journal of Political Science*, 37: 990–1007.

Gibbons, R. (2001) 'Trust in Social Structures: Hobbes and Coase meet Repeated Games', in K. S. Cook (ed.) *Trust in Society*, New York: Russell Sage Foundation.

Holmstrom, B. (1982) 'Moral Hazard in Teams', *Bell Journal of Economics*, 13: 324–340.

Horn, M. J. (1995) *The Political Economy of Public Administration: Institutional Choice in the Public Sector*, Cambridge and New York: Cambridge University Press.

Kiser, E. and Baer, J. (2001) 'The Bureaucratization of States: Toward an Analytical Weberianism', unpublished paper.

Kiser, E. and Hechter, M. (1998) 'The Debate on Historical Sociology: Rational Choice Theory and its Critics' *American Journal of Sociology*, 104 (3): 785–816.

Kreps, D. (1990) 'Corporate Culture and Economic Theory', in J. Alt and K. Shepsle (eds) *Perspectives on Positive Political Economy*, Cambridge: Cambridge University Press.

Miller, G. (1992) *Managerial Dilemmas: The Political Economy of Hierarchy*, Cambridge: Cambridge University Press.

Miller, G. (2001) 'Why is Trust Necessary in Organizations? The Moral Hazard of Profit Maximization', in K. S. Cook (ed.) *Trust in Society*, New York: Russell Sage Foundation.

Miller, G. and Andrew, B. W. (2002) 'Trust and Incentives in Principal–agent Negotiations', *Journal of Theoretical Politics*, 14 (2): 231–267.

Miller, G. and Falaschetti, D. (1999) 'Tying the Owner's Hands: The Moral Hazard of Profit Maximization', paper presented at the annual meeting of the International Society of New Institutional Economics, Washington DC.

Miller, G. and Falaschetti, D. (2001) 'Constraining Leviathan: Moral Hazard and Credible Commitment in Institutional Design', *Journal of Theoretical Politics*, 13 (4): 389–411.

Moe, T. M. (1984), 'The New Economics of Organization', *American Journal of Political Science*, 28: 739–777.

Moe, T. (1990) 'The Politics of Structural Choice: Toward a Theory of Public Bureaucracy', in Oliver Williamson (ed.) *Organization Theory*, Oxford: Oxford University Press.

Peters, B. G. (2001) *The Politics of Bureaucracy*, 5th edn, London: Routledge.

Przeworski, A. (1996) 'On the Design of the State: a Principal–Agent Perspective', unpublished paper.

Schelling, T. (1960) *The Strategy of Conflict*, Cambridge MA: Harvard University Press.

Schnapp, K-U. (2001) 'Influence of Ministerial Bureaucracies and Political Decision Making: Three Models', paper presented at the first general conference of the ECPR, University of Kent at Canterbury, 5–8 September.

Silberman, B. S. (1993) *Cages of Reason: The Rise of the Rational State in France, Japan, the United States, and Great Britain*, Chicago: University of Chicago Press.

Tilly, C. (1990) *Coercion, Capital, and European States, 990–1990*, London: Blackwell.

Tirole, J. (1994) 'The Internal Organization of Government', *Oxford Economic Papers*, 46: 1–29.

Tsebelis, G. (1995) 'Decision Making in Political Systems: Veto Players in Presidentialism, Parliamentarism, Multicameralism and Multipartidism', *British Journal of Political Science*, 25: 289–325.

Tsebelis, G. (2002) *Veto Players: How Political Institutions Work*, Princeton NJ: Princeton University Press and New York: Russell Sage Foundation.

Weber, M. (1978) *Economy and Society*, Berkeley CA: University of California Press.

Williamson, O. E. (1984) 'The Economics of Governance: Framework and Implications', *Journal of Institutional and Theoretical Economics*, 140: 195–223.

Williamson, O. E. (1990) 'A Comparison of Alternative Approaches to Economic Organization', *Journal of Institutional and Theoretical Economics*, 146 (1): 61–71.

Part II

The next steps in delegation

Independent agencies, interest organizations, and the European Union

6 Delegation to independent regulatory agencies in Western Europe

Credibility, political uncertainty, and diffusion

Fabrizio Gilardi

In a report on regulatory reforms the OECD wrote that 'One of the most widespread institutions of modern regulatory governance is the so-called independent regulator or autonomous administrative agency with regulatory powers' (OECD, 2002: 91). This observation is correct. Independent regulatory agencies (IRAs) have been established in all West European countries and beyond. For example, all EU countries have an independent authority regulating telecommunications markets. What is striking, however, is that only ten years ago the OECD would have not been able to write that sentence. Figure 6.1 shows the evolution of the number of IRAs in economic and social regulation[1] from 1950 to 2002. Two trends appear clearly. The first is that IRAs are more numerous in economic rather than social regulation. The second is that IRAs have become widespread only since the late 1980s. Why, in the late 1980s, did only a few independent regulators exist,[2] while now these institutions have become so common that the OECD can refer to them as 'one of the most widespread institutions of modern regulatory governance'?

Independent regulators are widespread indeed. As shown in Figure 6.1, they have been set up in such diverse regulatory domains as telecommunications, food safety, and competition. All West European countries have established them in at least some sectors. What sets these institutions apart from the rest of public bureaucracy is that, as their name indicates, they are 'independent'. That is, they are independent from direct political control. For example, the Swedish telecommunications regulator has been designed so that its director-general's term of office is over six years, and the incumbent cannot be dismissed for reasons related to his or her policy choices. The regulator can autonomously determine its internal organization, as well as the allocation of its staff. Its budget is partly independent from the general state budget, and only a court can overturn its decisions. These factors mean the government's capacity to control what this regulator does is much lower than for the rest of the bureaucracy. On the other

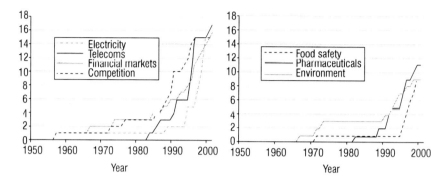

Figure 6.1 Evolution of the number of IRAs in seventeen countries, 1950–2002.

hand, the Portuguese competition authority's budget comes entirely from the government, which also decides its internal organization. The government can overturn the authority's decisions, though with some constraints. The director-general has a fixed term of three years, but the minister who appointed him or her can fire him or her without restriction. In this case, the government has several instruments that enable it to influence the behaviour of the regulator. Finally, in other cases, no independent regulator exists, and regulatory policy is carried out within the normal administrative structures that the government can directly control.

Figure 6.2 gives a synthetic view of the formal independence of regulators in seventeen countries and seven sectors. Dots indicate mean formal independence in a given category (countries or sectors), while lines extend from minus to plus one standard deviation, and show heterogeneity inside each category. It can be noticed that there is considerable variation in the formal independence of regulators, both cross-nationally and by sector. Why in some cases is there a quite independent IRA, in other cases a much less independent IRA, and in still other cases, no IRA at all? How can variations in the formal independence of regulators be explained?

This chapter summarizes the findings of my doctoral research (Gilardi, 2004a), and answers two questions. First, how can we explain the fact that most IRAs were established during the 1990s? Second, why are some IRAs more independent than others?

Delegation to IRAs: credibility, political uncertainty, and diffusion

The new institutionalism, and in particular its rational choice and sociological variants, are a useful starting point to approach delegation to

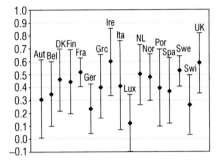 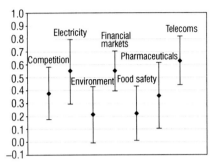

Figure 6.2 Mean and standard deviation of the formal independence of regulators in seventeen countries and seven sectors. Dots indicate mean values; lines extend from minus to plus one standard deviation (source: Gilardi, (2004a)).

IRAs (Gilardi, 2004b). Rational choice institutionalism points to the fact that delegation to IRAs is related to two aspects of choice over time. Regulatory policy making, like policy making more generally, does not consist of discrete, one-off decisions, but of decisions that have to be taken, confirmed, and implemented over time. The first consequence of this fact is that policy choices may be time-inconsistent because of change over time. A government may prefer option A at time t but option B at time t + 1. There are at least three reasons why this can happen. The first is simply that, at time t + 1, new contingencies, facts or information may emerge, leading governments to revise the original decision. For example, a government may choose a restrictive monetary policy at time t but prefer to sustain growth at time t + 1 if there are dangers of recession.

A second reason for time-inconsistent preferences is that, even if nothing changes in the context, actors that are targets of the policy may anticipate the government's time inconsistency and act accordingly. The standard example (Kydland and Prescott, 1977) is that of a government that does not want houses to be built on a flood plain and therefore makes a commitment not to build protections in case houses are built. If some actors anticipate this, and houses are actually built, then the government will be inclined to build protections to prevent a tragedy, and the final outcome is that both houses and protections are built. The government's preferences here are time-inconsistent: at time t, it does not want to build protections; at time t + 1, it prefers to build them. The anticipation of relevant actors is the cause of time inconsistency in this case. If they believed the government's commitment, they would not build houses and the government would not have to build protections at time t + 1.

The third source of time inconsistency is the shape of the discount function of policy makers. Actors discount the future: they give the present more weight than the future. The way this operation is done matters. Economists usually assume that the discount function is exponential. In this case, time inconsistency is ruled out. If A is preferred to B at time t, then it will always (i.e. at any t) be preferred. However, if the discount function is not exponential but hyperbolic, as experimental studies suggest, then temporary preference reversals may occur. In this case, an actor may prefer A to B at most t, but prefer B to A during a few periods. This type of time discounting causes time inconsistent preferences (Frederick *et al.*, 2002).

Time inconsistency is problematic for policy makers because it leads to lack of credibility. Policy makers may announce a decision at time t, but the relevant actors know that the decision could be changed at time t + 1. This has adverse consequences for some types of regulatory policies, notably those where one of the main goals is attracting investment. A case in point is post-liberalization utilities regulation. The government has to set up investor-friendly regulation and protect them from expropriation.

If the promise of fair regulation the government makes at time t is not credible, a lack of investment may result. Time inconsistency therefore prevents governments from achieving their objectives. Institutions, however, help achieve credible commitment capacity. Veto players, for example, hinder policy change (Tsebelis, 2002). While they do not prevent time-inconsistent preferences, they make it more difficult to translate those preferences in actual decisions. As a result, policies are more credible. Another political institution that increases the credibility of commitments is market-preserving federalism (Weingast, 1993, 1995), a particular form of federalism that is often associated with fiscal federalism. Governments may also design specific institutions to increase credibility. IRAs are a case in point. By delegating authority, policy makers bind themselves and therefore increase the credibility of their commitments. In this view, IRAs are therefore a means to improve the credibility of regulatory commitments (Levy and Spiller, 1994; Majone, 2001). This is the first hypothesis.

The second rational choice institutionalist argument is that delegation to IRAs is a means not to improve credibility, but to cope with political uncertainty. Political uncertainty derives from the fact that authority over policy is given up when elections are lost. Any government is bound to be able to influence policy only temporarily. If a new coalition gains power, policies can be changed. If a government fears replacement by a coalition with different preferences and does not expect to regain power in the short term, then it may try to insulate policy from politics so as to make change more difficult (De Figueiredo, 2002; Moe, 1990). Existing institutions, such as veto players, hinder policy change, and therefore make the political uncertainty problem less severe. If policy change is easy, on the other hand, a government may try to insulate policies through delegation to IRAs. The second hypothesis is thus that delegation to IRAs is a means to mitigate political uncertainty.

These two explanations, credibility and political uncertainty, implicitly assume that each government decides whether to delegate to IRAs independently from the choices of other governments. There is, however, a growing body of literature on policy diffusion stressing that actors behave interdependently (e.g. Simmons and Elkins, 2004). The choice of actor A may have an impact on the choice of actor B. It is thus possible that the decision of a government to delegate powers to IRAs is not independent from similar decisions elsewhere, or, conversely, that the choice of a government to delegate powers to IRAs has an effect on the decisions of other governments. Policy diffusion occurs when choices are interdependent. It is, however, important to stress that diffusion-like patterns can appear even though actors decide independently, provided that they react to similar functional pressures at roughly the same time. In the case of IRAs, governments may respond to credibility and political uncertainty; if they do so at the same time, IRAs will spread as though diffusion was at work, though any apparent diffusion should be considered spurious. If diffusion does arise from the fact that actors are interdependent, on the other hand, then several diffusion mechanisms can be identified.

The main distinction is between diffusion mechanisms where problem solving is the primary rationale for action, and those where policies spread irrespectively from their problem-solving capacity. In the first category we find learning, which can be fully rational or only of bounded rationality. Rational learning is best conceptualized in Bayesian terms (Meseguer, 2003). Here, governments are assumed to act after updating their beliefs about the benefits of a given policy by looking at the experience of others, which is used to update prior beliefs and eventually orient action. Bounded learning, on the other hand, is a bounded rationality version of Bayesian learning. In this case, actors try to gather relevant information from the observation of the behaviour of others, but they rely on 'cognitive short cuts' (McDermott, 2001; Tversky and Kahneman, 1974) rather than on Bayesian updating. Learning here can be much less effective than in the Bayesian view. Actors do try to get new information from the experience of others, but use cognitive short cuts rather than Bayes's rule to update their beliefs. Conversely, in cooperative and competitive regulatory interdependence (Lazer, 2001) the logic of diffusion remains problem solving-oriented, but is not grounded in the desire or need of actors to gather new relevant information that can help them make better policy choices. Under cooperative interdependence, diffusion is driven by the benefits that follow from having compatible policies, and under competitive interdependence, by strategic responses to the behaviour of competitors.

The second broad category of diffusion mechanisms is based on sociological institutionalism, and is characterized by the fact that behaviour is not oriented toward problem solving. In coercive and normative isomorphism (DiMaggio and Powell, 1991), the spread of organizations and policies depends much more on advocacy for them by powerful or authoritative actors than on the problems they can solve.[3] Coercive isomorphism results from the presence of pressures, both formal and informal, exerted on organizations by other organizations on which they depend. Normative isomorphism, on the other hand, arises from processes of professionalization and socialization within networks, where persuasion may occur through the development of conceptual models that gain authority through advocacy for their use by prominent actors.

The last two mechanisms of diffusion are related to symbolic imitation. First, the setting up of an organization, or the adoption of a policy, can be a ceremony intended to provide legitimacy to certain decisions by diverting the attention from more substantial concerns (Meyer and Rowan, 1977). In the case of IRAs, governments may create independent regulators so as to legitimate other decisions, such as liberalization of utilities. As IRAs become valued by the broader institutional environment (which includes norms and values), establishing them may enhance the legitimacy of certain policy choices. Second, over time some organizational forms can be 'taken for granted', while others disappear from the 'domain of the possible' (Hannan and Carroll, 1992). In this perspective, organizations are established simply because they have become the normal or obvious thing to do in given contexts, while other options are not even considered.

The third main hypothesis is that diffusion processes have been at work in the spread of IRAs; in other words, the hypothesis is that diffusion has not been spurious. I will not be able to test for the presence of all diffusion mechanisms. I will rather focus on two of them, namely coercive isomorphism and symbolic imitation.

The next two sections present the empirical findings. Then the following section examines the pattern of the establishment of IRAs over time, while the last considers the determinants of their formal independence.

The diffusion of IRAs in Western Europe

The findings presented in this section are from a Weibull event history analysis model. The estimated parameters of the model are presented in Appendix 6.2, while the operationalization of variables and data sources are summarized in Appendix 6.1. The full analysis can be found in Gilardi (2004a).

The first thing to check in an empirical study of the diffusion of IRAs is to what extent their spread is due to similar variations in functional pressures for their establishment, namely credibility and political uncertainty. Where their spread is caused by these factors, diffusion should be considered spurious because is not related to the interdependence of governments.

Credibility is an important political asset in economic regulation in general, but is particularly crucial in the regulation of utilities, which are characterized by both high sunk investments and significant dangers of political biases in regulatory policy making (Levy and Spiller, 1994). Following this argument, credibility is most necessary when competitive markets are created in formerly nationalized utilities. The success of utilities liberalization and privatization depends crucially on the capacity to attract private investment, which requires from governments the capacity to credibly commit to fair regulation. Figure 6.3 shows that this argument is consistent with empirical evidence. Liberalization and privatization have a positive impact on the hazard of IRA creation.[4] IRAs are also more likely to be established in financial markets and competition policy than in social regulation or utilities without privatization or liberalization. The impact of liberalization, however, is conditional on the partisan composition of government. Taking as a reference point the hazard of IRA creation when there is neither privatization nor liberalization, privatization increases the likelihood of IRA creation for both centre-right and centre-left governments. Similarly, both types of government are more likely to establish an IRA in financial markets and competition policy. Liberalization, on the other hand, increases the likelihood for centre-right governments, but *decreases* it for centre-left governments. This is an indication that when centre-left governments liberalize telecommunications or electricity, they want to keep more direct control over these sectors than does the centre-right. They are more afraid of the possible negative effects of

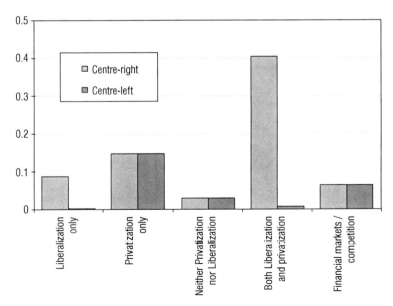

Figure 6.3 Hazard of IRA creations as a function of regulatory domain and government partisanship.

the free market, and are less willing to reduce their capacity to directly intervene in these sectors. When it comes to privatization, on the other hand, both centre-right and centre-left governments acknowledge that delegation is necessary for a credible commitment to those who buy shares in the privatized company, and who appreciate guarantees against expropriation dangers. In addition, if there is no liberalization, most of the fears associated with the free market do not emerge, which explains the willingness of centre-left governments to give up some of their direct control.

Figure 6.4 also shows the impact of the partisan composition of government, but more important, illustrates how the effect of liberalization depends on political constraints. Delegation is more likely when few political constraints are present, which means that political constraints are a functional equivalent of delegation for the achievement of credibility. When there are many political constraints, the system has intrinsic credibility as decisions can less easily be reverted once they are taken. Delegation is therefore less necessary. In the opposite case, few political constraints imply that decisions can quite easily be changed. The political system itself thus provides little credibility. When credibility needs to be achieved, other solutions must be found, and the establishment of IRAs is a possibility.

The second main source of spurious diffusion is political uncertainty, which is operationalized here, following Franzese (2002), as replacement risk, namely the risk for a government of being replaced by a coalition with different preferences.[5] Figure 6.5 consists of three figures for which the values of political constraints and replacement risk are the same, while mean replacement risk varies. Although the three variables are continuous, for interpretation purposes the impact of mean replacement risk and

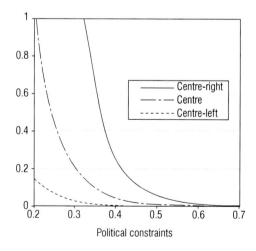

Figure 6.4 Impact of government partisanship and political constraints on the hazard of IRA creation, assuming utilities liberalization.

political constraints is examined only at 'high' and 'low' levels (as well as 'medium' for mean replacement risk). The findings on the role of political constraints receive strong confirmation in the context of political uncertainty. IRAs are more likely to be created if there are few political constraints. The reason is the same as for credibility: political constraints are a functional equivalent of delegation, rather than a precondition of it, as a means of preventing unwelcome policy changes. Replacement risk is a problem because if it is high, then policies are likely to be changed in unwanted ways. Delegation represents a means of preventing such changes. If there are many political constraints, however, delegation is redundant because change is already difficult. Figure 6.5 shows clearly that the impact of replacement risk on the likelihood of IRA creation is less important with many political constraints, and this is exactly what was expected. The second important insight in Figure 6.5 is related to the effects of mean replacement risk. Mean replacement risk is important because it can be seen as capturing the re-election chances of a government that has lost office. If mean replacement risk is high, then there are frequent alternations between different coalitions. Conversely, if mean replacement risk is low, it means that governments stay in place for a long time, or that governments change frequently, but differ little in their partisan composition. The consequences of replacement risk on incentives to delegate thus depend on mean replacement risk: a government will be less willing to pay the costs of delegation (mainly, in this context, self-binding) if in their country replacement risk is usually high (mean replacement risk is high), because even if it is replaced by a different coalition, the chances of it returning to office soon are high. In the opposite situation, if mean replacement risk is low, losing office means staying out for a long time, and therefore the incentives to bind the future government through delegation are higher. Figure 6.5 is consistent with this story. This can best be seen by looking at how the slope of the dashed line (which corresponds to the case of few political constraints) changes in the three graphs when mean replacement risk increases. The curve becomes less steep as mean replacement risk increases, meaning that replacement risk has a stronger impact when re-election prospects are poor (mean replacement risk is low) than when they are good (mean replacement risk is high).

So far we have refined our interpretation of the impact of spurious diffusion on the spread of IRAs. We can now move to the two diffusion mechanisms that have been found to be significant predictors of IRA creations, namely symbolic imitation and coercive isomorphism. Starting with the latter, Figure 6.6 shows that EU directive 97/51 had a very strong impact on the probability that IRAs were created for telecommunications regulation. The probability was over seven times higher for the period during which the directive required the separation of ownership and regulation of telecommunications companies, controlling for the impact of the other variables (including privatization and liberalization).

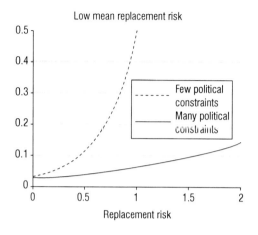

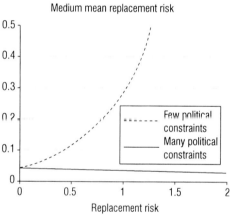

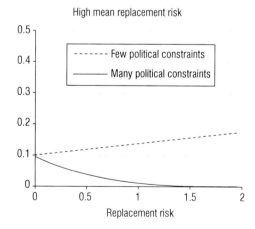

Figure 6.5 Impact of replacement risk and political constraints on the hazard of IRA creation.

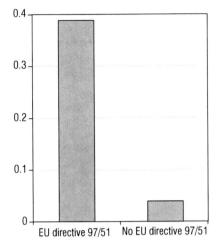

Figure 6.6 Impact of EU directive 97/51 (telecoms) on the hazard of IRA creations.

Second, Figure 6.7 illustrates how the probability of IRA creation in two domains (financial markets/competition policy and social regulation) increases with the number of IRAs of the same regulatory type (economic or social regulation) that have already been established. Following the organizational sociology literature (e.g. Hannan and Carroll, 1992), this simple indicator captures the extent to which a given policy or organizational form has achieved a 'taken for granted' status. While the validity of this measure is controversial, it is included in most sociological analyses of the diffusion of organizational forms, and is often found a good predictor of their adoption. Accordingly, and although I am aware of its limitations, I use the number of existing IRAs as a measure for symbolic imitation.

The curves are dashed when they refer to out-of-sample conditions: only thirty IRAs for social regulation have been established, though potentially up to fifty-one could be (i.e. three regulatory domains times seventeen countries). Further, the graph refers to the 1990s period, at the beginning of which five social and twenty economic IRAs already existed. The effect of symbolic imitation is strong: controlling for the other variables, including functional pressures, the probability that an IRA for financial markets or competition policy is established is over three times higher when IRAs exist in most economic regulatory domains in most countries than when only a few have been established. The effect is similar for social regulation, though at lower absolute levels because of differences in credibility pressures. Figure 6.7 thus clearly confirms the important role of symbolic imitation in the diffusion of IRAs. Should we want to

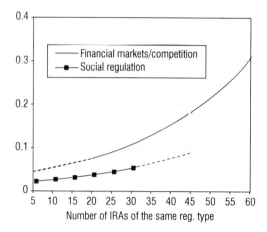

Figure 6.7 Impact of the number of IRAs existing at time t − 1 on the hazard of IRA creation.

quantify it, we would say that symbolic imitation multiplies the likelihood of IRA creation by three, keeping all functional pressures constant.

Variations in IRAs' formal independence

This section examines why some IRAs are formally more independent than others. The result presented here are from a Heckman selection model, whose estimated coefficients are in Appendix 6.3. The full analysis can be found in Gilardi (2004a).

Figure 6.8 shows how formal independence varies across regulatory domains. Two points are noteworthy. The first is that regulators engaged in economic regulation are more independent than those engaged in social regulation. The second is that utilities regulators are more independent than those in financial markets and competition policy. This is a strong confirmation of the credibility hypothesis. There are theoretical reasons to believe that governments need credibility in economic regulation in general, but particularly in utilities regulation. Figure 6.8 clearly indicates that these arguments are consistent with the empirical pattern of delegation to IRAs.

The third main insight of the analysis refers to the role of political uncertainty in explaining IRA independence. If they are afraid of losing office, governments may be inclined to grant more independence to IRAs, thereby trying to prevent their successors from changing their policies by delegating responsibility for them to IRAs. The measurement of replacement risk is here much more crude than in the longitudinal analysis: it is an average. Furthermore, in a purely cross-sectional analysis it is imposs-

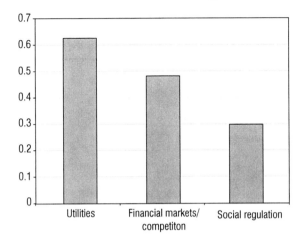

Figure 6.8 Formal independence of regulators in utilities, financial markets and competition, and social regulation.

Note
Unconditional expected value, Heckman model.

ible to test the hypothesis that the impact of replacement risk actually depends on the chances of a rapid return to office. Despite these limitations, replacement risk does have a significant impact on IRAs' independence, though only indirectly through the selection stage. Countries that, on average, are characterized by higher replacement risk tend to make IRAs more independent when they decide to establish them. On the other hand, institutions mediate the impact of replacement risk. Veto players operate as functional equivalents of delegation, since they promote the same policy stability that can be achieved through delegation. Therefore, replacement risk should be less of a problem in countries with many veto players. Figure 6.9 indicates that these arguments are consistent with empirical evidence. Replacement risk increases the formal independence of IRAs, but its impact is not linear: it is stronger at low levels of replacement risk. In other words, the difference is mainly between countries that are characterized by very little replacement risk and countries that experience moderate or high replacement risk. Moreover, veto players reduce the impact of replacement risk. In countries with many veto players, replacement risk does not increase IRAs' independence. This is consistent with theoretical expectations: since changing policies is difficult when many players have veto power, changes in the partisan composition of government are not associated with dramatic policy reversals. As a result, replacement risk is not significant in policy terms. Figure 6.9 shows exactly this: the impact of replacement risk on IRAs' independence decreases as the number of veto players increases.

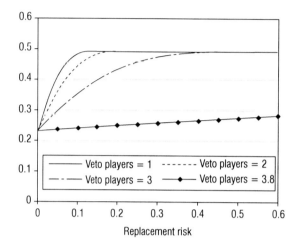

Figure 6.9 Impact of replacement risk and veto players on the formal independence of regulators.

Note
Unconditional expected value, Heckman model.

Delegation to IRAs in Western Europe: summary of the findings

We can now summarize the main findings of the empirical analysis. First, functional pressures matter. Delegation to IRAs is a response by governments to the twin problems of credibility and political uncertainty, which both arise from the fact that choices are made over time. Delegation is more likely, and formal independence more extensive, in economic than in social regulation; within the former, IRAs are more likely to be established and are formally more independent in utilities than in financial markets and competition policy. This reflects differences in credibility pressures, which are most acute in utilities, because of the sunk costs that investments involve, and more significant in other economic regulation than in social regulation. Liberalization and privatization of utilities sharply increase the probability that an IRA will be established. On the other hand, replacement risk increases both the likelihood of delegation and the extent of formal independence. Governments are more likely to delegate if they are at risk of being replaced by a coalition with different preferences, and the likelihood of this decreases congruently with the likelihood of them regaining power in the near future. If governments fear replacement but know the turnover rate in government is high, delegation means self-binding as much as binding others.

Second, institutions mediate functional pressures. Veto players and fiscal federalism are functional equivalents of delegation for the achievement of credible commitment capacity, as they prevent policy reversals and therefore improve the credibility of policy commitments. The formal independence of utilities IRAs is lower in countries characterized by market-preserving federalism, and the impact of utilities liberalization on the likelihood of IRA creation depends on veto players: IRAs are more likely to be created as a result of liberalization in political systems with few veto players. Veto players also moderate the effect of political uncertainty, as replacement risk has less impact on the probability that an IRA will be created in the presence of many veto players.

Credibility and political uncertainty partly explain the spread of IRAs in Western Europe, something which has occurred mainly since the late 1980s. The diffusion of IRAs has therefore been in part spurious, since it has been driven by the independent reaction of governments to similar functional pressures. None the less, governments also behaved interdependently. Symbolic imitation is one of the diffusion mechanisms that have been at work. IRAs are more likely to be established if many other IRAs already exist. This suggests that IRAs are established also because they have become a widely accepted and almost natural way to organize regulatory policies. While the functional properties of IRAs do matter, they are not the only factor that matters. IRAs are established not only because of the functions they perform, but also because they have been increasingly taken for granted as the normal thing to do when regulating markets. In addition, the European Union has exerted isomorphic pressures through some of its directives on common markets for electricity and telecommunications. IRAs were much more likely to be established following EU directives. Coercive isomorphism is therefore a second diffusion mechanism. It can be concluded, therefore, that delegation to IRAs is driven by a mix of functional pressures, which are mediated by institutions, and by diffusion mechanisms.

Conclusion

In the introduction I raised two broad questions on delegation to IRAs. These can now be answered. Why, in the early 1990s, did only a few independent regulators exist, while ten years after these institutions have become so common that the OECD can refer to them as 'one of the most widespread institutions of modern regulatory governance'? Because during the 1990s, as utilities were liberalized and privatized, the need for credible commitment capacity was raised, particularly in countries with few veto players. At the same time, the European Union actively promoted the establishment of IRAs. Replacement risk increased the probability of IRA creation throughout the period, but less in the presence of many veto players. As IRAs started to spread, it became increasingly difficult for governments *not* to establish IRAs, as they progressively became taken for granted as the appropriate way to organize regulatory policies.

Why, in some cases, are there quite independent IRAs, and in other cases, much less independent IRAs? The degree of independence depends on how much credible commitment capacity is needed. This in turn depends on the characteristics of the sector. Economic regulation in general, and utilities regulation in particular, needs more credible commitment capacity and therefore more independence. Replacement risk also leads to higher levels of independence. Veto players mitigate both pressures because, like IRAs, they make it more difficult for a government to change regulatory decisions.

The IRAs landscape, however, is not fixed, and is bound to change in complex ways over the next years. How will delegation to IRAs evolve? On the basis of this analysis, two main determinants of changes in delegation to IRAs can be identified. The first are functional pressures: as they change, delegation to IRAs can also be expected to change. Credibility and political uncertainty pressures are not constant over time, and though changes may not be immediately translated into new delegation arrangements, significant alterations in their importance can be expected to lead, eventually, to a reconsideration of IRAs' independence. The possibility that an IRA will be terminated altogether cannot be discarded either. Lewis (2002), for example, studied US agencies between 1946 and 1997 and found that more than 60 per cent were terminated, mainly as a result of political turnover. The symbolic dimension of IRAs can also be a cause of a trend reversal. IRAs are now widespread, and they are somewhat taken for granted as a good way to organize regulatory policy, but should a sizeable number of countries embrace a new model, or go back to regulation through ministries, a diffusion of the new arrangements could be expected, due notably to symbolic imitation. Other mechanisms, of course, could drive the diffusion of new regulatory institutions. It would not be the first time waves of policies could be observed; for example, utilities first underwent a wave of nationalization, then a wave of privatization. The same kind of waves could also characterize government approaches to regulatory institutions. IRAs are now widespread, but it would be a bold claim to say that they are here to stay.

Appendix 6.1. Summary of variables and measures

Variable	Measure	Source of data
Dependent variables		
Establishment of an IRA	Dummy taking the value of 1 if an IRA is established	Gilardi (2004a)
Formal independence of IRAs	Independence index (Gilardi 2002)	Gilardi (2004a)
Credibility		
Economic/social regulation	Dummy (1 for telecommunications, electricity, financial markets, competition; 0 for food safety, pharmaceuticals, environment)	Gilardi (2004a)
Utilities	Dummy (1 for telecommunications, electricity; 0 for financial markets, competition, food safety, pharmaceuticals, environment)	Gilardi (2004a)
Utility liberalization	Dummy (1 for years when market was opened in telecommunications or electricity)	Boylaud and Nicoletti (2000); Steiner (2000)
Utility privatization	Dummy (1 for years when telecommunications or electricity companies were privatized)	Boylaud and Nicoletti (2000); Levi-Faur (2003)
Political uncertainty		
Replacement risk	(Inverse of actual government duration)*(standard deviation of the partisan 'centre of gravity' of governments) (Franzese 2002)	Gilardi (2004a); Woldendorp *et al.* (2000)
Rapid re-election chances	Mean replacement risk	
Symbolic imitation		
Total No. of IRAs (t − 1)	–	Gilardi (2004a)
No. of IRAs of same reg. type (t − 1)	Reg. types: economic, social	Gilardi (2004a)
No. of IRAs in same reg. domain (t − 1)	Reg. domains: social reg., utilities, financial markets/competition	Gilardi (2004a)
Coercive isomorphism		
EU legislation requiring IRAs	Dummy (1 for years when an EU regulation requiring or promoting the set-up of IRAs was passed, or for years during which member states had to pass laws implementing EU directives requiring or promoting the set-up of IRAs)	Gilardi (2004a)
Institutions		
Veto players	Political constraints, checks, veto players	Beck *et al.* (2001); Henisz (2002); Tsebelis (2002)
Market-preserving federalism	Fiscal federalism	OECD
Consensus democracy	Consensus democracy, first dimension	Lijphart (1999)

Appendix 6.2. Determinants of the establishment of IRAs (event history analysis)

Diffusion: symbolic imitation	
No. of IRAs of the same reg. type	0.035**
	(0.015)
Diffusion: coercive isomorphism	
EU directive 92/44 (telecommunications)	0.468
	(0.737)
EU directive 96/92 (energy)	0.245
	(0.501)
EU directive 97/51 (telecommunications)	2.307***
	(0.405)
Spurious diffusion: credibility	
Financial markets/competition	0.717***
	(0.261)
Privatization	1.537***
	(0.584)
Liberalization	11.907***
	(2.557)
Liberalization × political constraints	−15.084***
	(4.726)
Partisan composition of government × liberalization	−1.995***
	(0.318)
Spurious diffusion: political uncertainty	
Replacement risk	1.605***
	(1.489)
Mean replacement risk	2.881***
	(0.855)
Replacement risk × mean replacement risk.	−5.463**
	(2.149)
Replacement risk × political constraints	−5.308***
	(1.873)
Spurious diffusion: mad cow	
Mad cow (BSE)	0.009***
	(0.002)
Institutions and parties	
Political constraints	1.088
	(1.422)
Partisan composition of government	−0.184
	(0.142)
Constant	−17.714***
	(4.456)
Alpha	4.067
Log likelihood (constant only)	−42.333
Log likelihood (full model)	−9.496
Wald chi^2 (d.f.)	613.5 (16)
No. of sectors/countries (IRA creations)	117 (77)
No. of observations	4,405

Notes
Weibull model. Robust standard errors in parentheses (for clustering on IRAs). *$z < 0.1$, **$z < 0.05$, ***$z < 0.01$.

Appendix 6.3. Determinants of the formal independence of IRAs (Heckman selection model)

	Selection	*Independence*
Utilities	8.361***	0.132***
	(1.875)	(0.023)
Financial markets/competition	1.822***	
	(0.32)	
Replacement risk (mean)	28.192***	
	(4.974)	
Consensus democracy		
Fiscal federalism	0.025***	−0.002**
	(0.009)	(0.007)
Veto players	0.49*	
	(0.25)	
Utilities × fiscal federalism	−0.098***	
	(0.026)	
Replacement risk (mean) × veto players	−7.315***	
	(1.334)	
Constant		
	−4.026***	0.563***
	(0.822)	(0.031)
Rho	−0.632**	
	(0.218)	
Sigma	0.114***	
	(0.008)	
Log likelihood	33.657	
Wald chi^2	32.76	
Censored observations	22	
No.	100	

Notes
Maximum likelihood estimation. Robust standard errors in brackets (for clustering on countries). *$z < 0.1$, **$z < 0.05$, ***$z < 0.01$.

Notes

1 Conventionally, regulation is termed 'economic' when it deals with the price, entry, exit and service of an industry, while it is termed 'social' when it concerns non-economic issues such as safety and health (see e.g. Meier, 1985: 3).

2 This does not mean delegation was necessarily absent. Self-regulation, for example, entails delegation to the private sector. On the other hand, independent agencies have long been present in research policy, notably in the form of funding agencies.

3 In the third form of isomorphism, mimetic isomorphism, copying occurs because of uncertainty. It can be conceptualized as a form of bounded learning, and is thus not treated separately.

4 'Hazards' are a concept used in event-history analysis. For the present purposes, the hazard can be considered equivalent to a probability (in this case, the probability that an IRA is established). For more details see Box-Steffensmeier and Jones (2004: 13–15)

5 More precisely, replacement risk is operationalized as the product of the inverse of actual government duration and of the standard deviation of the partisan 'centre of gravity' of governments over a certain number of years.

References

Beck, T., Clarke, G., Groff A., Keefer, P. and Walsh, P. (2001) 'New Tools in Comparative Political Economy. The Database of Political Institutions', *World Bank Economic Review*, 15 (1): 165–176.

Box-Steffensmeier, J. M. and Jones, B. S. (2004) *Event History Modeling. A Guide for Social Scientists*, Cambridge: Cambridge University Press.

Boylaud, O. and Nicoletti, G. (2000) *Regulation, Market Structure and Performance in Telecommunications*, Economic Department Working Papers, No. 237 ECO/WKP(2000)10, Paris: Organization for Economic Co-operation and Development.

De Figueiredo, R. J. P. (2002) 'Electoral Competition, Political Uncertainty, and Policy Insulation', *American Political Science Review*, 96 (2): 321–333.

DiMaggio, P. J. and Powell, W. W. (1991) 'The Iron Cage Revisited. Institutional Isomorphism and Collective Rationality in Organizational Fields', in P. J. DiMaggio and W. W. Powell (eds) *The New Institutionalism in Organizational Analysis*, Chicago: University of Chicago Press.

Franzese, R. J. (2002) *Macroeconomic Policies of Developed Democracy*, Cambridge: Cambridge University Press.

Frederick, S., Loewenstein, G. and O'Donoghue, T. (2002) 'Time Discounting and Time Preference: A Critical Review', *Journal of Economic Literature*, 40: 351–401.

Gilardi, F. (2002) 'Policy Credibility and Delegation to Independent Regulatory Agencies: A Comparative Empirical Analysis', *Journal of European Public Policy*, 9 (6): 873–893.

Gilardi, F. (2004a) 'Delegation in the Regulatory State. Origins and Diffusion of Independent Regulatory Agencies in Western Europe', PhD dissertation, Université de Lausanne.

Gilardi, F. (2004b) 'Institutional Change in Regulatory Policies: Regulation through Independent Agencies and the Three New Institutionalisms', in J. Jordana and D. Levi-Faur (eds) *The Politics of Regulation. Institutions and Regulatory Reforms for the Age of Governance*, Cheltenham: Edward Elgar.

Hannan, M. T. and Carroll, G. R. (1992) *Dynamics of Organizational Populations. Density, Legitimation, and Competition*, Oxford: Oxford University Press.

Henisz, W. J. (2002) 'The Institutional Environment for Infrastructure Investment', *Industrial and Corporate Change* 11 (2): 355–389.

Kydland, F. E. and Prescott, E. C. (1977) 'Rules rather than Discretion: The Inconsistency of Optimal Plans', *Journal of Political Economy*, 85 (3): 473–491.

Lazer, D. (2001) 'Regulatory Interdependence and International Governance', *Journal of European Public Policy*, 8 (3): 474–492.

Levi-Faur, D. (2003) 'The Politics of Liberalisation: Privatisation and Regulation-for-Competition in Europe's and Latin America's Telecoms and Electricity Industries', *European Journal of Political Research*, 42: 705–740.

Levy, B. and Spiller, P. T. (1994) 'The Institutional Foundations of Regulatory Commitment: A Comparative Analysis of Telecommunications Regulation', *Journal of Law, Economics, and Organization*, 10 (2): 201–246.

Lewis, D. E. (2002) 'The Politics of Agency Termination: Confronting the Myth of Agency Immortality', *Journal of Politics*, 64 (1): 89–107.

Lijphart, A. (1999) *Patterns of Democracy. Government Forms and Performance in Thirty-six Countries*, New Haven CT: Yale University Press.

Majone, G. (2001) 'Nonmajoritarian Institutions and the Limits of Democratic Governance: A Political Transaction-Cost Approach', *Journal of Institutional and Theoretical Economics*, 157: 57–78.

McDermott, R. (2001) 'The Psychological Ideas of Amos Tversky and their Relevance for Political Science', *Journal of Theoretical Politics*, 13 (1): 5–33.

Meier, K. J. (1985) *Regulation. Politics, Bureaucracy, and Economics*, New York: St Martin's Press.

Meseguer, C. (2003) *Learning and Economic Policy Choices: A Bayesian Approach*, EUI Working Paper No. 2003/05, Florence: EUI.

Meyer, J. W. and Rowan, B. (1977) 'Institutionalized Organizations: Formal Structure as Myth and Ceremony', *American Journal of Sociology*, 83 (2): 340–363.

Moe, T. M. (1990) 'Political Institutions: The Neglected Side of the Story', *Journal of Law, Economics, and Organization*, 6 (Special Issue): 213–253.

OECD (2002) *Regulatory Policies in OECD Countries. From Interventionism to Regulatory Governance*, OECD Reviews of Regulatory Reform, Paris: Organization for Economic Co-operation and Development.

Simmons, B. A. and Elkins, Z. (2004) 'The Globalization of Liberalization: Policy Diffusion in the International Political Economy', *American Political Science Review*, 98 (1): 171–189.

Steiner, F. (2000) *Regulation, Industry Structure and Performance in the Electricity Supply Industry*, Economics Department Working Papers, No. 238, ECO/WKP(2000)11. Paris: Organization for Economic Co-operation and Development.

Tsebelis, G. (2002) *Veto Players: How Political Institutions Work*, Princeton NJ: Princeton University Press.

Tversky, A. and Kahneman, D. (1974) 'Judgment under Uncertainty: Heuristics and Bias', *Science*, 185 (4157): 1124–1131.

Weingast, B. R. (1993) 'Constitutions as Governance Structures: The Political Foundations of Secure Markets', *Journal of Institutional and Theoretical Economics*, 149 (1): 286–311.

Weingast, B. R. (1995) 'The Economic Role of Political Institutions: Market-preserving Federalism and Economic Development', *Journal of Law, Economics, and Organization*, 11 (1): 1–31.

Woldendorp, J., Keman, H. and Budge, I. (2000) *Party Government in 48 Democracies. Composition – Duration – Personnel*, Dordrecht: Kluwer.

7 Delegation in the distributive policy arena

The case of research policy

Dietmar Braun

While other chapters of this book fill gaps by dealing with the 'delegation chain of parliamentary democracy' or by discussing delegation to independent regulatory agencies I intend to enlarge our view of delegation by choosing a different public policy field – research policy – which is generally considered to belong to the *distributive* policy arena. Similar to the regulatory policy field, in research policy we find a large degree of delegation to independent agencies, i.e. funding agencies. Although the widespread diffusion to these institutions took place some time ago, in contrast to independent regulatory agencies (Braun, 1997), by comparing regulatory and distributive policy, general conclusions can be drawn on similar and divergent patterns and dynamics of delegation in public policy making.

First, I will discuss how distributive and regulatory policies differ from each other and what this means for how to delegate. Next, it will be demonstrated that a specific type of distributive policies, namely policies taken under risk, show characteristics that fit with the discussion on delegation. The more thorough analysis of research policy as an example of such a risk policy shows that one should distinguish between trustor and trustee relationships between policy makers and target groups, e.g. scientists, and delegation relationships between policy makers and funding agencies. The discussion on delegation will deal with the question of discretion and control of funding agencies and the tensions funding agencies are confronted with as intermediaries between scientists and policy makers.

Distributive and regulatory policies

Most of the recent discussions of delegation in public policy making have dealt with regulatory policies, including an outflow of the increasing numbers of so-called independent regulatory agencies in this field (see Thatcher and Stone Sweet, 2002; Gilardi, 2002). Regulatory policies have distinctive characteristics compared to other public policy 'arenas', particularly with regard to distributive and redistributive policy fields (see for this distinction Lowi, 1972). To date, the discussion on delegation has not sufficiently taken these differences into account. Seldom do we find profound reflections on the relationship between the various character-istics of public policy areas and the usefulness or problems of delegation.[1] In this chapter, I will address this shortcoming by analysing a particular type of distributive policy, i.e. policies taken under risk like research pol-icies, to broaden our perspective on the usefulness of studies on delega-tion in public policy making.

There are some indications that delegation is embedded differently in environments of regulation and distribution. For systematic reasons the reader should remember that delegation in public policy fields, independ-ent from the policy arena, takes place within a configuration of actors that entail in its most basic form three parties, policy makers, target groups, and bureaucracy or in our case independent agencies. Often forgotten in discussions on delegation is that the basic relationship is the one between policy makers and target groups. Delegation to independent agencies is not unavoidable and it might be a temporary phenomenon as Gilardi sug-gests (see Gilardi in Chapter 6). It is my contention that the characteristics of the relations between policy makers and target groups play a major role in understanding the why and how of delegation to independent agencies.

Regulatory policies limit individual or group choices in order to restrict unacceptable behaviour or enhance a desired behaviour. In distributive policy, governments attempt to distribute money to some groups within the population and pay for those benefits from general tax revenues. This immediately reveals that the effects on target groups are different, with consequences for the degree of conflict and actor relations in both arenas. In distributive policies the benefits are visible whilst costs are hidden. In regulatory policies costs in terms of behavioural restrictions are most evident for target groups and benefits are usually visible only in the long term. This explains why there is usually greater conflict about formu-lating regulatory policy than distributive policy. Target groups in regula-tory policy endeavour to influence the policy design process. Often coalitions are formed that defend similar ideological and interest

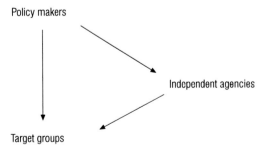

Figure 7.1 Basic actor configuration in public policy.

positions. As this policy arena is subject to strain and tensions, decisions are mostly taken in parliament with a high degree of visibility to the public. Regulatory policies are transparent, often cause conflicts and the political salience is high, which explains the dominant role of the legislator. It also explains why discussions on 'time inconsistency' of policy makers and credible commitment have such a high status in explaining the reasons for delegation in regulatory policy (see Majone, 2001a, b; Gilardi in Chapter 6) Parliaments and governments have good reason in this policy arena to believe that future governments may choose other options for dealing with regulatory matters. The degree of conflict between political parties on these matters may lead to the conclusion that it is better to delegate decisions to bureaucracy or independent regulatory agencies in order to avoid the high bargaining and transaction costs (see Epstein and O'Halloran, 1999 for a summary of the arguments).

Distributive policies are less subject to such tensions. In contrast to regulatory policies they have low visibility, are non-conflictive, and have a low salience in policy making. This is easily explained: as there are no visible costs involved, we seldom find coalition building to defend particular issues in this context. Mostly small and homogeneous groups profit from the public money. As political salience is low, decisions are usually taken at the level of ministries and public bureaucracy. Agency capture is an immanent danger in this field, much more so than in regulatory policies (see Gormley, 1979 and Cohen, 1986 for regulatory policies). Because small and homogeneous groups profit from government money they have a high incentive and the potential to act collectively in order to influence the decisions in this field. This leads to frequent contacts with agencies and ministries responsible for distributive policies. It is unsurprising that the 'iron triangle' metaphor has been developed in a distributive policy field, i.e. in relation to the promotion of health research (see Heclo, 1978) and that Olson speaks of 'distributive coalitions' to characterize economic inefficiencies (Olson, 1982). Instead of internal conflicts, one more often finds collusion between benefiting target groups, responsible agencies and ministries to defend the budget for the policy in question and to be in conflict against other policies (Epstein and O'Halloran, 1995: 230). The 'revolving doors' (Gormley, 1979) often play a role in distributive policies. Usually decisions are taken within the confines of ministries or by delegated agencies which are not visible to the public. The parliament is only generally involved in allocating general budgets to the distributive policy field and does not interfere in the daily affairs or legislate in this area. This suggests that delegation might have a different character in this policy arena. In regulatory policy, agencies need to maintain a certain distance from target groups to credibly develop and defend certain policies, whilst they are in constant struggle with parliament about the degree of discretion. In distributive policies, agencies have close links with target groups and are exempt from constant struggles about discretion. Such close links are not to be expected or desired in regulatory policies. Though independent regulatory agencies depend on the information of target groups, as in distributive policies, they must keep at distance so as not to undermine their position as authorities in the regulatory policy in question.

In addition, it is generally assumed that agencies in distributive policies need considerable room for manoeuvre and discretion to function effectively. Why is that so? Although policy makers may be able to define broad guidelines, the actual task of distributing money to target groups needs a lot of flexibility and day-to-day decision making that cannot be defined in advance. If the policy area in question is relatively restricted, then agencies are usually granted considerable room for manoeuvre by responsible ministries.

This overview based on literature about public policies demonstrates that starting with the assumption that delegation may have different characteristics in policy arenas is justified – relationships between actors differ; the role of target groups is significant in delegation, while the role of parliament seems to have a much lower status.

Trust in research policies

Until now I have discussed delegation in terms of political principals (government, ministry, parliament), independent agencies and target groups. The relationship between political principals and independent agencies is usually described in terms of delegation. So, how can we define the relationship between policy makers and target groups? We need to understand in a systematic way the whole 'triad' of actor constellations, before we can understand delegation in the distributive policy arena.

My proposition is that, for the specific type of distributive policies that I am interested in here, relations between policy makers and target groups can be better analysed in terms of *trustor and trustees* than in terms of delegation. However, trust and delegation have commonalities (see Coleman, 1990: 91). Both can be described as social structures that derive from decisions under risk taken by policy makers. In both cases policy makers invest resources 'based on a hope or expectation that the other's actions will satisfy his interests better than would his own actions' (ibid.). The incentive is the hope of future gains, in terms either of money or of a 'unilateral transfer of control over certain resources to another actor' (ibid.). Trust and delegation involve uncertainty about the future because the principal or the trustor depends on future actions of the agent or the trustee. The difference between the two types of decisions under risk and uncertainty, according to Coleman, consists of one feature: in delegation relationships which he considers as authority relations where property rights are transferred, *contracts* are usually used to reduce the risk to the principal. The use of contracts gives the opportunity of defining the discretion granted to agents and the control procedures involved. This is not the case for trust relationships which are not enforceable by law. Hence, discussions of discretion and control are relegated to the background. In this case the risk is incorporated into the 'decision of whether or not to engage in the action' (ibid.), which is equivalent to trust, and reducing risks entails carefully thinking about the possible losses and gains of the investment. In fact, policy makers as trustors need to feel that the probability of winning with their investment is greater than the possibility of losing. According to Coleman (1990: 99):

$$\frac{p}{(1-p)} > \frac{L}{G}$$

where the trustor invests in the activities of the trustee with the risk of losing his or her investments (L). If the trustee is trustworthy and successful, the trustor will receive gain from the investments (G). As investments into science are risk investments there is only a probability p that the trustor will indeed receive gain of investments. $1 - p$ is the chance that he or she will lose the invested money.

Delegation and trust relationships are both subclasses of decisions under risk with commonalities and differences. It is worthwhile keeping this difference in mind when discussing the social action structure between policy makers, independent agencies and target groups

Distributive policies are not generally considered policies under risk. Only if there is a transfer of money to target groups where services are to be provided in the distant future is there risk involved. We would not speak of a policy under risk in the case of distributing meal vouchers to the poor or when a subsidy is given to individuals without any obligation. This is different for research policy. In this case money is given to scientists on the base of a promise for future discoveries and inventions. Funds provided to scientists willing to investigate the genome of the worm are an investment in an uncertain future. Nobody knows whether there will be any useful result. Thus, there is a 'time lag' between the spending of the money and the return of knowledge. In order to reduce the risk policy makers must find out if scientists who receive the money are 'trustworthy', whether they will be good enough and are willing to do their best. Therefore, before policy makers will give money to scientists, they need some assurance mechanisms, signals and proofs of the trustworthiness of scientists in order to reduce the probable loss of their money (Coleman, 1990: 91). This problem, of course, is similar to the problem of adverse selection and moral hazard in delegation relationships. However, in delegation this problem can be addressed by using contracts, whereas in trust relationships it cannot.

Research policy is by nature a policy area based on trust because the characteristics spelled out above hold. Given this, then a crucial point in the trustor's decision to trust is to what extent he or she can trust scientists or how he or she can increase the probability that scientists will indeed deliver what they promise. If policy makers can be sure that they have chosen the best scientists and that these scientists will do their best to keep their promises, then the risks involved in the distribution of money to research can be considerably reduced and $(1 - p)$ will be low.

What are the options for policy makers to reduce the risk of research investments and make sure that they find trustworthy 'trustees' who do their best and are successful if they cannot use contracts? In the literature four *mechanisms* are mentioned that may help to improve the belief of policy makers in the trustworthiness of scientists.

Balancing out

The first mechanism aims to shave the sharp edges off the claims of policy makers and scientists in funding research that are often in conflict with each other, most notably with regard to the distribution of money for responsive and earmarked funding. The best outcome for scientists in the 'funding game' is to get money from the state and decide for themselves what to do with the money, whilst policy makers might prefer to spend as much as possible of the earmarked funding linked to their own purposes. There are several ways to reconcile the conflicting interests and find a balance that gives neither scientists nor policy makers an incentive to strain trust relationships.

First, Morris refers to the micro-level and, based on empirical research, contends that scientists are quite able to cope with the increasing demands of policy makers in research funding without losing their identity or sacrificing their interest (Morris, 2003). Scientists, she maintains, often do not take into account the attitude of an agent or a trustee at all. They consider themselves as 'independent contractors' and 'entrepreneurs' who are respecting demands of their 'stakeholders', but who nevertheless manage quite well to bring them into line with their own view of things, mostly by developing compromises between what policy makers want and their own objectives in their daily work as scientists. There is much more flexibility in the use of scientific norms and objectives than one usually thinks. This gives scientists the opportunity to 'reconcile the incompatibilities' (ibid.: 367) within the constant 'boundary process' that they are engaged in. In other words, though scientists feel the pressure, they have developed coping behaviours that plane off the sharp sides of the directed mode of funding. This prevents a general shift to shirking.

Van der Meulen adds a second argument (Meulen, 1998). He states that if policy makers and scientists can *build up a consensus on the objectives to be pursued in research policy*, then there will be no reason for either side to cheat. Institutional opportunity structures for consensus building vary between countries. The integration of scientific advisers in the government, the use of science councils or the Etats-généraux in France may serve this purpose. Bernal proposed early corporatist schemes to set up a joint research policy between scientists and policy makers (Bernal, 1939; see also Braun, 1997). Notwithstanding doubts on the feasibility of such a joint policy formulation, consensus building has often been an objective of policy makers in research policy and has without any doubt appeased occasional tensions between the scientific community and policy makers. Morris adds that there have always been research areas where scientists and policy makers' interests converged (for example in health research) and that today there may very well be more commonalities between scientists and policy makers than one might anticipate (Morris 2003). The scientific community today seems to have accepted the idea that science should demonstrate its usefulness to the public. This means that there is potential for reorganizing career structures of scientists in favour of innovation.

More recently, new institutions are used in funding policies that may serve to reconcile the interests of scientists with demands from the economy and society, i.e. *networks*, especially cross-systemic networks between industry and academia (for literature on 'triple helix' see Etzkowitz and Leydesdorff, 1998, 2000). The advantage of these networks, which are often in the form of public–private partnerships, is that they create 'interaction spaces' between basic research, applied research and development without obliging scientists to adapt to the objectives and culture of enterprises. In this way scientists can continue their academic career and enterprises may profit from the collaboration with scientists. The moral hazard for scientists can therefore be avoided in the institutional embedding of networks.

Changing career patterns

A much stronger way to avoid the shirking of scientists is to change their career patterns – building on the reputation mechanisms of the scientific community and encouraging them to accept research patterns dedicated to application and innovation as part of their scientific career. The new governance strategies inspired by new public management endeavour to attain such a fundamental change. The strategy is to use research institutions, like universities that already employ scientists. For this purpose contracts have been introduced that include broad objectives to diffuse basic knowledge for industrial and societal purposes as the 'third function' of universities. This has started and is continuing to change some of the career structures in academia. Reputations previously defined by contributions to basic science became contested or compromised within universities and research institutions by other activities, e.g. contributions to patents, participation in university–industry collaboration etc. In this way, scientists become increasingly motivated to regard knowledge production of useful applications favourably, as part of their career structure and not as 'wasted time'. Consequently the incentive for moral hazard decreases and government and scientist objectives begin to converge.

Intermediaries of trust

The next mechanism uses 'intermediaries of trust' (for an analytical description of this term see Coleman, 1990: 180–185). Such intermediaries enter the trust relationship between scientists and policy makers and serve to generate and maintain the trust of policy makers concerning the work of scientists. To do so, intermediaries of trust advise government or they may 'guarantee' the non-shirking of the trustee, although this is not a suitable procedure in research policy. The key point is that government has good reason to trust these intermediaries more than they can trust scientists. One reason may be that such intermediaries are specifically set up to take into account the interests of government while having an inherent interest in preventing scientists from shirking. Such an interest can originate from the fact that they would lose their position as intermediaries if the trustee, the scientist, shirked. Two institutions are discussed in the literature that can fulfil such a function.

The first institution is *peer review* where scientific experts are chosen as advisers. Policy makers trust the experts to have sufficient judgement about who to trust within the scientific community. On the base of their judgement money is distributed to scientists. The important point is that the scientific community itself has a vested interest in peer reviewing: it establishes a quality selection mechanism that the scientific community can use for its own purposes; it avoids political monitoring and provides the opportunity to allocate government money. Experts themselves have a motive to play the game and fulfil their function honestly, as they are selected on the basis of their reputation in the field. If the selected scientists shirk, this has immediate repercussions on their status not only in the eyes of policy makers but also within the scientific community. The more important question is whether policy makers will be able to find scientific experts who are willing to play the role of intermediaries of trust if strings are attached to funding measures and political objectives are more often imposed on research funding. In this case, it may be that peer review is unfeasible or, if scientific experts are used, they might not have sufficient standing in the scientific community to make accurate judgements on the quality of other scientists.

The second type of institution is a *research institution* such as a *university* which employs scientists, for example as professors, and indicates through their procedural requirements that these scientists are capable of doing good research. In this case, policy makers trust the judgment and procedures of universities as an institution in a similar way that they trust scientific experts.[2]

Delegation to funding agencies

A last mechanism is to use explicit delegation to (independent) funding agencies as a mechanism to make sure that scientists are trustworthy (see Morris, 2003; Braun, 1993, 1997, 1998; Guston, 1996, 2000, 2001; Meulen, 1998; Caswill, 1998, 2003). Delegation is a functional means to deal with the uncertainties involved in the direct relationship of policy makers and scientist target groups. This places funding agencies in the triad between policy makers and scientists. The next section discusses this delegation relationship embedded in the context of trust relationships in research policy.

In summary, there are a number of non-contractual mechanisms that can help to both maintain the trust of policy makers in scientists and convince scientists to use government money in line with political objectives. In this way, the probability of losing money can be considerably reduced. These mechanisms serve to maintain a sufficiently high belief in p by policy makers.

Delegation in research policies

Policy makers have usually established funding agencies with the aim of increasing the likelihood that investments in research will have beneficial outcomes, which is equivalent to saying that scientists are trustworthy. In this case contracts are defined which specify the tasks, the degree of discretion and the accountability of these agencies. As in all delegation relationships, 'shirking' is a possible strategy for funding agencies and policy makers must make provision to prevent such behaviour. Delegation is not for reasons of political uncertainty and problems of political credibility, as in the case of independent regulatory agencies, it is the uncertainties involved in the trust relationship with scientists. Delegation in research policy is, therefore, intimately connected to the trustor–trustee relationship between policy makers and scientists.

To grapple with the essential characteristics of delegation in research policy the following sections will deal with two topics: the contractual features policy makers can use to prevent shirking by funding agencies, in particular the amount of discretion they grant to funding agencies and the control mechanisms they have, and second, how funding agencies position themselves between the principal and the trustee and what kind of dynamics this creates.

Discretion and control in the delegation to funding agencies

The degree of discretion granted to agencies is, according to the literature on regulatory policies, a function of the degree of uncertainty, defined as the 'range of alternative policy choices over which the legislator has little or no information, and thus over which the legislator cannot discern a clear optimum' (McCubbins, 1985: 736) as well as of a conflict of interests in parliament. If principals are uncertain about their preferences, objectives and outcomes, it is reasonable to give agencies a high degree of autonomy in decision making so that they can flexibly react to developments in the field. In addition, it may be a useful strategy for avoiding blame for unfavourable outcomes in the policy domain that may have negative effects on electoral prospects of policy makers. What can we say about uncertainty and discretion in delegating research policies to funding agencies?

The first answer is that it depends. Usually, one regards the field of research policy as a domain where information is hard to come by and political objectives are difficult to develop, in comparison to many other policy areas. In addition, it is a distributive policy field where flexibility is seen as an advantage for the functioning of agencies. However, the story is more complicated, mainly because uncertainty about outcomes varies with the kind of research that is done. In other words, uncertainty is correlated with different stages of research, normally distinguished as basic, strategic, and applied research.[3] While it is hard to specify where basic research will lead to and whether/when we can expect a discovery, strategic research attempts to build a bridge between basic and applied research and set objectives which basic research should lead to (Irvine and Martin, 1984). Applied research is the most advanced in this respect as it is inspired by concrete problems in the economy, society or politics and tries to find answers to these problems. Though it remains difficult to guarantee any specific outcomes or be sure about positive results at any stage of research, applied research is less beset with risk than basic research is. For this reason industrial enterprises often prefer to delegate investments in basic research to the state.

To sum up the argument, one can state that uncertainty decreases from basic to applied research and policy makers are more able to develop preferences in applied than in basic research. The consequences for policy makers can be expressed in terms of an *expectation rate* linked to future gains from investments in research (G in the formula above). In basic research future gains are far away and not yet visible. The expectation rate can therefore be considered small. From strategic to applied research, uncertainty decreases and future gains are more attainable and thus the expectation rates rises and therefore G. Policy makers become increasingly able to define preferences and objectives in research and also limit the number of alternatives funding agencies can decide upon. According to the insights of McCubbins, this means that one can expect that agencies specialized in the funding of basic research will have high discretion, while more applied-oriented technological funding agencies will have less discretion.

It seems, therefore, that the trust of policy makers and the structure of delegation depend on characteristics of the subject in question, i.e.

knowledge production. Yet this is too simple. It is not only the 'field' that structures delegation but also *institutional capabilities* of the political system and *ideational* factors. Discussing the latter first, models of innovation that prevail at certain points of time can have an important influence on the perception policy makers have about how to delegate. The 'interaction model of innovation' developed in the 1980s links applied research more closely to basic research with effects on the expectations about the discount rate of future gains in research investments, while the 'science push model' after the Second World War, still supported by many actors (see above all Stokes, 1997; Guston and Keniston, 1994; Elzinga and Jamison, 1995), petrified the image of the three separate stages of research. Consequently, in the interaction model it becomes difficult to uphold the clear demarcation of types of funding agencies and their degree of discretion. Second, institutional capabilities are affected by whether and to what extent the political system has developed an expertise of its own in developing research policies. Until the 1960s such expertise was simply lacking, with the consequence that political objectives could not be defined nor preferences developed. Though limits remain concerning the three stages of research, there is more capacity today to define political preferences and objectives and, therefore, expectations of future gain become more concrete. As neither the innovation model nor institutional capacities existed at the establishment of the funding agencies – before and shortly after the Second World War (see Braun, 1997) – nevertheless one can maintain the assumption that one will find differences in the constitutional setup of funding agencies with regard to discretion.

However, it would be too simple to discuss delegation to funding agencies only in terms of discretion. Discretion is seldom granted without some safety nets, i.e. control procedures. There are several mechanisms discussed in the literature on regulatory policy that serve to prevent or at least to mitigate the shirking of agencies:

The strongest mechanism is the 'veto power' of policy makers, which can reverse any decision that funding agencies have taken (for the regulatory policy domain see Epstein and O'Halloran, 1999). As has already been said, funding decisions of agencies are usually not discussed in parliament or in government. Parliamentary discussion usually – except for laws on structural changes in the system – deals with the budget dedicated to research and it is here that sanctions may be taken. However, this is not equivalent to veto power. While parliament does not hold such a veto power, this is different when considering the interventions of the responsible minister. Depending on their legal status, the decisions of funding agencies may be liable to approval by the minister, though this would be exceptional, as the autonomy of funding agencies is sufficient enough to make day-to-day decisions on their own, although the minister might be involved when budget questions or strategic decisions are under review.

A weaker mechanism is *sanctions*. First, the most effective sanctions are budget cuts or the earmarking of government money to politically defined goals (and thereby reducing the discretion of funding agencies). The use of the budget as a sanctioning mechanism is highly relevant in the United States, where the appropriation committees of Congress have an important policy position. It is feasible and has often happened that Congress used the budget to sanction previous policies of funding agencies or to earmark government money. This is a less frequent occurrence in the European context, where the money for funding agencies is often part of a general package of money distributed to research and presented to the parliament without major discussions on particular items. In Europe, it is usually government that has the power to sanction funding agencies by curtailing or by granting funds. Such power is not exercised over individual items in the decisions of funding agencies but rather takes into account the overall performance of funding agencies. More often than not, however, budget decisions in the European context are not based on any particular evaluation of the performance of funding agency, they are simply the result of the degree of support for research in government on the one hand and parliament and budgetary constraints on the other. Second, government can use the appointment and dismissal of key personnel in the funding agency as a sanction mechanism. Sanctions can have a preventive effect in respect of shirking, when they are clearly and credibly announced. More often they serve to correct inefficient use of government money by funding agencies. When it comes to appointments and dismissals, the right to use this sanction depends on the legal status of the funding agency. If funding agencies are established as private or quasi-public foundations, government will find it difficult to use this measure and it may also be subject to negotiation during the constitution-building period, as the example of the National Science Foundation in the United States demonstrates. In this case, the President has the legal right to nominate the director. In contrast, at the German Science Foundation policy makers cannot interfere. Third, the strongest sanction is the right of the government to close down or merge funding agencies. Again, this depends on the legal status of the agency.

Sanctions cannot be used without a preceding process of *monitoring* (Fiorina, 1981, Weingast, 1984). Usually one distinguishes in the literature on principal–agent theory between 'police patrol oversight' and 'fire alarm' (McCubbins and Schwartz, 1984: 166) where police patrol oversight means more central and direct monitoring of activities of the agency and fire-alarm oversight establishes a decentralized system of control where 'third parties' like citizens and interest groups have the opportunity to report on the behaviour of agencies. Both monitoring procedures can help policy makers to prepare sanctions. The usefulness of such monitoring devices in research policy depends on the ability of policy makers to define their preferences and objectives at the particular research stage. The more uncertain the future in research becomes the less it seems possible to install a central and directed monitoring policy. In basic research the only means for monitoring that policy makers usually have are the scientists themselves expressing their content or discontent with the activities of the funding agency. This could operate as a kind of 'third party' fire alarm for policy makers if one could assume no collusion or 'revolving door' policies between scientists and funding agencies. Given the close relationship between basic research funding agencies and scientists, the fire alarm may often fail In strategic and applied research the actors that might directly profit from research, like industrial enterprises and citizens, are considered as adequate third parties. In fact, though such fire alarms have become more institutionalized in recent years by integrating 'stakeholders' in advisory boards of funding agencies and by demanding more frequent exchange between funding agencies and the public, it remains extremely difficult for outsiders to judge the activities of funding agencies. As there is uncertainty about future outcomes even at the applied research stage, different investments might lead to success and it is difficult to tell from the outside (or from the inside) what would be the best strategy. Police patrol oversight procedures are usually not implemented except for the hearings in the appropriation committees of the US Congress, where funding agencies must defend their policies and in particular the use of earmarked funds.

While veto power and sanctions are *ex post* measures, the last mechanism, *procedural requirements*, can be defined as an *ex ante* mechanism, applied during the constitution-building period, though one might introduce other elements later on. McCubbins (1985) mentions as examples of procedural requirements the institutional setting, like decision-making rules, as well as informational requirements, like reporting. Though funding agencies are usually required to prepare their accounts and reports in the context of budget decisions, informational requirements are usually not severe or extensive. Annual reports give an overview of activities and the use of funds. The institutional setting depends on what kind of research the agency is supposed to fund. In general, however, one seldom finds a decisive voting position of government officials within funding agencies, as scientists usually prevail. On the other hand government has the power of the purse and this ensures that it can negotiate effectively when it comes to discussions on the budget. Such discussions may take place with governing boards of the funding agency or, as in the United States, in the appropriation committees of Congress. Internally, decisions in funding agencies are seldom constrained by clearly defined voting procedures as there is a preference for consensus building (see Braun, 1998).

This limited overview demonstrates that discretion granted to funding agencies often cannot be effectively counteracted by preventive mechanisms for shirking, although there are some differences between types of funding agencies (see below). A veto power in research funding is almost non-existent, monitoring devices are difficult to develop, and procedural requirements do constrain funding agencies, but not too much. The most important corrective measures for discussing detailed funding decisions seem to be sanctions by budget. However, these are seldom used in the European context. More often, they serve to influence the general strategic orientation of funding agencies, above all the distribution of money to earmarked and non-earmarked research funding. They are not applicable, moreover, when monitoring devices are weak.

The granting of discretion and the introduction of control mechanisms differs, however. In Table 7.1 I have summarized three types of funding agencies that demonstrate variations in discretion and control mechanisms.

The first type of funding agency can be defined as 'all-purpose agencies' (Price 1954). They are usually responsible for setting up basic research and are not restricted to one discipline or specific research domain. Examples are the National Science Foundation in the United States, the French Centre national de la recherche scientifique,[4] the German Deutsche Forschungsgemeinschaft and the Swiss Nationalfonds.

The second group consists of funding agencies that have been established to fund research in certain problem domains like health or environment and are supposed to make a link between basic and applied research. They are required to comprehend the whole chain of research in order to provide answers to the basic problems in applied fields. In this sense they can be regarded as being active in strategic research. Examples are the National Institutes of Health in the United States, the Institut national de la santé et de la recherche médicale in France and the various research councils one finds in Great Britain. One might call them 'mission-oriented agencies'.

The last type encompasses funding agencies at the execution of politically defined applied research programmes, often in the technological field. These agencies are usually closely connected to ministries responsible for technological research, for example the so-called *project agencies* in Germany. One could call this type 'applied-oriented agencies'.

Table 7.1, based on my empirical research (Braun, 1997; see also Braun, 1993), demonstrates in a broad manner how the different criteria discussed so far are valued in each type of funding agency. The table demonstrates that, as expected, the stage of research determines the constitutional setup of funding agencies, although there are problems of clearly demarcating the groups and of country-specific variations in each group.[5] Basic research agencies usually have considerable leeway to develop their policies and are seldom constrained by extensive mechanisms to prevent shirking. The opposite holds for applied-oriented agencies, although there is considerable variation within this type. From the example I have chosen, the 'project agencies' in Germany, it becomes clear that the room for manoeuvre of this kind of agency remains clearly

Table 7.1 Discretion and control in funding agencies

	All-purpose agencies	Mission-oriented agencies	Applied-oriented agencies
Discretion	Very substantial	Substantial	Very limited
Veto power	No	No	Yes, the ministry
Sanctions	Budget in a limited way	Budget, appointments, closing down, merging	Budget, appointments, other measures, closing down, merging
Oversight	Fire alarm by scientists	Fire alarm by scientists and increasingly by stakeholders; in the US police patrol by Congress	Police patrol by ministry; fire alarm by stakeholders
Procedures	Limited influence on funding decisions	Voice of policy makers in budget discussions; limited influence on funding decisions	Substantial reporting and information procedures; usually government has final voice in funding decisions

limited: discretion is poor and there are substantial control procedures established that reduce the risk of shirking. Policy makers keep their eyes on these agencies. In the middle we find the mission-oriented agencies who usually have some room to decide on alternatives in the funding of their research area. They are clearly under more scrutiny, though, as policy makers expect them to report on their performance in matters of application. Stakeholders can raise the fire alarm and budget discussions serve to redirect the general orientation of these agencies. In comparison to independent regulatory agencies (see Chapter 6 in this book), these variations cannot be explained by different degrees of political uncertainty, but are a function of the degree of uncertainty about future outcomes.

The differences between agencies, especially between basic research and strategic research agencies, should not be exaggerated, though. The discussion above demonstrates that often control mechanism do not really interfere with the daily work of funding agencies and that preventive mechanisms have for a long time been rather ineffective, although this has changed since the 1990s, when control measures received more attention.

Funding agencies between science and politics

All funding agencies are somewhere in between policy makers and scientists. No funding agency can survive without government money, nor be successful without convincing scientists to participate in funding programmes and to make their best effort to produce new knowledge. As I explained elsewhere (Braun, 1993), this may create tensions in loyalties and conflicts in coming to terms with demands from both sides. The analysis above demonstrates that such conflicts may have different dynamics and implications for the different types of funding agencies. I would now like to discuss the conflicts of interests that funding agencies are subject to and that may influence their attitudes towards shirking by considering a *policy space* where policy makers and scientists have their own interest in distributing government money both to basic and applied research.[6] Let us assume that there is a fixed amount of money available for research and that policy makers and scientists have their own ideal preferences in relation to the amount of money that should be given without any strings attached to basic research and how much money should be earmarked for applied purposes. Figure 7.2 demonstrates probable preferences of scientists and policy makers in the policy space.

For reasons of simplicity let us visualize the policy space as the direct line between S and P in the following figures. Let us further assume that both scientists and policy makers as collective actors have their ideal position as demonstrated in Figure 7.2 and that they are indifferent to a number of other solutions close to their ideal point. This is usually

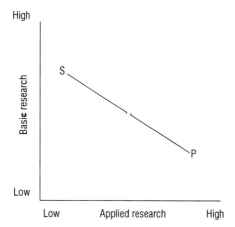

Figure 7.2 Policy space in research policy.

expressed by indifference curves. Where do the different types of funding agencies position themselves in this policy space?

Starting from the assumption that funding agencies have to meet objectives, then, first, they want to fulfil their function as defined in their constitution. This links them in different ways to the principals: all-purpose agencies directly to science, applied-oriented agencies to policy makers and mission-oriented agencies to both principals. The best way to fulfil the function is to not lose the trust of the principals, which means *minimizing the distance* between the ideal point of principals and the ideal point of the funding agencies. Second, funding agencies need to maximize resources, which invariably binds them to policy makers who hold the 'power of the purse'. The preference points chosen by the various types of funding agencies are therefore *not independent* of the ideal points of their principals. They are constrained by the choices of the principals. The funding agencies are required to choose their preference point in relation to how they want to distribute the money internally, either to non-earmarked or to earmarked projects.[7]

Let us assume that the ideal point science chooses reflects a distribution of government money of 80 per cent for basic research and 20 per cent for applied research, while for policy makers the ideal point is 80 per cent distribution for applied research and 20 per cent for basic research. Science will not opt for 100 per cent basic research funding, as parts of the scientific community are intrinsically interested in applied research money. Government recognizes that basic research has some value and will never opt for a 100 per cent distribution in favour of applied research. If science, as a collective actor, achieves its preference point, then most of the money would flow to those funding agencies that are implementing investigator-initiated grants, i.e. all-purpose agencies and, in part, mission-oriented agencies. If most of government money was spent in an ear-marked way then applied-oriented agencies would profit at the cost of the other agencies.

As stated above, all agencies will endeavour to minimize the distance from their principals, but the principals differ. All-purpose agencies depend on close collaboration with scientists to foster basic research and must choose a position as close as possible to the ideal position of science without completely rejecting policy makers' demands concerning applied research. The position S′ in Figure 7.3, which minimizes the distance from the scientists' ideal point S, and which is still on the indifference curve of policy makers, seems to be the best choice for all-purpose agencies. The reverse is true for applied-oriented agencies. These agencies, constrained by low discretion and control, are obliged to be as near as possible to the ideal point of policy makers and vote to maximize applied research without rejecting the claims of scientists for the funding of basic research. Applied-oriented funding agencies depend on scientists to do research. Position P′, which minimizes the distance to the ideal point of policy makers and which is still on the indifference curve of scientists, seems to be the optimal position for these agencies. Mission-oriented agencies need to combine both basic and applied research and cannot afford to estrange scientists or policy makers. Their best strategy seems to be to minimize the distance from both scientists and policy makers, which is equivalent to the mean and is point D in Figure 7.4.

According to the example above this would mean that all-purpose-agencies would vote for a 60–40 per cent distribution in favour of basic research, applied-oriented agencies for a 60–40 per cent distribution in

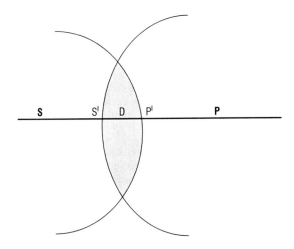

Figure 7.3 Funding agencies' best positions in policy space.

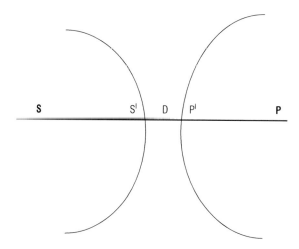

Figure 7.4 Ideal positions of research actors in a policy space without intersect-
ing interests.

favour of applied research and mission-oriented agencies for a 50–50 per
cent distribution.

Now, imagine that policy makers shift their position in the direction of
the ideal position of science while the scientists' indifference curve
remains stable. In this case, all-purpose-agencies and mission-oriented
agencies can move in the direction of the ideal position of scientists as
long as they stay on the indifference curve of policy makers. The position
of applied-oriented agencies would be unchanged.

What happens if the indifference curves of scientists and policy makers
do not intersect, perhaps because policy makers have decided to radically
change their spending patterns and demand more applied-oriented
research? All funding agencies are then in trouble, as they lose either the
trust of scientists or that of policy makers or – in the case of mission-
oriented agencies – the trust of both actors. If this happens, it is in the
interest of all agencies to bring both indifference curves to the point
where they intersect. At this point, the interests of funding agencies in the
policy space would converge.

What can we learn from this description? It is important to note that
funding agencies cannot freely choose their position in the policy space;
they are bound by the preferences of both scientists and policy makers.
Independent agencies in research policy are subject not to a dyadic relationship, but rather to a triadic one. This means they have to demonstrate
their loyalty to both sides, to differing degrees. In regulatory policy the
discussion of delegation is, with some exceptions, inspired by a dyadic
concept. In distributive policies under risk, like research policy, the triadic

configuration prevails because independent agencies depend on actions of the third party in order to fulfil their task. In regulatory policy, independent agencies must keep their distance from target groups, although they also need some cooperation. However, their task is already fulfilled when they have applied norms independent of the actions of the third party.

Another significant insight is that the 'binding' is different for the various types of agencies. The discussion of the distributive policy arena reveals that features of the policy field – such as institutional capacities and ideational factors – influence characteristics of delegation. Discretion and control vary – *ceteris paribus* – with the stage of research. The more uncertain the outcome of research the more policy makers are inclined to grant substantive discretion to funding agencies. Therefore, it is not the distributive policy arena as such which determines the degree of discretion, but the degree of uncertainty and the (in)capacity to define political preferences and the optimal strategy that are decisive for the structure of delegation. These characteristics allow all-purpose agencies to deviate substantially from ideal positions of policy makers, though the position must still be within the 'preferential continuum' of policy makers, while applied-oriented agencies are more tightly bound by the preferences of policy makers.

Interestingly, as the last figure demonstrates, even all-purpose agencies can accept a distribution of money largely in favour of applied research if need be, with evident consequences for their own funding patterns. It is one thing to say that most funding resources must go to applied research and then accept that one's own resources will be cut substantially and it is another to respond to these constraints by changing internal funding patterns. In fact, internal funding patterns will be influenced by such a shift to the right of the policy space. If resources for basic research become scarce, all-purpose agencies that are rational and want to have sufficient competences and resources to maintain their standard interests must attempt to change their patterns and integrate applied research topics. This is indeed what has happened in most countries where such shifts have occurred: the National Science Foundation was compelled to accept a more applied-oriented funding programme as early as the 1960s; the Swiss National Science Foundation finally integrated several national priority programmes in the 1970s; the Deutsche Forschungsgemeinschaft has been continually under pressure to accept earmarked money from policy makers and there are many other examples. The more pressure policy makers put on funding agencies, and the more credibly this is presented, the more incentives there are for funding agencies not only to accept a revised formula of the distribution of money across funding agencies, but also to modify internal funding patterns.

The converging preference points of funding agencies in Figure 7.5 demonstrate that one might expect an assimilation of funding patterns

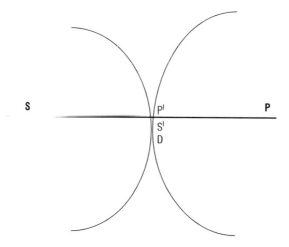

Figure 7.5 Converging positions of funding agencies.

and less clear distinctions between funding agencies, because all-purpose and mission-oriented agencies are shifting their positions. This was different in the 1950s and 1960s, when policy preferences were influenced by the science-push model, congruent with science preferences and scientists' indifference curves clustered closely around the ideal point presented above. At this time most funding agencies were integrating basic research funding schemes into their funding repertoire and it was hard to tell if a mission-oriented agency was not in fact an all-purpose agency in its orientation and funding pattern.

This demonstrates that the dynamics of delegation are highly influenced by the preferences of both scientists and policy makers alike; however, the policy makers are the agenda setters, as they finally decide where to distribute the money. This explains why it is important for scientists to convince policy makers by argument and lobbying where to allocate the money.

Another point I would like to raise is that no funding agency can be satisfied when the preferences of science and politics widely diverge, because then all funding agencies lose. Thus, they have a common interest and may resort to collective action in order to bring scientists and policy makers together to find a common point of understanding, a focal point that can serve as a new equilibrium in the distribution of government money. Where this equilibrium is situated depends on time, circumstances and perceptions of knowledge production.

Finally, the analysis also allows some preliminary conclusions to be drawn concerning the shirking of funding agencies. Shirking in terms of respecting policy preferences is not an issue in the relationship between all-purpose agencies and policy makers because policy makers do not usually have clear demarcated preferences or objectives in basic research. For this reason there is also substantial discretion and lack of control for these agencies. Conflicts between these two actors can arise only over the amount of money that should be spent with and without strings attached, but this is not linked to shirking. However, shirking can be important in the relationship between policy makers and applied-oriented agencies, as political preferences exist in this situation. The opportunity for applied-oriented agencies to choose shirking is extremely limited, given the reduced room for discretion and the tight control measures that exist. Mission-oriented agencies probably have the most delicate position, because they must to some extent fulfil political demands without rejecting the claims of scientists. In this case, there is constant pressure to move between the two sides and shirking can happen in both directions. This is facilitated by the more substantial freedom these agencies have and the only limited possibilities to control.

Conclusion

In this chapter I have tried to demonstrate that it is useful to distinguish between policy arenas, in this case between regulatory and distributive policies. For a subgroup of distributive policies, risk policies, it was demonstrated that both the rationale to delegate as well as the rationale to grant discretion and exercise control differ from what can be learnt from studies on regulatory policies. Research policies, the example chosen here, reveal a more complex actor structure. In order to understand the structure and dynamics of delegation one must put funding agencies in the context of a more general trust relationship between scientists and policy makers. Trust and delegation demonstrate similar action structures but also significant differences. The position as an intermediary between the trustee, science, and the trustor, policy makers, explains the particular dynamics of action that funding agencies are subject to. It was also demonstrated that different degrees of independence or autonomy are strongly linked to uncertainties of policy makers regarding the outcomes of the action of scientists. If there is high uncertainty and the likely gains of research investments are in the distant future, delegated agencies may have both substantial discretion and be exempt from political control. The more visible and likely research results become the more policy makers attempt to reduce discretion and exercise control over funding agencies. Given the structure of the policy arena, it is not political uncertainty that influences this variation in the constitution of funding agencies but the uncertainty about political outcomes. Finally, there are different types of funding agencies linked to different stages of research. Their constitutions bind them in different ways to policy makers and scientists, with implications for their ideal preference points. This demonstrates that an analysis of delegation relationships in the distributive policy arena cannot deal in a simple way with agencies. The embeddedness in overarching trust relations and the characteristics of the public good in question, knowledge, contributes to complex and differentiated delegation patterns, the analysis of which needs further refinement. Finally, research in other 'risk areas' and other policy arenas is necessary to carry the argument further and demonstrate that it is the structure of the policy field that influences the structure and dynamics of delegation in public policies.

Notes

I would like to thank Fabrizio Gilardi and David Guston for their useful remarks on an earlier version of this chapter. Special thanks to Chris Caswill, who not only helped to improve the chapter but who also has been the driving force to develop the perspective of principal–agent theory in research policy in general.

1 One might mention though that Epstein and O'Halloran (1999) have looked into the degree of discretion granted by Congress in the United States to different policy fields. They also discussed the particular characteristics of distributive policies (1995: 230). In addition, within regulatory policies there has been attention to different policy areas like economic versus social regulation (e.g. Gilardi 2004). There is, however, no systematic discussion on the three major policy arenas Lowi has used to develop his hypothesis on the influence of policies on politics. This seems to me, therefore, to be a useful starting point for discussion.

2 It is interesting to notice that Coleman does not foresee such a type of 'intermediary of trust'. He distinguishes between the adviser, the guarantor and the entrepreneur (1990: 180–185). Institutions as they are introduced here belong to neither category. Policy makers trust the procedural requirements of institutions that have a reputation for selecting good scientists. There is no advice, no guarantee is given nor is there an entrepreneurial function.

3 In the field of the sociology of science there is a lot of discussion on the usefulness of these terms and about the characteristics to be attributed to each category (see only Godin 2001). For our purposes, the categorization, which is usually used in OECD publications, most notably in the Frascati-Manual, will suffice.

4 The CNRS was set up to also build a bridge between basic and applied research but developed more strongly in the direction of basic research after the Second World War.

5 One should also note that not all types of agencies are actually present in each country. In the United Kingdom for example we only find mission-oriented agencies, with implications for their role in the funding of research, as they need a much wider range of funding than agencies in countries where a clear functional differentiation exists and all three types are present, as for example in the United States. In Germany mission-oriented agencies are lacking, which unfolds other dynamics and problems of delegation. Given the limited room at my disposal, I am unable to elaborate on these interesting aspects.

6 For simplicity reasons I leave aside strategic research and focus only on basic and applied research. Mission-oriented agencies must then have a certain combination of basic and applied research to fulfil their function of bridging both research types.

7 Note that this can be controlled by policy makers in relation to what funding

agencies actually do. Here, funding agencies must announce publicly how they will use their money in terms of basic and applied research and earmarked and non-earmarked funding. This at least becomes visible to policy makers. For this reason funding agencies cannot choose a certain point in the space and hope that policy makers will not notice because they lack monitoring capacities or do not have defined objectives.

References

Bernal, J. D. (1939) *The Social Function of Science*, London: Routledge.

Braun, D. (1993) 'Who Governs Intermediary Agencies? Principal–Agent Relations in Research Policy-Making', *Journal of Public Policy*, 13 (2): 135–162.

Braun, D. (1997) *Die forschungspolitische Steuerung der Wissenschaft*, Frankfurt am Main: Campus.

Braun, D. (1998) 'The Role of Funding Agencies in the Cognitive Development of Science', *Research Policy*, 27: 807–821.

Braun, D. (2003) 'Lasting Tensions in Research Policy-Making. A Delegation Problem', *Science and Public Policy*, 30 (5): 309–322.

Caswill, C. (1998) 'Social Science Policy. Challenges, Interactions, Principals and Agents', *Science and Public Policy*, 25 (5): 286–296.

Caswill, C. (2003) 'Principals, Agents, and Contracts', *Science and Public Policy*, 30 (5): 337–346

Cohen, J. E. (1986) 'The Dynamics of the "Revolving Door" at the FCC', *American Journal of Political Science*, 30 (4): 689–708.

Coleman, J. S. (1990) *Foundations of Social Theory*, Cambridge MA: The Belknap Press of Harvard University Press.

Elzinga, A. and Jamison, A. (1995) 'Changing Policy Agendas in Science and Technology', in S. Jasanoff *et al.* (eds) *Handbook of Science, Technology, and Society*, Beverly Hills CA: Sage.

Epstein, D. and O'Halloran, S. (1995) 'A Theory of Strategic Oversight. Congress, Lobbyists, and the Bureaucracy', *Journal of Law, Economics and Organization*, 11: 227–255.

Epstein, D. and O'Halloran, S. (1999) *Delegating Powers. A Transaction Cost Politics Approach to Policy Making under Separate Powers*, Cambridge: Cambridge University Press.

Etzkowitz, H. and Leydesdorff, L. (1998) 'The Endless Transition. A Triple Helix of University–Industry–Government relations', *Minerva*, XXXVI: 203–218.

Etzkowitz, H. and Leydesdorff, L. (2000) 'The Dynamics of Innovation. From National Systems and "Mode 2" to a Triple Helix of University–Industry–Government Relations', *Research Policy*, 29: 109–123.

Fiorina, M. P. (1981) 'Congressional Control of the Bureaucracy: A Mismatch of Incentives and Capabilities', in L. C. Dodd and B. Oppenheimer (eds) *Congress Reconsidered*, 2nd edn, Washington DC: Congressional Quarterly Press.

Gilardi, F. (2002). 'Policy Credibility and Delegation to Independent Regulatory Agencies. A Comparative Empirical Analysis', *Journal of European Public Policy*, 9 (6): 873–893.

Gilardi, F. (2004) 'Delegation in the Regulatory State. Origins and Diffusion of Independent Regulatory Agencies in Western Europe', PhD dissertation, Université de Lausanne.

Godin, B. (2001) 'Defining R&D. Is Research Always Systematic?' *Project on the History and Sociology of S&T Statistics*, Paper No. 7, University of Montréal; http://www.inrs-urb.uquebec.ca.

Gormley, W. T. (1979) 'A Test of the Revolving Door Hypothesis at the FCC', *American Journal of Political Science*, 23 (4): 665–683.

Guston, D. H. (1996) 'Principal–Agent Theory and the Structure of Science Policy', *Science and Public Policy* 23 (4): 229–240.

Guston, D. H. (2000) *Between Politics and Science. The Integrity and Productivity of Research*, Cambridge: Cambridge University Press.

Guston, D. H. (2001) 'Boundary Organizations in Environmental Policy and Science. An Introduction', *Science, Technology, and Human Values*, 26 (4): 399–408.

Guston, D. and Keniston, K. (eds) (1994) *The Fragile Contract. University Science and the Federal Government*, Cambridge MA: MIT Press.

Heclo, H. (1978) 'Issue Networks and the Executive Establishment', in A. King (ed.) *The New American Political System*, Washington, DC: American Enterprise Institute.

Irvine, J. and Martin, B. R. (1984) *Foresight in Science. Picking the Winners*, London: Pinter.

Lowi, T. J. (1972) 'Four Systems of Policy, Politics, and Choice', *Public Administration Review*, July/August: 298–310.

Majone, G. (2001a) 'Two Logics of Delegation. Agency and Fiduciary Relations in EU Governance', *European Union Politics*, 2 (1): 103–121.

Majone, G. (2001b) 'Nonmajoritarian Institutions and the Limits of Democratic Governance. A Political Transaction-Cost Approach', *Journal of Institutional and Theoretical Economics*, 157: 57–78.

McCubbins, M. D. (1985) 'The Legislative Design of Regulatory Structure', *American Journal of Political Science*, 29: 721–748.

McCubbins, M. D. and Schwartz, T. (1984) 'Congressional Oversight Overlooked. Police Patrols versus Fire Alarms', *American Journal of Political Science*, 28 (1): 165–179.

Meulen, B. J. R. (1998) 'Science Policies as Principal–Agent Games. Institutionalization and Path-Dependency in the Relation between Government and Science', *Research Policy*, 27: 397–414.

Morris, N. (2003) 'Academic Researchers as "Agents" of Science Policy', *Science and Public Policy*, 30 (5): 359–370.

Olson, M. (1982) *The Rise and Decline of Nations. Economic Growth, Stagflation, and Social Rigidities*, New Haven CT and London: Yale University Press.

Price, D. K. (1954) *Government and Science. Their Dynamic Relation in American Democracy*, New York: New York University Press.

Stokes, D. E. (1997) *Pasteur's Quadrant. Basic Science and Technological Innovation*, Washington DC: Brookings Institution.

Thatcher, M. and Stone Sweet, A. (2002) 'Theory and Practice of Delegation to Non-majoritarian Institutions', *West European Politics* 25 (1): 125–147.

Tsebelis, G. (2002) *Veto Players. How Political Institutions Work*, Princeton NJ: Princeton University Press.

Weingast, B. R. (1984) 'The Congressional–Bureaucratic System. A Principal–Agent Perspective (With Application to the SEC)', *Public Choice*, 44: 147–191.

8 Consequences of legitimizing independent regulatory agencies in contemporary democracies

Theoretical scenarios

Gül Sosay

Although it has been prevalent in the United States since the nineteenth century, the practice of delegation to independent regulatory agencies (IRAs) and its consequences have not attracted much scholarly attention elsewhere until the more recent proliferation of IRAs in other contemporary democracies. Several decades ago, these institutions were often associated with the 'regulatory state', that is, 'a neologism of American origin and of dubious relevance to the European context' (Majone, 1999: 1). As this is no longer the case, delegation to IRAs and its effects need to be studied within the context of democratic systems other than that of the United States.

From among the problems regarding the consequences of delegation to IRAs, those related to legitimacy and democracy are of particular significance, since they can affect the fundamental nature of political systems. Currently, the legitimacy problems of delegation to IRAs seem to be resolved by adopting 'substantive (output) legitimacy' in combination with 'procedural legitimacy' as standards.[1] Such *ex post facto* legitimacy can be interpreted as an effort to justify practices that are believed to resolve governments' credibility problems, and increase decision-making expertise and efficiency. Without disparaging the gains from such practices, this chapter focuses on the possible consequences of legitimizing IRAs in contemporary democratic regimes.

After a brief discussion of how delegation to IRAs is legitimized in contemporary democracies, two theoretical scenarios, which should not be taken to represent deterministic paths, will be developed. Although the scenarios are based on similar requirements of legitimacy, they emphasize different aspects. In the first scenario, the establishment of a strictly rule-based system relying increasingly upon knowledge and expertise in a complex and fragmented environment leads to bureaucratic or technocratic rule. The second scenario accentuates the diffusion of power and the potential for increased public participation as significant attributes of delegation to IRAs and involves a shift towards a more participatory form of democracy than majoritarian institutions would allow. The choice of which theoretical scenario is more likely to be played out in contemporary democracies experimenting with IRAs is still a largely open-ended question,[2] as tendencies towards both directions seem to exist.[3]

Rather than trying to develop scenarios based on actual practices of delegation to IRAs in contemporary democracies, this chapter builds theoretical scenarios. As such, it does not aspire to answer empirical questions, such as whether and/or to what extent the existing IRAs have been able to fulfil specified standards of procedural and output legitimacy, nor does it aim to show the empirical accuracy of the scenarios developed. The objective of this chapter is *to discuss the potential effects of embedding IRAs as legitimate institutions in democratic political systems on the nature and functioning of these systems.*

Legitimization of IRAs and democracy

Legitimacy and accountability issues for IRAs pose serious challenges for democratic regimes that are based on the principles of majoritarian democracy and electoral accountability. As governmental entities that possess and exercise public authority separately from other institutions, but are neither directly elected by the people nor directly managed by elected officials, IRAs can be viewed as 'constitutional anomalies which do not fit well into the traditional framework of controls, checks, and balances' (Veljanovski 1991: 16). Consequently, IRAs can be judged to lack democratic legitimacy and accountability.[4] Based on this understanding, it can be argued that delegation to IRAs represents a move away from basic principles of democracy and, hence, constitutes a serious challenge to established democracies. This line of argument does not leave room for reconciliation between the expansion of IRAs in Europe (and in some developing countries) and principles of democratic legitimacy. Is this the end of the debate? The answer is evidently negative as there is no single standard of legitimacy and no single unanimously agreed definition of democracy. Without going into a normative debate about what democracy is and what its requirements are, this chapter presents a thoughtful exercise on the possible effects of legitimately integrating IRAs into contemporary democratic political systems.

The focus of this chapter will be on the particular standards of procedural and output legitimacy that are employed to justify delegation to IRAs. First, procedural legitimacy fundamentally implies that IRAs are created by democratically enacted statutes, which define the legal authority and objectives of these institutions; that those who occupy positions within these institutions are appointed by elected officials; that decision making by IRAs follows formal rules which often require public participation; and that IRA decisions must be justified and open to judicial review (Majone, 1997: 160). Second, the legitimacy of IRAs also depends on 'their capacity to engender and maintain the belief that they are the most appropriate ones for the functions entrusted to them' (Majone, 1998: 22).

This is the very basis of what Majone calls substantive standards of legitimacy. The relevant criteria for substantive legitimacy involve policy consistency; the expertise and problem-solving skills of those who occupy positions in IRAs and their ability to protect diffuse interests; professionalism; and a clear definition of the objectives of the independent non-majoritarian institution and of the limits within which it is expected to operate (Majone 1997: 161). As this type of legitimacy also subsumes accountability or legitimacy by results (output legitimacy), it requires that the outcomes of IRA decisions and actions can be objectively measured in order to evaluate whether the clearly specified objectives have been accomplished.

Both sets of criteria seem to make up coherent, neatly defined and rigorous standards of legitimacy that can be acceptable and even desirable within the framework of democratic regimes. However, such a perspective ignores or at best underestimates the inherent tensions and contradictions among some of these criteria.

One significant tension can be discerned by considering why delegation to IRAs occurs in the first place. Merging two logics of delegation,[5] IRAs are granted independent authority due to demand for both policy-relevant expertise and credible commitment (Majone, 2001). The motive of the principals is to isolate those with policy-relevant expertise and problem-solving skills from the political influence of majoritarian institutions, which ensures policy efficiency and credibility. This rationale is behind the legitimacy criteria that constitute the basis of the first scenario developed in this chapter. Majone treats these criteria as if they are easily compatible with the requirement for public participation which drives the second scenario. Independent authority is delegated to experts and technocrats not to diffuse political power or increase public participation, so including a criterion of legitimacy to that effect may go against the rationale behind such delegation. Opening IRA decision making to public access and participation means exposing it to the political influence of non-experts. In this case, rather than their political representatives in majoritarian institutions, private actors themselves can directly exert influence on public agencies. While this may be regarded as a gain for democratic standards, it may not be so in terms of policy consistency and efficiency as these standards are expected to be fulfilled by the experts occupying positions in IRAs.

Scharpf's (1999) distinction between input-oriented and output-oriented legitimacy, based on normative political theory, can be used to further clarify the aforementioned tension. As he explains in his study of the multi-level European polity,

> [i]nput-oriented democratic thought emphasizes 'government *by the people*'. Political choices are legitimate if and because they reflect the 'will of the people' – that is, if they can be derived from the authentic preferences of the members of a community. By contrast, the output

perspective emphasizes 'government *for the people*'. Here, political choices are legitimate if and because they effectively promote the common welfare of the constituency in question.

(1999: 6)

Consistent with the line of argument in this chapter, Scharpf recognizes that these two perspectives 'differ significantly in their preconditions and in their implications for the democratic legitimacy of European govcrnance, when each is considered by itself' (1999: 6).

While input-oriented legitimacy relies on participation, output-oriented legitimacy demands the capacity to solve problems requiring collective solutions. Scharpf identifies 'independent expertise' (e.g. of judges, central bankers, regulators) as one of the mechanisms by which the output-oriented criterion of problem-solving effectiveness is thought to be fulfilled. If the policy areas in which the independent experts of IRAs operate can be presumed to aim for collective efficiency as opposed to redistribution, the tension between input-oriented and output-oriented standards may diminish, but it does not disappear. As Papadopoulos remarks, 'even if analysts perceive some choices as most likely to yield Pareto-optimal outcomes, not all interested parties might agree with such a framing because policy properties are differently constructed by social actors' (2003: 484). As will be highlighted below, even efficiency-enhancing policies have some redistributive effects that can make them politically controversial. Therefore, enhancing input legitimacy by opening IRA decision making to the participation of ordinary citizens may make the realization of Pareto-optimal solutions, as determined by the experts of IRAs, more difficult, and hence compromise output legitimacy.

Whilst not claiming that the comprehensive criteria adopted for legitimizing IRAs are completely incompatible with one another, the two scenarios developed in the next section acknowledge the inherent tensions among them and build on the prediction that these tensions will be resolved by prioritizing some criteria over others.

Two theoretical scenarios

The decision to legitimize delegation to IRAs in contemporary democracies may mark a critical turning point in the evolution of democratic political systems. In other words, adoption of new standards of legitimacy to resolve the problems of 'securing public support'[6] is a relatively recent development that may entail a fundamental change in the form of contemporary democracies.

Based on the belief that legitimization of IRAs by new standards of procedural and substantive (outcome) legitimacy opens up new possibilities in democracies, this chapter proposes two theoretical scenarios for the future. These scenarios should not be interpreted as deterministic paths, since what will evolve is likely to depend on many factors ranging from the formal statutes of IRAs to the organization of societal interests. In agreement with Dryzek (1996: 4), I conceive of democracy as an open-ended project that is not heading for a single destination. But, the choices that are made on the way may close the routes to some destinations while increasing the likelihood of heading towards others (i.e. path dependence).

Scenario 1: towards bureaucratic/technocratic rule

In the first scenario, legitimization of delegation to IRAs can potentially lead to a bureaucratic/technocratic type of rule, weakening the democratic basis of contemporary political systems. One critique of the persistent application of the standards of majoritarian democracy to evaluate the 'regulatory state' is that while the crisis of the welfare state has reduced the political significance of redistribution relative to policies aiming to increase aggregate welfare, the normative standards have not been reset accordingly. The contention of those who advance this critique is that redistribution and efficiency issues can and should be distinguished from one another. Based on this distinction, in the sphere of efficiency, issues tied to the maximization of aggregate welfare need to reset the standards of legitimacy so as to democratically justify delegation to IRAs aiming to correct market failures.[7] This argument can be interpreted as another ramification of the increasing pervasiveness of economic rationality and the trend towards the rationalization of society in an increasingly complicated environment.[8]

Weberian thinking, based on an observation of the longer-term trend toward the rationalization of society as early as the beginning of the twentieth century, is highly relevant to the context of the first theoretical scenario. In other words, one direction which the legitimization of IRAs based on standards of procedural legitimacy may lead to is a political system grounded on a set of common assumptions, views and practices elaborated by Weber and, as will be demonstrated below, by Schumpeter and von Hayek.

First of all, pessimistic assumptions about human nature in general, and about voters in particular, underlie the systems of thought developed by the aforementioned thinkers. Weber (1972) has a low estimation of the mass electorate, whom he characterizes as being emotional and unable to understand or judge public affairs. Similarly, Schumpeter (1976) portrays the electorate as generally weak, prone to strong emotional impulses, intellectually unable to be decisive on its own, and susceptible to outside forces. Based on such premises, although they uphold representative democracy in principle, all three conceive of political life where there is little scope for democratic participation and envisage democracy, at best, as a means of choosing leaders and curbing their excesses (Held, 1996).

Moreover, Weber is critical of majoritarian democracies based on parliamentary accountability. He considers the idea of parliament as a centre of rational argument and debate as a misrepresentation of the nature of modern parliamentary affairs (Weber, 1972: 102). As emphasized by Held, 'Weber argued that the extension of the franchise and the development of party politics undermined the classic liberal conception of parliament as a place where national policy is settled by rational reflection, guided only by the public or general interest' (1996: 169). For Weber, modern mass democracies take the form of plebiscitary democracy where parliamentary democracy is reduced to party politics.

Ruling out the possibility of defining a 'common good' based on rational argument, Schumpeter sees claims to that end as a danger that may lead to the dismissal of all dissension as sectarian and irrational. His assertion that when the 'will of the majority' is taken to be the 'will of all' it is by no means guaranteed that classical democracy will achieve 'what people really want' (Held, 1996: 254) echoes Madisonian statements against the 'tyranny of the majority'.[9] Hence, Schumpeter holds, 'if results that prove in the long run satisfactory to the people at large are made the test of government *for* the people, then government *by* the people, as conceived by the classical doctrine of democracy, would often fail to meet it' (Held, 1996: 256). In Schumpeterian thought, democracy can be a breeding ground for administrative inefficiency and a hindrance to good management (Schumpeter, 1976: 284–289). Schumpeter even claims that decisions by non-democratic agencies may sometimes prove more acceptable to people generally than 'democratic decisions', for such agencies can use their unique position to produce policies which the various affected parties either would have failed to agree upon, or would have rejected on the grounds that they entailed unacceptable levels of sacrifice.

Scepticism towards majoritarian democracy is also evident in von Hayek's thought. He sees the propensity for arbitrary and oppressive majority rule and the progressive displacement of the rule of the majority by the rule of its agents as two dangers in the dynamics of contemporary mass democracies (Hayek, 1978). According to von Hayek, 'too much faith in a majoritarian "will of the people" leads to tyranny and economic disaster' (Centeno, 1998: 45).

In summary, one of the main threads that bind Weber, Schumpeter and von Hayek to contemporary advocates of delegation to IRAs is their critical view of majoritarian institutions and their ability to generate outcomes that maximize aggregate welfare. Another thread is the reliance on procedural standards for legitimacy.

According to Weber, legitimacy involves acceptance of the validity of an order of rules (Lassman, 2000). The absence of the normative question of whether or not that body of rules should be considered legitimate from this definition clearly reveals Weber's view of political life in the age of modernity that is characterized by competing values, where none can be regarded as objectively valid. Within this context, the idea that political life is founded on a given or agreed morality cannot be maintained (Held, 1996: 160). Instead, in an era identified by increasing rationalization of society, legitimacy can be defended only on procedural grounds (Roth and Schluchter, 1979). Weber maintains that, in this age, there is public obedience to authority by 'virtue of "legality", by virtue of the belief in the validity of legal statute and functional "competence" based on rationally created *rules*' (Weber, 1972: 79). Although the resemblance between this conception of legitimacy and procedural legitimacy defined by scholars attempting to legitimize IRAs within the framework of contemporary democracies is quite striking, it has to be underlined that, for Weber, there is no form of democratic legitimization. As it does not fit readily into his classification of political forms of legitimization, Weber discusses modern democracy under the heading of charismatic rule.

In contrast, Schumpeter specifies procedures, i.e. elections, as the foundation of democracy, but does not explicitly provide standards of legitimacy. In Held's (1996) interpretation, Schumpeter assumes that voting entails a belief that the polity or political institutions are accepted and legitimated. Decisions and decision makers enjoy *de facto* legitimacy as a result of the periodic election of competing political elites. However, Schumpeter does not further distinguish the grounds on which compliance is achieved.

Based on his concern with the 'tyranny of the majority', von Hayek holds that legitimacy of laws should not be confused with majority rule (Hayek, 1973–1979). He makes a critical distinction between law and legislation. Law, which is essentially comprised of fixed general rules that determine the conditions of individuals' actions, including constitutional rules, circumscribes the power of those making legislation, i.e. routine changes in the legal structure. In other words, the legislative scope of governments is and must be restrained by the rule of law. The rule of law defines the legitimate range of activities of democratic governments. Von Hayek also echoes Weber, with his emphasis on legal rule and acceptance of the authority of a system of abstract rules as the source of legitimacy.

Having laid down the relevant common assumptions, views and standards of legitimacy by Weber, Schumpeter and von Hayek, the next step is to try to articulate the type of political system that can be built upon these foundations. In such a system the voters' intellectual abilities are seriously doubted, the form and operation of majoritarian institutions are judged to be essentially dysfunctional for the efficient management of public affairs, and procedural standards are used to justify political institutions. A critical reading reveals that all these elements are present in the writings of those promoting IRAs as legitimate institutions capable of generating 'superior' outcomes to those of majoritarian institutions. Hence, it is not unrealistic to propose a scenario based on the line of thought developed by Weber, Schumpeter and von Hayek.

As mentioned above, Weber perceives rationalization as a phenomenon permeating all the major institutions of capitalist society. In Weber's view, the rationalization of the modern world involves the extension of calculative attitudes of a technical character to more and more spheres of activity, epitomized by scientific processes and given substantive expression in the increasing role that expertise, science and technology play in modern life (Giddens, 1972). Rationalization is inevitably accompanied by the spread of bureaucracy that is regarded as the most suitable form of administration in a political system based on legal-procedural legitimacy. Furthermore, according to Weber, a bureaucratic organization is *technically superior* to other forms of organization. Owing to their training, expertise, specialization and objectivity, bureaucrats become increasingly indispensable as economic and political life become more rational, complex and differentiated (Weber, 1968).

Schumpeter, like Weber, observes the application of a rational, calculating attitude to ever more sectors of life and argues that such rationalization requires impartial and functional ordering. For Schumpeter, 'the services of a well trained bureaucracy' are necessary for modern management and democratic government.

> Such a bureaucracy is the main answer to the argument about government by amateurs. Potentially, it is the only answer to the question so often heard in this country: democratic politics has proved itself unable to produce decent city government; how can we expect the nation to fare if everything . . . is to be handed over to it.

Hence, it is essential that the bureaucracy is 'in a position to evolve principles of its own and sufficiently independent to assert them' (Schumpeter, 1976: 293).

Schumpeter's views of human beings as being incapable of knowledgeable action and of the 'will of the people' as a social construct with little, if any, rational basis are, according to Held, 'but a short step to thinking that all that "people" need as "governors" are engineers capable of making the right technical decisions about the ordering of human affairs. Schumpeter's "competitive elites" are only one small step removed from this technocratic vision – a vision that is both anti-liberal and anti-democratic' (Held, 1996: 193).

Von Hayek, with a similar distrust of democratic participation, gets even closer to the technocratic vision. His, as Centeno calls it, 'neo-liberal technocratic ideology' holds that there are superior forms of knowledge transfer than political debates and politics should not be allowed to interfere with the natural functioning of the market as the best means to gain such knowledge (Centeno, 1998: 47). By seeking to minimize the involvement of the public and its political representatives in the administration of public affairs, von Hayek aims to protect the public from its worst political instincts. This perspective can also be interpreted as a call for an increased role for the technocrats, whose expertise is required to achieve market efficiency, discipline and confidence, economic policy credibility and consistency.

Similarly, those who defend the legitimacy of IRAs also emphasize their advantage in knowledge, expertise, specialization, professionalism and insulation from political influences. In this vein, Majone holds that the administrative demands of rule making 'are best met by flexible, highly specialized organizations enjoying autonomy in decision making: the independent regulatory agencies' (1997: 152). Their power of technical expertise which neither legislators nor bureaucratic generalists possess is believed to be the engine of social improvement. In other words, the administrators/regulators of IRAs are *technically superior* not only to elected politicians, but also to traditional bureaucrats. Majone suggests that the distinguishing features of the agency model when applied to IRAs 'is the combination of expertise and independence, together with specialization in a fairly narrow range of policy issues' (Majone, 1997: 154). Despite this differentiation, similarities between the attributes of bureaucracy listed by Weber and those of administrators/regulators of IRAs are striking. Weber attributes several characteristics to bureaucratic organizational structures: the existence of impersonal and written rules of procedure; strict limits on the means of compulsion at the disposal of each official; the appointment of officials on the basis of their specialist training and qualifications; clearly demarcated specialized tasks demanding full-time employees; and the separation of officials from ownership of the means of administration (Weber, 1968: 220–221). None of these attributes seems to contradict those ascribed to IRAs. Moreover, IRAs enjoy independence that Schumpeter argues bureaucrats should have, but cannot as they are formally situated within the democratic chain of delegation. *Thus, it may be plausible to interpret the proliferation of IRAs as a stage in the bureaucratization process that is associated with the rationalization of an increasingly complex society.*

Majone's reliance on the distinction between efficiency-enhancing and redistributive policies in order to provide substantive legitimacy and democratic justification for delegation to IRAs and hence resolve the normative problem of the 'regulatory state'[10] is a strategy that allows for the legitimate expansion of economic rationality into wider areas of policy. Although he acknowledges that regulatory policies have redistributive consequences, he presumes that the administrators/regulators of IRAs are capable of isolating themselves from concerns about these consequences. As he says, 'for the regulator, such consequences should represent potential policy constraints rather than policy objectives. Only a commitment to efficiency, that is, to the maximization of aggregate welfare, and to accountability by results, can substantively legitimize the political independence of regulators' (Majone, 1996: 295). Such a normative basis appears to reflect the fundamental belief of the technocratic vision – that technocrats can make socially neutral decisions and generate Pareto-optimal solutions for the collective well-being. Utilizing insights drawn from von Hayek, whose neo-liberal ideology has had a more direct impact on the rise and development of the regulatory state, this could potentially be the path that leads to bureaucratic/technocratic rule. The standards of substantive legitimacy which Majone offers to bolster the procedural legitimacy of IRAs do not provide effective conditions that can curb this tendency, but rather, may actually reinforce it.

If all standards of procedural and substantive legitimacy are properly met, then delegation to IRAs can be claimed to provide for 'good governance', which the neo-liberal orthodoxy has been promoting at global, regional, national and subnational levels for a while.[11] However, good (or better) governance may come with a price tag, as it reduces politics to the administration or management of the public and its affairs with a view to achieving market efficiency, discipline and confidence, economic policy credibility and consistency.[12] As such, 'good governance' requires the increased involvement of technocrats whose expertise is crucial for the realization of these objectives and minimum involvement of elected politicians, whose priorities may lie elsewhere. Legitimizing the discretionary rule-making, executive and judicial powers of IRAs in the name of 'good governance' may mean the triumph of technocratic, economic rationality over politics and of technocratic rule over democracy.

What are the necessary empirical conditions that would increase the likelihood of the realization of this theoretical scenario? I contend that this scenario is most likely to be played out in the following circumstances: when the IRAs perfectly meet the required standards of procedural and substantive legitimacy; when they unquestionably prove themselves to be 'the most appropriate ones for the functions entrusted to them'; when they legitimately become the fourth branch of government; and when such a consensus forms around their performance that controls become irrelevant and are rarely exercised, i.e. when IRAs become so successful in what they do that their existence, decisions and actions are no longer questioned by the public, their elected representatives or the judiciary. As Thatcher and Stone Sweet emphasize, 'the legitimacy of [non-majoritarian institutions] is only at issue when agents are corrupted, or fail to deliver adequate levels of promised benefits' (2002: 18).[13]

Furthermore, the outstanding performance of established IRAs is also likely to lead to an expansion in their zones of discretion and/or to the establishment of IRAs in new policy areas. This is a plausible prediction, as policy learning and institutional isomorphism have already been one of the most important factors behind the spread of IRAs (Thatcher, 2002). In the final analysis, if IRAs gain indisputable legitimacy in contemporary democracies, regulation by independent technocrats may eventually turn into rule by technocrats where public participation is by *de facto*, limited to voting in regular elections.

Scenario 2: towards a (more) participatory democracy

Although increasing public participation is not an objective of delegation to IRAs, the second scenario regards legitimization of IRAs as a path that can potentially lead to a more participatory form of democracy. Similar to the first scenario, the starting position is that such legitimization is possible based on standards of procedural and substantive legitimacy. If delegation to IRAs is, as Majone (1996) claims, a means of diffusing power, then IRAs may contribute to the development of more egalitarian and participatory processes of decision making.

The increasing complexity of contemporary societies is also acknowledged by those who advocate a participatory form of democracy. However, unlike those in the Weberian tradition, who regard specialization along bureaucratic/technocratic lines as an inevitable and necessary consequence of this increasing complexity, and defend a type of democracy where public participation is restricted to voting in regular elections, Macpherson (1977), for instance, emphasizes the possibility and necessity of establishing more participatory institutions within the same context. If delegation to IRAs is interpreted as a strategy that protects these institutions from the 'tyranny of the majority' while providing openings for public participation, then IRAs may emerge as such participatory institutions. This requires a view of IRAs not as bureaucratic/technocratic agencies that are 'above' or 'outside' politics, but as *political* institutions providing new channels of political participation by the public.

In order to highlight the merits of public participation, rather than the disadvantages, the Weberian/Schumpeterian assumptions about voting citizens should be modified. In this respect, those arguing for participatory democracy, such as Pateman (1970), concede to the Weberian/Schumpeterian view that average citizens will never be as interested in decisions made at national level, as they would be in those decisions that immediately and directly affect their lives. Nevertheless, Pateman holds that, by starting to participate directly in decision making at sub-national levels, individuals can enhance their sense of political efficacy, increase their ability to judge national questions, assess the performance of political representatives, and participate in decisions of national scope as active and knowledgeable citizens. Thus, Weber's disenchanted citizens of the rationalized society are replaced with ones who have a reduced sense of estrangement from power centres and an increased concern for collective problems as well as some competence to tackle them. By decentralizing power and opening new channels of access and participation to decision making for such citizens, IRAs may pave the way toward a more participatory form of governance than contemporary majoritarian institutions allow.

One of the procedural standards adopted to legitimize IRAs is that the regulatory decision making follows formal rules that require public participation and deliberation, as well as peer and judicial review. Although the inclusion of this requirement agrees with the basic notion of procedural legitimacy developed by Weber and Schumpeter, it does not seem to be consistent with their systems of thought based on limited public participation. This implies there is no single definition of procedural legitimacy. For example, Habermas, like Weber and Schumpeter, relies on principles of procedure for legitimacy, but, his requirements of legitimacy are different from those presented in the previous section. According to Habermas, one of the standards of legitimacy is that procedures should guarantee collective deliberations based on open, unrestricted and egalitarian discourse. For such legitimacy, rule of law is a necessary, but insufficient basis (Peters, 1996). This chapter does not claim that legitimization of IRAs can open the way towards the type of deliberative democracy which Habermas advocates. In this scenario, even if legitimization of IRAs based on procedural standards may not lead all the way up the Habermasian road to deliberative democracy, it can theoretically help bring about a more participatory democracy that enhances public debate and encourages participation in decision-making processes[14] whilst avoiding the pitfalls of the majoritarian model.

As specified by Held, 'an open information system to ensure informed decisions' by citizens is one of the general conditions of participatory democracy (1996: 271). As long as IRAs are established by democratically enacted statutes which clearly demarcate their zones of discretion and objectives and they are bounded by requirements of justification and transparency in order to facilitate public participation and judicial review, they will be able to meet this condition more satisfactorily than majoritarian institutions. This is one of the reasons that the process of decision making by IRAs is 'better than the insular, often secret deliberations of cabinets and executives' (Thatcher and Stone Sweet, 2002: 19). Thus Rose-Ackerman asks: 'if the courts require the regulatory process to be open to public inputs and scrutiny and to act on the basis of competent analyses, are the regulators necessarily less accountable than elected politicians?' (1992: 34).

Furthermore, it is understood that IRAs favour public participation, 'while the opportunity for consultations by means of public hearings is often denied to government departments because of the conventions under which they operate' (Majone, 1994: 84). Another benefit of IRAs is that they 'can protect citizens from bureaucratic arrogance and reticence, and are able to focus public attention on controversial issues, thus enriching public debate' (Majone, 1994: 85). In other words, they are able to create an institutional environment more conducive to public participation and to offer new opportunities to challenge public decisions compared with majoritarian institutions and traditional bureaucracies. Hence, IRAs are viewed as being instrumental to increased rights protection of individuals against states.

However, this is an idealistic scenario based on assumptions that can not be taken for granted. The following assumptions underlying this scenario may be challenged both in theory and in practice; a pluralist model of interest representation and the low cost of obtaining information, participating in and overseeing of IRA decision making.

When decision making by IRAs is opened to public participation and deliberation, it is not known *a priori* whom the *actual* participants will be. A pluralist model of interest representation presumes that political power is widely and equally distributed among all citizens in a given polity. Thus, given that formal procedures instituting a process of decision making open to all are established, every citizen can participate and act to protect their own rights and interests in the regulated areas within the framework of a participatory form of governance. Yet this is not a highly probable outcome, for various reasons.

Clearly, even if the assumptions of the pluralist model hold, not all citizens are expected to closely monitor the regulatory activities of IRAs, as there are significant costs of collecting and deciphering policy-relevant information, which is often highly specific and technical. Therefore, unless regulatory decisions entail concentrated costs or benefits for them, rational citizens are not likely, individually or collectively, to pay close attention to or oversee IRA activities. The high costs of gathering and analysing policy-relevant information and overseeing procedures will deter or discourage such efforts by a majority of citizens.

In a more realistic scenario, actual participants in decision making by IRAs are going to be those who either have to pay concentrated costs or will receive concentrated benefits from regulation and thus are willing to pay the costs of information collection and analysis as well as of oversight. Consistent with the logic of collective action, as argued by Olson (1971), those same individuals will also engage in organized action to exert more influence on regulatory decisions by IRAs.

The institutional design of IRAs often privileges particularistic, organized interests from the outset. As McCubbins *et al.* suggest, agencies are first designed to ensure that interests who are active participants in the debate over the original legislation on delegation are given representation through the structure and process of the agency.

> Second, the structure and process of an agency should *stack the deck* in favor of the groups who, among those significantly affected by the policy, are also favored constituents of the coalition that caused the policy to be adopted. And third, agency policies should exhibit an *autopilot* characteristic in the sense that as the preferences of the constituencies enfranchised in the agency's structure and procedure change so too will the agency, freeing Congress and the President from having to enact new legislation to achieve this end.
>
> (McCubbins *et al.*, 1989: 444)

Thatcher and Stone Sweet (2002) also observe that, in order to increase their own influence, interest groups reorient their activities to the regulatory agencies after authority is delegated to them.[15] In summary, it can be claimed that regulation by IRAs incorporates specific interests, rather than all equal citizens, as active participants in the full range of decisions from institutional design to oversight.

A possible consequence is that IRAs become captured by sectional interests, particularly in regulated industries. The 'capture' hypothesis with regard to IRAs is found in the literature since the 1960s.[16] Whilst this approach has been challenged on both empirical and theoretical grounds; it has never been totally ruled out as having no empirical relevance or explanatory value.[17] The implication is, that despite all the measures taken to prevent it, there are still areas of regulation and IRAs that are prone to 'capture'.[18] Thus capture is always a potential problem.

This discussion suggests that the politics of regulation by IRAs involves the politics of interest groups, as usual, but filtered through different channels and in a different institutional context.[19] In contemporary democracies, interest group politics are definitely not peculiar to regulation by IRAs as institutions of decision making. However, the prevalence of interest group politics in this arena may have more undesirable consequences than in others, given that these agencies are independent from the majoritarian institutions consisting of the political representatives of the broader public.

From among the standards of substantive (output) legitimacy listed by Majone (1996, 1997), there is the condition that IRAs must be able to protect diffuse interests and ensure fairness among the inevitable winners and losers from regulatory decisions. For reasons discussed above, as the societal actors that participate more effectively in decision making by IRAs are most likely to be stronger and better informed particularistic interests, IRAs will be unable to meet this condition. The incommensurable influence of organized interests in specific regulated policy areas and sectors may create a bias that cannot be counterbalanced by that of all those influenced by regulatory decisions and their elected representatives. Moreover, the growth in the number and scope of regulated areas and IRAs as legitimate institutions of decision making creates further incentives for *politics around organized minorities* and entails an extension of such bias to new areas of political life in democratic systems.

To summarize, in a realistic scenario accentuating legitimacy criteria that aim to ensure public participation in decision making by IRAs, there may be enhanced public participation. However, this would require more participation by an increasing number of minorities organized around their particularistic interests in regulated areas. Even if formal procedures allow equal access and participation by all citizens, their involvement in regulatory activities by IRAs is likely to remain marginal. As voting in regular elections will continue to be the major instrument through which the majority of citizens exert political influence, delegating powers of elected institutions to IRAs will actually diminish the political power of the general public by their *de facto* exclusion from regulated policy domains. Granting incontestable legitimacy to IRAs, as if their decisions are made based on the equal access and participation of all citizens who formally have the right of equal access and participation and are affected by these decisions, may have broader implications for democratic regimes, particularly with regard to their ability to achieve equality and fairness. These are democratic principles that must be safeguarded not only on paper, but also in practice. Therefore, given their present stage of development, the legitimacy of IRAs should remain an issue to be questioned and debated, especially as it relates to these general principles.

Conclusion

The objective of this chapter has been to reflect upon the possible consequences of legitimizing IRAs for contemporary democratic regimes. The theoretical scenarios developed in previous sections should be considered as 'ideal types' that do not perfectly correspond to real-life practices and outcomes. Both scenarios are based on similar standards of legitimacy as applied to IRAs, yet each has emphasized different aspects of these standards. The empirical accuracy of these scenarios deserves further debate focusing on the actual practices of delegation to IRAs. This requires a research agenda that explores types of delegation (principal–agent or fiduciary), level of agency independence and loss, types of IRAs (economic or social regulation), systems of interest representation, state structures, and institutional legacies as intervening variables that can influence the type of rule that emerges out of these practices.

This chapter has not questioned whether IRAs should be legitimized. Nor have the democratic credentials of the standards of procedural and substantive legitimacy that are used to legitimize IRAs been explicitly challenged on normative grounds. Yet these issues require critical consideration.

In the realm of IRAs, legitimization has followed practice, after the establishment of IRAs as a part of regional and national institutional structures. This can be viewed as an effort to reset normative standards to the structural requirements of strategies that have been adopted since the 1980s. In other words, structure has followed strategy, as Chandler (1962) theorized, and legitimization or the resetting of normative standards has followed structure. The new strategies were developed by the neo-liberal orthodoxy prioritizing efficiency over redistribution and rationalizing it as a necessary consequence of the crisis of the welfare state. Majone's legitimization of IRAs, based on a distinction between efficiency-enhancing and redistributive policies, is in harmony with the orthodoxy. From such a perspective, delegation to IRAs becomes basically a technical question about how to ensure efficient outcomes.

However, efficiency is a value of the markets, not of political institutions. The task at hand is not how to manage a private firm so as to maximize profits by discovering the most efficient means. Even Majone recognizes the difference:

> It is of course true that efficiency-enhancing policies, like all public policies, will normally have redistributive impacts. This is not a serious problem if the efficiency gains are large enough to compensate the losers, and if it is politically feasible to do so. However, it is well known that compensation is often difficult at national level because of the veto power of special interests.
>
> (1998: 28)

Hence, delegation to IRAs cannot and should not be reduced to a technical problem. On the contrary, it is a highly political issue with significant effects on political systems and communities. Delegation itself is a political decision that affects distribution of power and creates winners and losers. Therefore, isolating IRAs in a realm of economic rationality and efficiency may be neither possible nor desirable.

The main challenge in specifying and applying standards of procedural legitimacy for IRAs is to achieve a balance between economic rationality and democratic politics. On one hand, creating institutions of strictly apolitical and technocratic decision making, completely immune from legitimate democratic demands, is to be avoided. On the other hand, opening these institutions to public participation carries the risks of high politicization and ungovernability that go against the rationale for delegation in the first place. Finally, outcome legitimacy should never be allowed to overshadow compliance with such balanced standards of procedural legitimacy. As Papadopoulos underlines, outcome legitimacy 'is not democratic in and of itself. Goods and service provision can in principle be judged satisfactory regardless of the democratic character of decision making, and dictatorships too produce policies that are perceived as adequate by some of their recipients'(Papadopoulos 2003: 473). As the uncoupling of democratic standards and assessment of outcome legitimacy is not possible in regimes that claim to be democratic, Pareto-optimal solutions should not be sought at the expense of democratic principles which Western contemporary democracies are proudly exporting to the rest of the world.

Notes

1 See, for instance, Thatcher and Stone Sweet (2002), Levy and Spiller (1996), Majone (1996, 1997).
2 This open-ended question is further complicated in the European context, where delegation to IRAs has taken place at the regional and national levels and is characterized by a diversity of regulatory regimes as well as variance in

actual practices of delegation to IRAs across countries and sectors. Thatcher (2002) underlines the difficulty of defining an 'independent regulatory agency' in Western Europe due to the diversity of agencies. For a comparative analysis that reveals the similarities and differences in regulatory regimes in Europe see, for instance, Böllhoff (2002). For general analyses of IRAs in Europe see Geradin and Petit (2004) and Yataganas (2001) and Gilardi's Chapter 6 in this book. The democratic accountability and legitimacy of the IRAs of the European Community/Union, as a 'mixed polity' involving multi-level governance, is often analysed in connection with its alleged 'democratic deficit'. See, for instance, Majone (1998, 2002), Papadopoulos (2003), Héritier (2001a) and Lord and Magnette (2004). Zweifel (2003) presents a comparative analysis of merger regulation in the European Union, the United States and Switzerland in regard to the question of democratic deficit. For a study at the national level see Wälti *et al.* (2004).

3 For a study of delegation to IRAs in the United States revealing the existence of both tendencies see an earlier version of this chapter by Sosay (2003).

4 For an evaluation of the Central Bank of Turkey as an independent non-majoritarian institution, on these grounds see Sosay (2002).

5 Epstein and O'Halloran (1999) also point out that the informational and cred-ibility rationales may overlap so that delegation may reflect a demand for both expert information and credible commitment.

6 This is how Baldwin (1996: 83) defines legitimacy.

7 See Majone (1996, 1997).

8 See Dryzek (1996) for an elaborate discussion regarding the tension between democracy and economic rationality.

9 See *The Federalist Papers*, Nos 10, 48 and 51. For a more elaborate discussion on this see Bellamy (1996).

10 This is the term used by Majone (1996, 1997).

11 For example, see the EC/EU, OECD, IMF and World Bank documents on gov-ernance.

12 For similar arguments see Cox (1997), Kiely (1998) and Pereira (2001).

13 Also see Majone (2000).

14 Normative models of deliberative democracy presume public participation. As Cooke states, in these models 'all citizens have an equal opportunity, and are equally encouraged to contribute to public deliberation on matters of common concern' (2000: 956).

15 On access to regulators see Héritier (2001b).

16 Kolko (1965) presents the best known of this line of argument. Stigler (1971) reformulated the hypothesis.

17 For a brief review of related literature see Lamoreaux (1984).

18 Namely, in the United States, the Civil Aeronautics Board (CAB), the Federal Communications Commission (FCC) and the Federal Trade Commission (FTC) are those that have been commonly cited as examples of such agencies. For a study of capture in Britain, France, Germany and Italy see Thatcher (2005).

19 In the United States the creation of public lobby groups in the 1970s with the intention that they would act as watchdogs on behalf of those who could not organize themselves to protect the public interest in social regulation, includ-ing issue areas such as environmental protection, consumer affairs or public health, was significant in opening up the regulatory process to participation beyond that of particularistic interests. However, public lobby groups have not achieved the ideals of citizen participation formulated by theorists of participa-tory democracy. In this respect, Harris and Milkis (1996) doubt that the public lobby regime has become more accessible to the public *per se* than the regime it

replaced. Lowi (1979) even claims that this regime has actually created elitist institutions even more dominated by organized interests and insulated from the people. The contention is that public lobby groups have been integrated into specific issue networks in Washington DC and insulated policy-making processes that take place outside the realm of public debate. According to Lowi, this has been just an extension of interest group liberalism. In other words, public lobby groups have become new actors on the familiar American political stage. Moreover, Harris and Milkis contend that since they have not always been in harmony with the public they profess to represent, public lobby groups have usually preferred to work through administrative and legal challenges that were insulated from majoritarian institutions. Hence the public lobby regime has actually sheltered regulatory policy from broader democratic influences such as the presidency or electoral politics. In the European context, the formation of policy networks may constitute a comparable development. See Majone (2000) and Papadopoulos (2003).

References

Baldwin, R. (1996) 'Regulatory Legitimacy in the European Context: The British Health and Safety Executive', in G. Majone (ed.) *Regulating Europe*, London and New York: Routledge.

Bellamy, R. (1996) 'The Political Form of Constitution. The Separation of Powers, Rights and Representative Democracy', *Political Studies*, 44 (3): 436–456.

Böllhoff, D. (2002) 'Developments in Regulatory Regimes. An Anglo-German Comparison on Telecommunications, Energy and Rail', *Preprints aus der Max-Planck-Projektgruppe Recht der Gemeinshaftsgüter*, Bonn.

Centeno, M. A. (1998) 'The Politics of Knowledge. Hayek and Technocracy' in M. A. Centeno and P. Silva (eds) *The Politics of Expertise in Latin America*, Basingstoke: Macmillan.

Chandler, A. D. (1962) *Strategy and Structure*, Cambridge MA: MIT Press.

Cooke, M. (2000) 'Five Arguments for Deliberative Democracy', *Political Studies*, 485: 947–969.

Cox, R. (1997) 'Economic Globalization and the Limits to Liberal Democracy', in A. McGrew (ed.) *The Transformation of Democracy? Globalization and Territorial Democracy*, Cambridge: Polity Press.

Dryzek, J. (1996) *Democracy in Capitalist Times. Ideals, Limits, and Struggles*, New York and Oxford: Oxford University Press.

Epstein, D. and O'Halloran, S. (1999) *Delegating Powers: A Transaction Cost Politics Approach to Policy Making under Separate Powers*, New York: Cambridge University Press.

Geradin, D. and Petit, N. (2004) 'The Development of Agencies at EU and National Levels: Conceptual Analysis and Proposals for Reform', Jean Monnet Working Paper 01/04, New York: Jean Monnet Center, School of Law, New York University, available online: www.jeanmonnetprogram.org/papers/04/040101.pdf.

Giddens, A. (1972) *Politics and Sociology in the Thought of Max Weber*, London: Macmillan.

Harris, R. A. and Milkis, S. M. (1996) *The Politics of Regulatory Change: A Tale of Two Agencies*, 2nd edn, New York and Oxford: Oxford University Press.

Hayek, F. A. von (1973–1979) *Law, Legislation and Liberty*, 3 vols, Chicago: University of Chicago Press.

Hayek, F. A. von (1978) *New Studies in Philosophy, Politics, and Economics and the History of the Ideas*, London: Routledge.

Held, D. (1996) *Models of Democracy*, Cambridge: Polity Press.

Héritier, A. (2001a) 'Composite Democratic Legitimation in Europe: the Role of Transparency and Access to Information', *Preprints aus der Max-Planck-Projektgruppe Recht der Gemeinschaftsgüter*, Bonn.

Héritier, A. (2001b) 'Regulator–Regulatee Interaction in the Liberalized Utilities: Access and Contract Compliance in the Rail Sector', *Preprints aus der Max-Planck-Projektgruppe Recht der Gemeinschaftsgüter*, Bonn.

Kiely, R. (1998) 'Neoliberalism Revised? A Critical Account of World Bank Concepts of Good Governance and Market Friendly Intervention', *Capital and Class*, 64: 63–88.

Kolko, G. (1965) *Railroads and Regulation, 1877–1916*, New York: Norton.

Lamoreaux, N. R. (1984) 'Regulatory Agencies', in J. P. Greene (ed.) *Encyclopedia of American Political History: Studies of the Principal Movements and Ideas*, New York: Scribner.

Lassman, P. (2000) 'The Rule of Man over Man: Politics, Power, and Legitimation', in S. Turner (ed.) *The Cambridge Companion to Weber*, Cambridge: Cambridge University Press.

Levy, B. and Spiller, P. (eds) (1996) *Regulation, Institutions and Commitment*, Cambridge: Cambridge University Press.

Lord, C. and Magnette, P. (2004) 'E pluribus unum? Creative Disagreement about Legitimacy in the EU', *Journal of Common Market Studies*, 42 (1): 183–202.

Lowi, T. J. (1979) *The End of Liberalism*, New York: Norton.

Macpherson, C. B. (1977) *The Life and Times of Liberal Democracy*, Oxford: Oxford University Press.

Majone, G. (1994) 'The Rise of the Regulatory State in Europe', *West European Politics*, 17 (3): 77–101.

Majone, G. (1996) *Regulating Europe*, London: Routledge.

Majone, G. (1997) 'From the Positive to the Regulatory State: Causes and Consequences of Changes in the Mode of Governance', *Journal of Public Policy*, 17 (2): 139–167.

Majone, G. (1998) 'Europe's "Democratic Deficit": The Question of Standards', *European Law Journal*, 4 (1): 5–28.

Majone, G. (1999) 'The Regulatory State and its Legitimacy Problems', *West European Politics*, 22 (1): 1–24.

Majone, G. (2000) 'The Credibility Crisis of Community Regulation', *Journal of Common Market Studies*, 38 (2): 273–302.

Majone, G. (2001) 'Two Logics of Delegation: Agency and Fiduciary Relations in EU Governance', *European Union Politics*, 2 (1): 103–121.

Majone, G. (2002) 'Delegation of Regulatory Powers in a Mixed Polity', *European Law Journal*, 8 (3): 319–339.

McCubbins, M. D., Noll, R. G. and Weingast, B. R. (1989) 'Structure and Process, Politics and Policy: Administrative Arrangements and the Political Control of Agencies', *Virginia Law Review*, 75: 431–482.

Olson, M. (1971) *The Logic of Collective Action*, Cambridge MA: Harvard University Press.

Papadopoulos, Y. (2003) 'Cooperative Forms of Governance: Problems of Democratic Accountability in Complex Environments', *European Journal of Political Research*, 42: 473–501.

Pateman, C. (1970) *Participation and Democratic Theory*, Cambridge: Cambridge University Press.

Pereira, A. W. (2001) 'Democracies: Emerging or Submerging?', *Dissent*, 48 (1): 17–23.

Peters, B. (1996) 'On Reconstructive Legal and Political Theory', in M. Deflem (ed.) *Habermas, Modernity and Law*, London: Sage Publications.

Rose-Ackerman, S. (1992) *Rethinking the Progressive Agenda*, New York: Free Press.

Roth, G. and Schluchter, W. (1979) *Max Weber's Vision of History*, Berkeley CA: University of California Press.

Scharpf, F. W. (1999) *Governing in Europe: Effective and Democratic?* Oxford: Oxford University Press.

Scharpf, F. W. (2000) 'Notes toward a Theory of Multilevel Governing in Europe', Max-Planck-Institut für Gesellschaftforschung Discussion Paper, No. 5/2000.

Schumpeter, J. (1976) *Capitalism, Socialism and Democracy*, London: Allen & Unwin.

Sosay, G. (2002) 'The Tension between the Institutional Requirements of Neoliberal Globalization and of Participatory Democracy: The Challenge of Economic Development in Democratizing Countries', paper presented at the forty-third annual meeting of the International Studies Association, New Orleans LA, 24–27 March 2002.

Sosay, G. (2003) 'Legitimation of Delegation to Independent Non-majoritarian Institutions and its Consequences for Contemporary Democracies', presented at the European Consortium for Political Research, Joint Sessions of Workshops, Workshop 15: Delegation in Contemporary Democracies, Edinburgh, 28 March–2 April, 2003.

Stigler, G. (1971) 'The Theory of Economic Regulation', *Bell Journal of Economics and Management Science*, 62 (2): 114–141.

Thatcher, M. (2002) 'Delegation to Independent Regulatory Agencies: Pressures, Functions, and Contextual Mediation', *West European Politics*, 25 (1): 125–147.

Thatcher, M. (2005) 'The Third Force? Independent Regulatory Agencies and Elected Politicians in Europe', *Governance*, 18 (3): 347–373.

Thatcher, M. and Stone Sweet, A. (2002) 'Theory and Practice of Delegation to Non-majoritarian Institutions', *West European Politics*, 25 (1): 1–22.

The Federalist Papers, Nos 10, 48 and 51.

Veljanovski, C. (1991) 'The Regulation Game', in C. Veljanovski (ed.) *Regulators and the Market*, London: Institute of Economic Affairs.

Wälti, S., Kübler, D. and Papadopoulos, Y. (2004) 'How Democratic is "Governance"? Lessons from Swiss Drug Policy', *Governance*, 17 (1): 83–113.

Weber, M. (1968) *Economy and Society*, 3 vols, New York: Bedminster Press.

Weber, M. (1972) 'Politics as a Vocation', in H. H. Gerth and C. W. Mills (eds) *From Max Weber*, New York: Oxford University Press.

Wilson, J. Q. (1989) *Bureaucracy: What Government Agencies Do and Why They Do It*, New York: Basic Books.

Yataganas, X. A. (2001) 'Delegation of Regulatory Authority in the European Union: The Relevance of the American Model of Independent Agencies', Jean Monnet Working Paper No. 3/01.

Zweifel, T. (2003) 'Democratic Deficits in Comparison: Best (and Worst) Practices in European, US and Swiss Merger Regulation', *Journal of Common Market Studies*, 41 (3): 541–566.

9 Whose agents?

Non-governmental organizations in policy-proposing commissions: agents of government or opposition parties?

Peter Munk Christiansen and Asbjørn Sonne Nørgaard

The relationship between government and parliament is crucial to the functioning of parliamentary democracy. In parliamentary regimes parliaments control the government. However, the value of parliamentary control varies with the strength of government. Majority governments control a majority in parliament and often reduce the role of parliament to a simple rubber-stamping of the government's policy. Under minority government the legislative majority in parliament can be actively involved in policy making and possibly 'defeat the executive on a wide range of specific policy issues' (Laver and Shepsle, 1991: 267). But in order to make 'durable deals' and solve future commitment problems, even majority governments have incentives to accommodate the preferences of opposition parties (Moe and Caldwell, 1994). Thus, in both cases, the opposition in parliament has some bargaining power vis-à-vis the government.

Regardless of the type of government the executive has certain advantages vis-à-vis parliament because it can design the policy making process in different ways (Strøm, 1990; Laver and Shepsle, 1991; Tsebelis, 1999; Heller, 2001). One way to structure the process is to delegate policy-proposing authority to a commission with organized interests, which may include traditional allies of the opposition. It is usually held that delegation to non-allies is not a good idea, because the non-ally will submit information that is distorted and untruthful (Bendor *et al.*, 2001: 250–252; cf. Epstein and O'Halloran, 1999). However, by delegating powers to a commission, which is in fact a composite agent that includes multiple agents with heterogeneous preferences, the behaviour of the non-allies is more uncertain. Members of such a policy-proposing commission will face penalties if they are found to be lying. False information is – at least partially – subject to verification, and commission members will have to provide lengthy justifications and undertake other costly efforts to convince the rest of the commission (cf. Lupia and McCubbins, 1998: 52–60).

If non-ally organizations accept the invitation to sit on a policy-proposing commission there is a good chance that the commission members, the allies and non-allies alike, become supportive agents of the government and obstructive agents of the parliamentary opposition.

Focusing on whether or not to include non-governmental interest organizations in the policy-making process, the questions addressed in this chapter are: who is more positive about the role of non-governmental organizations when they are included in commissions that have been dele gated policy-proposing powers, the government or the opposition parties? How does this kind of delegation affect the role of organizations as agents?

The principal–agent (PA) literature on delegation has only quite recently begun to focus on issues relevant to parliamentary democracies (Huber, 2000; Huber and Lupia, 2001; Müller, 2000; Strøm, 2000). Some delegation problems in the American division of powers system are not relevant to West European countries and others need to be modelled in a different way (Pollack, 2002; Moe, 1990; Moe and Caldwell, 1994). Quite surprisingly, no delegation study to date has addressed the role of non-governmental interest organizations in policy making in European parliamentary democracies. In consensual European democracies non-governmental organizations with strong vertical links to political parties have traditionally been closely involved in policy making and implementa-tion through various forms of corporatist arrangements and consultative institutions (Schmitter, 1974; Lehmbruch, 1984; Lijphart and Crepaz, 1991). This practice has been particularly widespread in the highly inclu-sive Scandinavian countries (Strøm, 1990: 86–90; Rokkan, 1966; Johansen and Kristensen, 1982; Hermansson *et al.*, 1999; Christiansen and Rom-metvedt, 1999; Blom-Hansen, 2001; Christiansen and Nørgaard, 2003).

Usually the close involvement of interest organizations in policy making has been modelled as a kind of political exchange involving bargaining and compromise with government (Molina and Rhodes, 2002). But the inclusion of non-governmental organizations in policy-proposing commis-sions may not involve actual bargaining with the cabinet or with individual ministers (Christiansen and Nørgaard, 2003: 79). Governments often change and amend the policy proposals formulated in the commissions before presenting the proposal as a bill in parliament (Christiansen *et al.*, 2004). Thus, the use of commissions that include non-governmental organizations may be seen as a case of delegation of power to propose policy and to provide information on policy consequences. As government does not need to accept the proposed policy and can amend it in any way it wants, the delegation of powers to commissions with non-governmental organizations resembles a 'signalling model' (Bendor *et al.*, 2001: 249, 252).

The idea that non-government interest organizations can be interested third parties that provide 'fire alarms' (McCubbins and Schwartz, 1984;

Lupia and McCubbins, 1994) or act as 'speakers', who help principals select agents or decide whether to accept agent offers (Lupia and McCubbins, 1998; Balla and Wright, 2001), is also relevant in consensual parliamentary democracies. However, with the inclusion of non-government organizations in policy-proposing commissions, the role of organizational agents may also differ from what is seen in an American context (Moe and Caldwell, 1994). Sometimes traditional allies of the opposition parties may be reluctant to 'push the alarm button' and 'speak up' as the non-governmental organization may have won concessions in the commission. If the proposal-cum-compromise made in the commission and forwarded to the government is accepted or only slightly amended the organizations may be reluctant to pass on information to their traditional parliamentary allies out of fear that the compromise negotiated with the commission will be at risk. Only if the organizations believe that their parliamentary allies in opposition are able to gain more concessions from the government will they provide trustworthy information to the parliament. Interest organizations *may* act as agents of their allies in parliament, but if they are included in policy-proposing commissions the organizations may find it advantageous not to reveal information to political allies in parliament. Thus, ultimately, the role of organizations as agents of government and oppositions parties is an empirical question.

It has been widely recognized that agents often face multiple principals (e.g. Waterman and Meier, 1998). Studies of the relationship between agents and their multiple, competing principals have focused on separation of powers systems, notably the United States (see Calvert *et al.*, 1989; Hammond and Knott, 1996; Bendor *et al.*, 2001; Volden, 2002). The traditional view taken in studies of parliamentary democracies is that government commands a majority in parliament and therefore can be seen as one principal (Moe, 1990), where government is 'fused or united' and 'each agent is accountable to one and only one principal' (Strøm, 2000: 264, 269). Principal–agency studies of the issue of multiple principals in parliamentary systems focus on coalition governments and the institutional possibilities for mutual checks within governing coalitions (Thies, 2001; Heller, 2001). Heller discusses the situation where a minority government faces opposition majorities in parliament on certain policy issues (2001: 791–792; cf. also Laver and Shepsle, 1991; Strøm, 1990; Huber, 1996; Tsebelis, 1999). Following Heller, the government can use 'last offers' to break up potential opposition coalitions. Furthermore, according to Tsebelis, minority governments usually enjoy a positional advantage that makes it possible for the government to 'lean slightly one way or another and find allies ready to support different pieces of legislation' (Tsebelis, 1999: 594; cf. Strøm, 1990). A complementary strategy for governments in parliamentary systems, particularly minority ones, is to involve interest organizations, including traditional allies of opposition parties, in policy-proposing commissions. As indicated, this strategy may have consequences for the role of non-governmental organizations as agents.

Focusing on the potential problems of agency loss and information asymmetry, the question in this chapter is: how do members of parliament (MPs) from the governing and the opposition parties perceive the role of non-governmental organizations as agents, depending on whether organizations have been involved in policy-proposing commissions or not?

In the next section we will discuss how the delegation game can be modelled when government confronts the choice of whether to include important non-governmental organizations which may be non-allies in a policy proposing commission. We will focus on the possible relations between the members of governing parties and opposition parties as principals on the one hand and organizations as agents on the other. Two theoretical propositions are presented, with the development of the argument focusing on minority governments and the case of majority governments discussed briefly.

In the following section, we will discuss Denmark as a case for testing the propositions. In the late 1970s, Danish governments often delegated the power to propose policy to commissions that comprised non-governmental organizations and included non-ally organizations. By the late 1990s this kind of delegation practice was much less utilized. Government prepared its own bills and policy proposing commissions were only rarely involved. Following a brief introduction, we outline four empirical theses on the role of organizations as agents of governing and opposition parties. Finally, the empirical theses will be tested. The data are based on two questionnaires sent to Danish MPs in 1980 and 2000 (cf. Appendix 9.1; cf. also Christiansen and Nørgaard, 2003) that enabled one index to be constructed to measure MPs' perception of agency loss and another one measuring information asymmetry/loss. The data covers two instances of minority governments that, as argued below, have the strongest incentives to delegate powers to policy-proposing commissions, including non-governmental organizations. However, majority governments may have an incentive to delegate in the same way as minority governments. In conclusion, we return to this issue along with the wider implications of the study for the theoretical issues discussed above.

The argument: delegation of policy-proposing powers to commissions with non-government organizations

The basic conceptual grammar of delegation problems from a principal–agent perspective has been summarized in numerous publications (e.g. Moe, 1984; Waterman and Meier, 1998; Bendor *et al.*, 2001). Because a principal lacks time or expertise to act on his own he may delegate to agents the authority to take actions (delegation-of-authority models), provide information or make proposals (signalling models) (cf.

Bendor *et al.*, 2001). In the case of policy-proposing commissions we find a signalling model, because government does not need to either outright reject or accept the proposal forwarded by the commission but can amend it, before introducing a bill in parliament. Due to agents' informational advantage and the potential problem of diverging preferences between principal and agent (which may or may not be fully known to the principal), there is a risk that delegation may fail and that the commission or individual commission members convey untrustworthy information to government. The principals run the risk of choosing the wrong agent (adverse selection) or that the agent, once selected, will not work loyally for the principal (moral hazard, shirking). In the case of policy-proposing commissions, commission members, notably non-allies of the government, may turn to the opposition in parliament.

We start by spelling out the argument in the case of minority governments where we have two principals. The government, or an agent of the government, usually formulates policy and prepares legislation which then needs to be passed by a parliamentary majority that includes parties who are not part of the governing coalition. However, the argument may have implications beyond the case of minority governments as majority governments in parliamentary systems face the general problem of making durable deals that can outlast a change in government power (Moe and Caldwell, 1994).

A minority government must enjoy the confidence of a majority of the parliament in order to operate effectively, but this does not imply that the government enjoys parliamentary support on all policy issues (Strøm, 1990; Laver and Shepsle, 1991; Heller, 2001; Thies, 2001). The supporting parties that have put the government into power – perhaps choosing the lesser of two evils – have their own constituencies and policy agendas. There are limits on how far a government will go in making concessions to a parliamentary majority. The government can make threats and define legislative defeat as a cabinet issue – i.e. a vote of confidence (Huber, 1996; Laver and Shepsle, 1996) – and it may also enjoy some procedural advantages with respect to making last offers, which can discipline insurgent coalition and support parties who are unable to identify a better alternative (Heller, 2001). Similar to the threat that a presidential veto can discipline a congressional majority of the opposition party, a minority government has certain instruments to discipline legislative majorities and opposition parties. Whilst divided government in the American context is due to *constitutional independence*, divided government under a parliamentary system 'is maintained by the *strategic behaviour* of the main actors' (Laver and Shepsle, 1991: 267, emphasis in original; Moe and Caldwell, 1994). A minority government cannot continually exploit the political sympathy of its supporting parties without ultimately facing the threat of a no-confidence vote. The government must be willing to accept some legislative defeats or amendments in order to stay in power and pursue more strategically important policies. Although different ways of building majority policy coalitions can be identified under minority government, they all involve making concessions to parties not holding government portfolios (Strøm, 1990: 98).

When the issue is policy formulation and legislative action, parliament is not restricted to either accepting or rejecting the government proposal, and the parties can amend government bills and obtain concessions. In effect, government and parliament negotiate and bargain over policy. Thus, although governments enjoy some privileges with respect to structuring the policy process, both parliament and government are *de facto* veto players that can formulate, amend and block policy initiatives.

The game played between government and potential strategic alliances in parliament, who might oppose government policy, is characterized by unpredictability. Government cannot predict whether a strategic alliance against its policy will materialize (cf. McKelvey, 1976). Policy and vote-seeking parties will try to get policy outcomes that satisfy their own policy goals to the highest degree at the lowest electoral cost. Leaving aside traditions of party cooperation, a political party will make bargains with the parties that are willing to make the most concessions. Because numerous policy deals can be struck there will be multiple equilibria. The unpredictability of the policy coalition that will be established – and indeed cabinet instability – increases when electoral competition and policy dispersion among issue dimensions increase (Strøm, 1990: 107). Thus, government cannot be sure of the reversion point if its policy is defeated by a strategic alliance in parliament. Will it be *status quo* or a new policy that is further away from the government's ideal policy?

Realizing that a parliamentary majority may form a strategic alliance to make amendments contrary to government policy (Laver and Shepsle, 1991: 262–265), a policy and vote-seeking government will try to minimize the risk that this eventuates.[1] By involving non-governmental organizations that represent and articulate significant voter preferences in a policy-proposing commission, and including organizations that organize segments of voters that usually align with parties of the opposition, a minority government reduces the risk that parties in parliament can form a strategic alliance against government policy. If the commission is able to agree internally and put forward a policy proposal that is accepted or only slightly amended by the government, then the organizations sitting on the commission may withhold information from the opposition parties in parliament. Even traditional allies of the opposition parties may forgo the opportunity to pass on true information to parliament because they fear that the concessions they have won in the commission can be jeopardized when the compromise is politicized in parliament.

If traditional allies of the opposition forgo their opportunity to inform and lobby the opposition parties in the parliamentary arena, then the opposition parties have little to gain by opposing government policy and majority support for the government bill is easier to establish. The opposition in parliament is unable to argue that government is partisan or failing to accommodate important social and economic interests. This raises the following question: why would non-governmental organizations that are traditional allies of the opposition give up the opportunity to pass on information to the opposition parties?

Organizations also face unpredictability. They have to choose the most effective means to influence policy outcomes. Organizations that are allies of the incumbent government, e.g. unions under a social democratic government, will have no difficulty with becoming an agent of government and join a policy-proposing commission because the government usually trusts these organizations (Bendor *et al.*, 2001). For non-allies the choice is more difficult. One strategy is to provide information to traditional allies in parliament and hope that the opposition parties will become part of the ruling coalition and be able to win concessions through bargaining with the government. But there is no guarantee that their political friends will become part of such a coalition, and in any case the opposition parties will only be able to win some concessions due to the disciplining powers enjoyed by the government.

Another strategy for these organizations is to accept an invitation to sit on a policy-proposing commission along with organizations that are allies of the government. In this situation, the non-allies may be able to negotiate concessions within the commission and have some influence on the policy proposal that the commission recommends to the government. The government can then choose to accept, reject or amend the proposal. If the government rejects the proposal or amends it in ways that take away the concessions non-ally organizations have previously won in the commission, the non-ally organizations will have an incentive to submit truthful information to their parliamentary allies in opposition. However, if the government fully or partially accepts the commission proposal then the non-ally organizations may not exploit this opportunity, because the concessions won in the commission and accepted by the government can be jeopardized. Even if some organizations have stronger alliances with the parliamentary opposition, the opposition parties may not be able to secure a better policy outcome. In a situation of repeated delegation, the government may deter organizations from going to their friends in parliament, in particular if the future is important for both sides (Bendor *et al.*, 2001: 256). Members of a policy-proposing commission will also face penalties for lying and there may be other opportunities for verifying the information and credibility of threats. Thus, even non-allies may become good agents of government.

Government understands the strategic calculation that non-ally organizations make. To circumvent or reduce parliamentary unpredictability the government has an incentive to accept some of the demands of the non-allies that have been included in the commission's proposal. The number of concessions a government is willing to make to organizations and the number of concessions organizations are willing to concede vary in time and space.[2]

The problem for the opposition parties is that the non-governmental organizations, including their own allies, may turn out to be poor agents, as the organizations may not pass on accurate information. Thus, the opposition perceives that the organizations' involvement in the policy-proposing commission results in an agency loss

Similar to committees in the US Congress that withhold information from the floor (Epstein and O'Halloran, 1999: 70–71), organizations that are members of policy-proposing commissions appointed by the government may find it unwise to pass on information to parliament. This is due not to ideological compatibility with the commission or the minority ruling government but because such organizations may calculate that their friends among the opposition parties will not be able to reach a better policy outcome.

The implication of the argument is that non-governmental organizations may be agents of the governing as well as the opposition parties, depending on whether the organizations are members of a policy-proposing commission appointed by government. Theoretically, we hypothesize that *if a minority government delegates policy-proposing powers to commissions with non-governmental organizations, the governing parties perceive those organizations as better agents than the opposition parties do*. This implies that the governing parties perceive organizations as providing reliable information and the agency loss resulting from the involvement of organized interests in policy making to be low. To rule out the fact that these perceptions result only when government allies are included in the policy proposing commission, it has to be demonstrated that non-allies are included in the commissions on an equal footing.

We further surmise that *if the government does not delegate policy-proposing powers to commissions with non-governmental organizations, the governing parties and the parties of the opposition have similar perceptions of interest organizations as agents*. Due to being excluded from the commissions non-governmental organizations have an incentive to pass on information to all parties in parliament to try to get concessions. Because of multiple equilibria, i.e. more possible winning policy coalitions, the organizations will have a strong incentive to contact all parties that may become part of a winning coalition. As all parties will receive a larger amount and more accurate information, the parties in parliament will have similar assessments of the information and agency loss resulting from the interplay with organizations.[3]

The implications of government delegation to policy-proposing commissions containing non-governmental organizations is most clearly spelled out under minority government, as this situation demonstrates the inherent unpredictability of the winning policy coalition. However, the model of two principals may also be relevant in the case of majority governments, although for different reasons.

First, political uncertainty about the outcome of future elections may encourage majority governments to seek super-majorities by including one or more opposition parties that may become part of a future government. Including organizational allies of opposition parties in policy-proposing commissions is a way to avoid future reversals of policy. 'If cooptation is to serve as a basis for durable deals, then proponents need to *include the losers* in their design, and thus provide enough balance to avoid massive pressures for change in the future' (Moe and Caldwell, 1994: 181). A government seeking truly consensual, and thus non-ideological, structures of delegation will not simultaneously be able to realize its own policy objectives. The party or parties in a majority government are faced with a trade-off between making durable deals or pursuing their own policy agenda.

Second, majority *coalition* governments may be faced with similar cross-cutting incentives as minority governments. The challenge of the coalition leader in this situation is not to muster a majority with parties outside government but to ensure that potentially insurgent coalition members stick to the agreed policy. The control over spoils and shared authority is one such incentive (Thies, 2001: 583), but delegation of policy-proposing powers to commissions that include non-governmental organizations may be another kind of *institutional check*. On some issue dimensions junior members of the governing coalition may have preferences that are closer to the minority opposition. By delegating powers to commissions that include non-governmental allies of the opposition and insurgent coalition members, the coalition leader may be able to discipline the insurgent coalition members. Thus, methods similar to those used by minority governments may be effective.

The case: delegation of policy-proposing powers to commissions with non-government organizations in Denmark

At the so-called earthquake election in 1973 the number of parties in the Danish parliament, the Folketinget, doubled from five to ten and has remained fairly constant since. The electoral backing of the four old parties, one of which has held the post of prime minister throughout the twentieth century, was reduced from about 85 per cent to less than 60 per cent (cf. Miller, 1996). Since 1973 all governments except one (in 1993–1994) have been minority governments. The characterization of Denmark as 'the epitome of a political system given to minority governments' (Strøm, 1990: 105; Damgaard, 1999) has much to recommend it. In the aftermath of the oil price shock in 1973, stagflation and rising unemployment rates were the order of the day. These trends, in combination with demands for more publicly funded welfare services, placed increasing pressure on the weak, predominantly Social Democratic minority governments of the 1970s. Effective governing became increasingly difficult.

Denmark's tradition of including well organized interests with strong preferences in policy proposing commissions and policy implementation dates back to before the First World War (Christiansen and Nørgaard, 2003). This practice was expanded and consolidated in the 1930s and after the Second World War, peaking during the 1970s. The number of extraparliamentary commissions and committees sponsored by the central government (by way of statute, executive order, or other kinds of governmental action) reached a record high of 715 in 1980. See Table 9.1.

Not only did the number of government-sponsored policy-proposing commissions peak in the late 1970s, the inclusion of organized interests also reached unprecedented levels. In 1975 interest organizations participated in some 150 commissions proposing policy, and in 1980, the number reached 185. Not only allies of the ruling Social Democratic Party sat on these committees. The number of trade associations that were members of committees and commissions was much higher than the number of unions. More than 300 trade associations were members of committees and commissions in 1981 according to the best estimate, compared to roughly 225 blue and white-collar unions (Christiansen and Nørgaard, 2003: 102, 235).

This raises the question of whether business associations had any influence on these commissions and whether their interests were visible in the policy proposals forwarded to the government. There is strong evidence indicating that organizational allies and non-allies of the Social Democratic governments participated on an equal footing in the policy-proposing commissions. In a questionnaire sent to all Danish non-governmental organizations in 1981 (Christiansen and Nørgaard, 2003: appendix), the organizational executives were asked how often their organizations had an influence on the content of the mandate of government commissions and committees. Seven unions reported 'very often' and twenty-nine answered 'quite often'. In contrast, more business and trade associations reported having influence on government commissions, with fourteen responding 'very often', and an additional thirty-four said 'quite often'. Thus, organizations not allied to the Social Democratic minority government were also able to have some bearing on the policy proposals that the commissions forwarded to the government.

By the late 1990s things had changed dramatically. The number of committees and commissions had dropped (although it began to increase again between 1995 and 2000, rising from 368 to 513), and – more significantly – the proportion of policy-proposing commissions was more than halved. The number of policy-proposing commissions that included non-governmental organizations was between fifty-five and sixty in the late 1990s, or roughly a third of what it was fifteen to twenty years earlier.

Table 9.1 Number of committees and commissions, share of policy-proposing commissions and participation of non-governmental interest organizations in policy-proposing commissions, 1946–2000

	1946	1955	1965	1975	1980	1985	1990	1995	2000
No. of committees and commissions	413	547	673	667	715	516	388	368	513
Percentage of committees and commissions proposing policy	37	40	44	46	37	33	20	23	18
Percentage of committees and commissions proposing policy of which non-governmental organizations were members of	40	53	51	50	70	70	74	71	60

Source: Christiansen and Nørgaard (2003: 60–61).

Note
Policy-proposing commissions include commissions that make proposals in the form of drafts bills as well as commissions that 'prepare' bills. In both cases, government can amend the proposals.

The economic context had changed considerably since the 1970s. In the late 1970s governments struggled with double-digit unemployment rates, looming inflation, and recurrent government deficits, but by the late 1990s unemployment was less than 5 per cent, inflation was under control, and the government budget was in surplus. Minority governments headed by the Social Democrats were dominant in both the late 1970s and the late 1990s. Except for a brief period in 1978–1979 when the Social Democratic Party was in coalition with the major bourgeois party, the Liberals, the governments from 1975 to 1982 were single-party minority governments. From 1994 to 2001 the Social Democrats led shifting minority coalitions and after 1998 in conjunction with a single small centre party, the Social Liberals. The Social Democrats controlled all the portfolios that most often delegate policy-proposing powers to committees in which organizations participate, namely Labour, Trade and Industry, Food and Agriculture, and Environment. The parliamentary situation in the periods 1979–1982 and 1998–2001 is summarized in Table 9.2.

These two minority governments in Denmark offer a unique opportunity for investigating whether organizations are agents of the government or of the opposition when government delegates the power to propose policy to a commission. In the late 1970s, the Social Democratic minority government often delegated policy-proposing authority to committees and commissions that included non-governmental organizations. Twenty years later things had changed substantially. Although delegation still occurred, it was much less frequent, and no organization could take for granted that it would be given a privileged role in preparing policy prior

Table 9.2 Distribution of seats in the Danish parliament, 1979 and 1998 elections

Election	Socialist opposition	Social Democratic minority government	Support parties[a]	Bourgeois opposition	Total no. of MPs[b]
1979	17	68	21[c]	69	175
1998	–[d]	70[e]	26	79	175

Source: www.folketinget.dk.

Notes

a Support parties have either made some kind of agreement with the government or helped ensure that the government was not subjected to legislative defeats on cabinet issues such as votes of confidence.

b In addition to the 175 Danish MPs, two from the Faroe Islands and two from Greenland have a seat in the Danish Folketing.

c The three centre parties, the Christian People's Party, the Centre Democrats and the Social Liberals.

d Both small socialist parties formally backed the government, and are included under support parties along with the Centre Democrats.

e The minority government headed by the Social Democrats was a coalition government that included the small centre party, the Social Liberals.

to the introduction of a bill in parliament. In a context of more plural relations between government and organizations, the latter had to struggle more intensely and use different routes and strategies to influence policy making. Not surprisingly, the proportion of organizations that contacted members of parliament at least on a monthly basis more then tripled, from 7 per cent to 24 per cent (Christiansen and Nørgaard, 2003: 179). This close contact by organized interests targeted a larger and broader segment of MPs from different political parties.

As the governing Social Democratic Party had involved non-government organizations so closely in policy proposing commissions in 1980, we suggest that the Social Democratic MPs are, for the reasons discussed in the preceding section, more likely to perceive organizations as better agents than MPs of the bourgeois opposition parties. The perspective of the support parties and the socialist opposition parties is more uncertain. The support parties have often been involved in the preparation of government bills and negotiated with the government prior to the introduction of a bill in parliament. Therefore, they have had access to the information submitted to the government by policy-proposing commissions. It is quite possible that the support parties of the centre are sometimes reluctant supporters of government policy and would prefer to align with the bourgeois opposition, but at the same time they are unwilling to use the no-confidence weapon and bring the government down (Huber, 1996). With regard to the socialist opposition parties the Social Democratic government enjoys a strong positional advantage (Strøm, 1990; Tsebelis, 1999). Although the socialist parties do not formally back the government, they can hardly hope for a better policy outcome than the one delivered by the Social Democratic government, since no realistic policy coalition can be established to the left of government. Furthermore, in bargaining with organizations that loathe uncertainty the government may be able to push policy further in the direction of its own ideal point, i.e. further to the left, than if policy is negotiated more openly in parliament.

Thus, we propose that the governing and the bourgeois opposition parties' perception of the organizations as agents will be highly different in 1980. The governing Social Democratic Party sees organizations as better agents than the bourgeois parties do. The perceptions of the support parties and the socialist opposition parties are more uncertain. More specifically, we suggest the following two testable propositions:

1a *Information asymmetry.* In 1980, MPs of the governing Social Democratic Party perceive organizations to be better providers of reliable and useful information than do MPs belonging to the bourgeois opposition parties. The perception of support parties and socialist opposition parties about organizations is uncertain.
  b *Agency loss.* In 1980, more so than the MPs of the governing Social

Democratic Party, MPs of the bourgeois opposition parties perceive that organizations have too much influence on policy and prevent urgently needed policy reforms. The perception of support parties and socialist opposition parties about organizations is uncertain.

In 2000 organizations are not as often involved in policy-proposing commissions and they contact MPs from all parties more frequently. On that basis, we suggest that all MPs have similar perceptions of organizations as agents, and that there will be no significant differences between MPs of the government and the opposition. We test the following two propositions:

2a *Information asymmetry.* In 2000, MPs of all parties (governing parties, support parties, and bourgeois opposition) have roughly similar perceptions of organizations as providers of reliable and useful information.

  b *Agency loss.* In 2000, MPs of all parties (governing parties, support parties, and bourgeois opposition) have roughly similar perceptions of the extent to which organizations have too much influence on policy and prevent urgently needed reforms.

The test: consequences of delegation of policy-proposing powers to commissions with non-governmental organizations

To test the propositions we use data on MPs' perception of organizations as agents. In 1980 and in 2000 a questionnaire sent to all Danish MPs included a section on the costs and benefits of contact with interest organizations.[4] Some of these items tapped into the issue of informational advantages and drawbacks, whereas others concerned the dangers of organizations biasing and blocking needed policy changes, i.e. agency loss. Two indexes on a scale of 0–20 have been constructed to measure the degree of informational advantages and the degree of agency loss caused by interaction with organizations (See Appendix 9.1 for details about the data set and the construction of the indices.)

In 1980 the hypothesis that members of the governing party are less concerned about information asymmetry than members of the bourgeois opposition is confirmed (see the Table 9.3).

Members of the governing Social Democratic Party are most satisfied with the information they get from non-government organizations (14.25). Although a substantial number of members in all parties find the information obtained from organizations valuable, the bourgeois opposition is significantly more concerned about the risk of informational bias (11.29), i.e. asymmetry (proposition 1a). The support parties and the socialist opposition to the left of the government defend an intermediary position.

Table 9.3 MPs' perceptions of non-governmental organizations as agents, according to political party membership in Parliament, 1980 (one-way ANOVA)

Party	Informational advantages ('inform')		Agency loss ('IO bias')	
Mean score (SD)				
Governing party, $n = 32, 33$	14.25	(3.57)	5.52	(4.48)
Support parties, $n = 13$	12.76	(2.91)	11.00	(6.11)
Socialist opposition parties, $n = 8$	13.25	(2.55)	5.13	(3.09)
Bourgeois opposition parties, $n = 38, 41$	11.29	(3.62)	12.61	(6.19)
Mean differences, Scheffe's test (SE)				
Governing *v.* support parties	1.48	(1.13)	−5.48*	(1.78)
Governing *v.* socialist opposition parties	1.00	(1.36)	0.39	(2.14)
Governing *v.* bourgeois opposition parties	2.96**	(0.82)	−7.09***	(1.27)

Note
Significance of difference of means: *0.05 level; **0.01 level; ***0.001 level.

However, the differences in perceptions of informational advantages vis-à-
vis the government are not significant, and an assumption of equal variance cannot be rejected at the 0.05 level.[5] The differences between the
support parties and the socialist parties are also insignificant when compared to the perception of the bourgeois parties (figures not shown).

The proposition on agency loss is also supported (proposition 1b). The
bourgeois opposition is more concerned about the risk of agency loss than
the governing party (12.61 compared to 5.52 on the agency bias scale),
and the mean difference is significant at the 0.001 level. In addition, the
support parties are significantly more troubled about the risk of agency
loss than the governing party (11.00). There is no difference in assessment between MPs of the governing party and the socialist opposition
parties. Indirectly, this lends support to the argument on the positional
advantage enjoyed by the government vis-à-vis the socialist parties. On
most policy dimensions, the socialist parties to the left of the government
cannot hope for a better policy outcome than the one delivered by a
Social Democratic government that structures parliamentary politics to
include non-governmental organizations in policy-proposing commissions. The support parties are located at the centre of the political spectrum, and on a number of issues their ideal policy positions are closer to
the bourgeois camp (notably on how to manage the economy) than the
Social Democratic government. However, a vote of no confidence is a
strong and blunt instrument and should not be used against the government without carefully considering the consequences. The significant fear
of agency loss suggests that the centre parties are reluctant supporters of
the government, but that the minority government commands a number
of instruments with which it can discipline potentially insurgent support
parties (Heller, 2001; Tsebelis, 1999).[6]

By 2000 the Social Democratically led minority government had changed its practice of appointing policy-proposing commissions. As reported in Table 9.4, the evaluation of organizations as agents had also shifted. In particular the bourgeois parties' fear of agency loss has waned. There are no significant differences between the political parties in their perceptions of informational advantages and agency loss in 2000. The main reason appears to be that the bourgeois party's perceptions have shifted and they now are more comfortable with the role of organizations in the policy-making process. With organizations less closely involved in government-sponsored policy-proposing commissions and with much stronger interactions between organizations and parliament, the bourgeois opposition is less suspicious of organizations and sees them as more reliable agents than twenty years earlier. In 2000, the organizations served multiple principals. The two main principals – the governing party and the bourgeois opposition – now have highly similar views on organizations as providers of useful information, and the bourgeois opposition is much less concerned with the risk of agency loss.

As shown in the preceding section, both traditional allies of the Social Democratic Party and the bourgeois opposition are included in the commissions proposing policy in the late 1970s, and both have influence on commission recommendations. If business associations were merely hostages of a weak minority government, they would not continue to sit on the commissions. The questionnaire does not differentiate among types of organizations and thus the data on MP perceptions refer to organizations *as a whole*. It may be surmised that bourgeois MPs are thinking of the close ties between unions and the Social Democrats when they perceive organizations as poor agents in 1980. This interpretation suggests that such a bias is not as valid for the bourgeois opposition in 2000. Because the traditional allies of the Social Democrats – the unions – are

Table 9.4 MPs' perceptions of non-governmental organizations as agents, according to political party membership in Parliament, 2000 (one-way ANOVA)

Party	Informational advantages ('inform')		Agency loss ('IO bias')	
Mean score (SD)				
Governing party, $n = 42, 43$	13.55	(2.94)	5.93	(4.47)
Support parties, $n = 16$	14.31	(3.72)	5.31	(4.35)
Bourgeois opposition parties, $n = 50, 54$	13.28	(3.28)	6.96	(3.94)
Comparison of means, Scheffe's test (SE)				
Governing *v.* support parties	−0.76	(0.95)	0.62	(1.23)
Governing *v.* bourgeois opposition parties	0.27	(0.67)	−1.03	(0.86)

Note
Significance of difference of means: *0.05 level; **0.01 level; ***0.001 level.

not as closely involved in policy-proposing commissions, the bourgeois opposition perceive organizations *as a whole* to be more reliable agents.

The argument that the bourgeois opposition is thinking only of non-allies when evaluating the role of non-government organizations in 1980 cannot be rejected with the data at hand. However, this interpretation is unlikely. Those bourgeois MPs with the closest interaction with business and trade associations in 1980 fear agency loss the most. In contrast those with the most frequent contacts with unions are no more concerned with agency loss than those who only rarely have contacts with unions (Table 9.5). This pattern suggests that the bourgeois MPs are *also* thinking of their traditional allies in 1980 when they dread agency loss due to the inclusion of non-government organizations in policy-proposing commissions.

When the government does not delegate policy-proposing powers to non-governmental organizations, they have an incentive to lobby all parties that may become part of a winning policy coalition. Organizations that have not been invited to join a policy-proposing commission have more incentive to provide accurate information to MPs and to try to influence policy outcomes in the parliamentary phase.

Organizations as agents in parliamentary democracies

Principal–agent theorizing has only recently been applied in studies of parliamentary democracy (Pollack, 2002). Traditionally, parliamentary democracy has been studied from the perspective of representation theory rather than as a system of delegation and accountability (Strøm, 2000). One reason for this theoretical focus seems to be that political parties play a larger role in most parliamentary democracies (Saalfeld, 2000), and that political parties traditionally have had close ties to distinct social classes and their organizations (Rokkan, 1966; Strøm, 1990). This complicates the principal–agency reasoning because principal and agent are not entirely separate or distinct entities. An organization that acts as an agent

Table 9.5 Bourgeois MPs' perception of agency loss (IO bias), 1980: different groups of MPs

1980	IO bias (mean)	n
Monthly or more frequent contact with business associations	13, 29	17
Less than monthly contact with business associations	11, 48	21
Monthly or more frequent contact with unions (*and* business associations)	12, 00	5
Less than monthly contact with unions	12, 44	34
Monthly or more frequent contacts with trade associations in agriculture	14, 57	14
Less than monthly contacts with trade associations in agriculture	11, 16	25

of a party in government is simultaneously a representative of the class that constitutes the core of the same party. The prevalence of multi-party systems, coalition and minority governments further complicates the relationship between legislature, executive, and bureaucracy. The common use of informal norms rather than formal rules to regulate much of executive–legislative relations (Moe and Caldwell, 1994) only adds to the complexities involved in delegation and accountability. It is not surprising that the preferred approach to relations between government and organizations has been a political exchange perspective, stressing concertation and interdependences on the one hand and bargaining on the other (Schmitter, 1974; Lehmbruch, 1984; Molina and Rhodes, 2002). However, the principal–agency perspective may help us to reinterpret some of the features that have often been portrayed as unique to European parliamentary democracy.

Principal–agency theory insists that the formal chain of delegation and accountability should be our point of departure for theorizing about power relations and policy processes. Government power and formal authority matter, although various causal mechanisms may also be at work. The concertation approach misses an important point when holders of public office are reduced to simply one of the parties negotiating a deal. Pursuing a principal–agency perspective enables us to ask the following questions. Why does a principal not fully exploit his formal powers? Why do agents behave the way they do? What are the consequences of structuring relationships between principals and agents in different ways? Starting with a simple model, it is easier to appreciate why deviations frequently occur.

Thus, rather than seeing the frequent use of policy-proposing commissions with non-governmental organizations in Denmark in the late 1970s as merely a traditional practice in a Scandinavian consensual democracy with a stable cleavage social and political structure, we should explore why the fairly weak Social Democratic minority government *chooses* this kind of delegation. After all, this usage was far more widespread in the late 1970s than fifteen years earlier or five years later. This suggests that the structure of delegation *is* a deliberate choice. The answer proposed by the present analysis is that the weak minority governments deliberately tried to boost their power to make policy without incurring the otherwise predictable stern opposition in parliament and the ensuing electoral costs that this opposition might lead to. By including non-allies in commissions and by accepting or only slightly amending the commission's policy proposals, the government turned traditional non-allies into fairly good agents of the incumbent government. For strategic reasons the non-governmental organizations did not turn to their traditional allies among the opposition parties, because the organizations calculated – rightly or wrongly – that they would obtain the best and most predictable policy outcome with the government bill. It is therefore, not surprising that the opposition parties considered non-governmental organizations as a poorer agent than the governing parties did.

More non-allies to the government than allies sat on the commissions and more non-ally organizations than allies felt that they had a say in commission mandates. MPs from the bourgeois opposition who had the most frequent contact with their traditional allies perceived a greater agency loss from the role non-government organizations played in the policy-making process than those who had less contact. Arguably, they knew better than their party colleagues that their friends in business and agriculture were unwilling to politicize a government bill which through their membership on policy-proposing commissions they had already had some influence on.

The principal–agent perspective suggests that policy-proposing commissions, and the organizations that sit on them, can be seen as agents. In reality, governments and ministers very rarely negotiate directly with commissions, at least in Denmark (Christiansen and Nørgaard, 2003), and quite often they amend the policy proposals before introducing a bill in parliament (Christiansen *et al.*, 2004). The government also frequently ignores commission recommendations. Proposals are sometimes rejected by appointing a new commission with a similar mandate shortly after the old one has finished its work. Thus, commission negotiations take place in the shadow of hierarchy and the formal powers of government. However, policy-proposing commissions are typically not forums for policy bargaining with government.

Governments who do not have formal hierarchical authority over non-governmental organizations that sit on government-sponsored policy-proposing commissions cannot totally and repeatedly ignore organizational demands. In these circumstances organizations will soon become poor agents of the government and will eventually refuse to participate in future government commissions. There is an element of *quid pro quo* in the relationship between government and the non-governmental organizations that are members of policy-proposing commission, as the organizations have to gain something in return, at least in the long run. But the same is true for relations between government and parliament more generally – between the US Congress and the President, or between Congress and congressional committees. This does not prevent scholars from pursuing a principal–agent perspective on these and other relationships and gaining important insights from the narrow focus such analyses produce.

Our analysis shows that the role of non-governmental organizations as agents for the opposition in parliament is contingent upon the way government structures the early stages of the policy-making process. When non-governmental organizations are not provided with a privileged position on a policy-proposing commission, there is a good chance that they become better agents of the opposition in parliament. They have a strong incentive to try to influence policy later in the process, and in doing so they will pass on information to MPs who may become part of the winning coalition. They will pursue their interests more directly because they have been excluded from the policy-proposing commissions. In such a context, organizations will probably both police the government and push the fire alarm button more often (cf. McCubbins and Schwartz, 1984). Further- more, knowing the preferences of non-governmental organizations and observing their costly efforts to change the *status quo* or a government bill, the opposition parties in parliament see organizations as better and more trustworthy agents (Lupia and McCubbins, 1998). The Danish evidence indicates that the models developed to study the US Congress and the concepts which describe the role of external actors such as organizations seem more relevant in parliamentary democracies that do not include non-governmental organizations in government-sponsored policy- proposing commissions.

Of course, a lot has changed in Danish politics in two decades. The causes of the changes in the use of policy-proposing commissions as well as MP perceptions of non-governmental organizations as agents may be influenced by broader changes in the relationship between social classes, political parties, and non-governmental organizations. Both the Social Democratic policy agenda and voting patterns have changed. The tradi- tional allies of the dominant political parties are perhaps not such import- ant constituents as they were twenty years ago, and their support may be less critical for the parties' electoral fortunes. Still, it is not quite clear how the changing political influence of non-governmental organizations affects their role as agents for the parties in parliament – do they become more or less trustworthy? It should be recalled that the convergence in perceptions of non-governmental organizations as agents was due to a change in the bourgeois opposition's perception, not in the Social Demo- crats'. The declining importance of traditional organizational-cum-class allies seems to be more conspicuous for the Social Democrats than for the other political parties. But the Social Democrats have not changed percep- tions.

Our interpretation of the findings is consistent with a change in government policy preferences. A government may change its preferences for a number of reasons and choose not to appoint a policy-proposing commission which includes non-governmental organizations. Con- sequently, organizations will probably act as better agents for the opposi- tion parties in parliament, simply because they have good reason to do so. Whilst this is good for democratic accountability, the government will probably have a more difficult time and face a sterner and more informed opposition. Danish Social Democratic minority governments do not resemble a government of the Westminster type. However, if majority gov- ernments are highly future-oriented and seek super-majority support for their policy initiatives they may also want to court non-governmental organizations that are traditional allies of the opposition. In both cases, a successful government may be able to break up traditional alliances between the opposition and non-governmental organizations and safeguard its own policy agenda. Thus, even traditional organizational allies become poor agents of the opposition.

When comparing parliamentary government and the American division of powers system it is important to note that the relationship between non-governmental actors, government and parliament is a result of strategic action rather than constitutionally embedded incentives. The executive in parliamentary democracies, even in a minority government, has a strategic advantage vis-à-vis parliament which American Presidents do not enjoy vis-à-vis Congress to the same degree. The executive can structure the policy-making process in a more flexible way and this can change the incentives of political actors that may or may not be important agents for parliamentary actors. To paraphrase Strøm, government strategic choices may determine whether 'each agent is accountable to one and only one principal' (Strøm, 2000: 269). The simple one-agent, one-principal model should not be taken for granted in parliamentary democracies, particularly when the agents are non-governmental organizations.

Appendix 9.1

In 1980 and 2000, a questionnaire was sent to all 179 members of the Danish parliament, the Folketinget. From the data set we have excluded four members from Greenland and the Faroe Islands who do not have much contact with Danish non-governmental organizations. We have also excluded MPs who were ministers and therefore cabinet members. As political *and* administrative heads of the different branches of the state bureaucracy these MPs have a wide range of contacts with organizations with an intense interest in their field of authority. (In Denmark all administrative agencies are hierarchically organized and under ministerial authority.) In 1980 the remaining 159 MPs were sent questionnaires and 103 (65 per cent) responded. In 2000, 161 MPs were neither ministers nor North Atlantic members, of these 119 (74 per cent) answered the questionnaire. The sample is representative in terms of sex, education, occupation, seniority and party (Christiansen and Nørgaard, 2003: appendix, section 4). Thus there is no reason to fear systematic errors in the figures used in the analysis.

One section of the questionnaire included a number of questions about the advantages and disadvantage of the role non-governmental organizations play in the policy-making process. Four questions referred to the issue of *informational advantages* ('inform'). Contact with organizations:

1 'Provides information that is otherwise difficult to obtain.'
2 'Saves time and resources with regard to preparation, collection of information, etc.'

3   'You become too dependent on the information provided by organizations.'
4   'Is too time-consuming.'

Four questions tapped into the issue of *agency loss* ('IO bias'). Contact with organizations:

1   'Undermines the sovereignty of Folketinget.'
2   'Gives too much influence to special interests.'
3   'Results in short-sighted solutions, hinders reform and innovation.'
4   'Favours the strongest organized interests at the expense of the non-organized.'

The MPs could answer by marking one of five categories: (a) 'very important' (five points), (b) 'somewhat important' (three points), (c) 'not very important' (one point), (d) 'means nothing' (zero points), and (e) 'don't know' (zero points). Reversing the scale for item 3 and 4 in the 'inform' index, the range for both indexes is [0; 20].

The actual range for 'inform' in 1980 is [1; 20], the mean is 12.71, and the mode is 14. The actual range for 'IO bias' in 1980 is [0; 20], the mean is 9.21, and the mode is 4 and 20. There is a moderate negative correlation between 'inform' and 'IO bias'. Pearson's R = 0.552.

The actual range for 'inform' in 2000 is [6; 20], the mean is 13.54, and the mode is 12. Compared to 1980, MPs have a tendency to evaluate the informational advantages more positively.

The actual range for 'IO bias' in 2000 is [0; 20], the mean is 6.34; and the mode is 8 and 10. Compared to 1980, MPs are less anxious of agency loss in 2000. There is a weak negative correlation between 'inform' and 'IO bias'. Pearson's R = −0.344.

Notes

1   For the reasons discussed by Strøm (1990) policy- and vote-seeking rather than office-seeking parties are more likely if minority government is dominant.
2   The calculation depends e.g. on the government's policy agenda vis-à-vis other parties, the number of policy dimensions, and the number of parties in parliament.
3   This only holds if there are no significant differences in the interplay between organizations on the one hand and governing and opposition parties on the other.
4   The study has been made possible by a grant by the Danish Power and Democracy Study. Professor Erik Damgaard has provided the 1980 data.
5   This of course is partially because of the small *n* for support parties and socialist parties. In effect, this implies that the detected mean differences have to be greater and/or the intra-group variance smaller for an assumption of equal variance to be rejected.
6   As a historiographic footnote we might add that two of the centre parties

became members of the so-called four-leaf bourgeois coalition government two years later. The last centre party, the Social Liberals, also switched sides and became support party of the new bourgeois minority government.

References

Balla, S. J. and Wright, J. R. (2001) 'Interest Groups, Advisory Committees, and Congressional Control of the Bureaucracy', *American Journal of Political Science*, 45 (4): 799–812.

Bendor, J., Amihai, G. and Hammond, T. H. (2001) 'Theories of Delegation', *Annual Review of Political Science*, 4: 235–269.

Blom-Hansen, J. (2001) 'Organised Interests and the State. A Disintegrating Relationship? Evidence from Denmark' *European Journal of Political Research*, 39: 391–416.

Randall, C. L., McCubbins, M. D. and Weingast, B. R. (1989) 'A Theory of Political Control and Agency Discretion', *American Journal of Political Science*, 33 (3): 588–611.

Calvert, R. L., McCubbins, M. D. and Weingast, B. R. (1989) 'A Theory of Political Control and Agency Discretion', *American Journal of Political Science*, 33 (3): 588–611.

Christiansen, P. M. and Rommetvedt, H. (1999) 'From Corporatism to Lobbyism? Parliaments, Executives, and Organised Interests in Denmark and Norway', *Scandinavian Political Studies*, 22 (3): 195–220.

Christiansen, P. M. and Nørgaard, A. S. (2003) *Faste forhold – flygtige forbindelser: Stat og interesseorganisationer i Danmark i det 20. århundrede*, Aarhus: Aarhus University Press.

Christiansen, P. M., Nørgaard, A. S. and Sidenius, N. Ch. (2004) *Hvem skriver lovene? Interesseorganisationer og politiske beslutninger*, Aarhus: Aarhus University Press.

Damgaard, E. (1999) 'Parlamentarismens udvikling', in O. S. Andersen (ed.) *Folketingets festskrift I anledning af grundlovens 150 års jubilæum den 5. juni 1999*, Copenhagen: Folketingets Præsidium.

Damgaard, E. and Eliassen, K. (1978) 'Corporate Pluralism in Danish Law-Making', *Scandinavian Political Studies*, 1 (4): 285–313.

Epstein, D. and O'Halloran, Sh. (1999) *Delegating Powers: A Transaction Cost Politics Approach to Policy Making under Separate Powers*, Cambridge: Cambridge University Press.

Hammond, T. H. and Knott, J. (1996) 'Who Controls the Bureaucracy? Presidential Power, Congressional Dominance, Legal Constraints, and Bureaucratic Autonomy in a Model of Multi-institutional Policy-Making', *Journal of Law, Economics, and Organization*, 12 (1): 119–166.

Heller, W. B. (2001) 'Making Policy Stick: Why Government Gets What It Wants in Multiparty Systems', *American Journal of Political Science*, 45 (4): 780–798.

Hermansson, J., Lund, A., Svensson, T. and Öberg, P. (1999) *Avkorporativisering och lobbyism*, Stockholm: SOU.

Huber, J. D. (1996) 'The Vote of Confidence in Parliamentary Democracies', *American Political Science Review*, 92: 577–592.

Huber, J. D. (2000) 'Delegation to Civil Servants in Parliamentary Democracies', *European Journal of Political Research*, 37: 397–413.

Huber, J. D. and Lupia, A. (2001) 'Cabinet Stability and Delegation in Parliamentary Democracies', *American Journal of Political Science*, 45 (1): 18–32.

Johansen, L. N. and Kristensen, O. P. (1982) 'Corporatist Traits in Denmark, 1946–1976', in G. Lehmbruch and P. Schmitter (eds) *The Consequence of Corporatist Policy-making*, London: Sage.

Laver, M. and Shepsle, K. A. (1991) 'Divided Government: America is Not "Exceptional"', *Governance*, 4 (3): 250–269.

Laver, M. and Shepsle, K. A. (1996) *Making and Breaking Governments: Cabinets and Legislatures in Parliamentary Democracies*, Cambridge: Cambridge University Press.

Lehmbruch, G. (1984) 'Concertation and the Structure of Corporatist Networks', in J. H. Goldthorpe (ed.) *Order and Conflict in Contemporary Democracy*, Oxford: Clarendon Press.

Lijphart, A. and Crepaz, M. M. L. (1991) 'Notes and Comments: Corporatism and Consensus Democracy in Eighteen Countries: Conceptual and Empirical Linkages', *British Journal of Political Science*, 21: 235–256.

Lupia, A. and McCubbins, M. D. (1994) 'Designing Bureaucratic Accountability', *Law and Contemporary Problems*, 57 (1–2): 91–126

Lupia, A. and McCubbins, M. D. (1998) *The Democratic Dilemma: Can Citizens Learn What They Need to Know?* Cambridge: Cambridge University Press.

McCubbins, M. D. and Schwartz, T. (1984) 'Congressional Oversight Overlooked: Police Patrols versus Fire Alarms', *American Journal of Political Science*, 28 (1): 165–179.

McKelvey, R. D. (1976) 'Intransitivities in Multidimensional Voting Models and Some Implications for Agenda Control', *Journal of Economic Theory*, 12: 472–182.

Miller, K. E. (1996) *Friends and Rivals. Coalition Politics in Denmark, 1901–1995*, Lanham MD: University Press of America.

Moe, T. M. (1984) 'The New Economics of Organization', *American Journal of Political Science*, 28: 739–777.

Moe, T. M. (1990) 'Political Institutions: The Neglected Side of the Story', *Journal of Law, Economics, and Organization*, 6: 213–253.

Moe, T. M. and Caldwell, M. (1994) 'The Institutional Foundation of Democratic Government: A Comparison of Presidential and Parliamentary Systems', *Journal of Institutional and Theoretical Economics*, 150/1: 171–195.

Molina, O. and Rhodes, M. (2002) 'Corporatism: The Past, Present, and Future of a Concept', *Annual Review of Political Science*, 5: 305–331.

Müller, W. C. (2000) 'Political Parties in Parliamentary Democracies: Making Delegation and Accountability Work', *European Journal of Political Research*, 37: 309–333.

Pollack, M. A. (2002) 'Learning from the Americanists (Again): Theory and Method in the Study of Delegation', *West European Politics*, 25 (1): 200–219.

Rokkan, S. (1966) 'Norway: Numerical Democracy and Corporate Pluralism', in R. A. Dahl (ed.) *Political Oppositions in Western Democracies*, New Haven CT: Yale University Press.

Saalfeld, Th. (2000) 'Members of Parliament and Governments in Western Europe: Agency Relations and Problems of Oversight', *European Journal of Political Research*, 37: 353–376.

Schmitter, Ph. C. (1974) 'Still the Century of Corporatism?' *Review of Politics*, 36: 85–131.

Strøm, K. (1990) *Minority Government and Majority Rule*, Cambridge: Cambridge University Press.

Strøm, K. (2000) 'Delegation and Accountability in Parliamentary Democracies', *European Journal of Political Research*, 37: 261–289.

Thies, M. F. (2001) 'Keeping Tabs on Partners: The Logic of Delegation in Coalition Governments', *American Journal of Political Science*, 45 (3): 580–598.

Tsebelis, G. (1999) 'Veto Players and Law Production in Parliamentary Democracies: An Empirical Analysis', *American Political Science Review*, 93 (3): 591–608.

Volden, C. (2002) 'Delegating Power to Bureaucracies: Evidence from the States', *Journal of Law, Economics, and Organization*, 18 (1): 187–220.

Waterman, R. W. and Meier, K. J. (1998) 'Principal–Agent Models: An Expansion?' *Journal of Public Administration Research and Theory*, 8 (2): 173–202.

10 Delegation in the European Union

Debates and research agenda

Fabio Franchino

Since the 1990s, the application of the theory of delegation to the European Union (EU) has produced a considerable amount of interesting, rigorous and systematic work which has helped our understanding of how this political system operates and strengthened the explanatory potential of the theory.

We can identify two processes of delegation in the European Union. They differ with regard to the procedures and the actors that are involved in the delegation decisions. In the first process, which can be labelled *Treaty delegation*, member states delegate powers to supranational institutions. They hold intergovernmental conferences (IGCs) where they unanimously agree amendments to the Treaty that then need to be ratified by national parliaments. Member states act as principals while the European Commission, the European Parliament and other supranational institutions are the beneficiaries of delegation and subject to control. The second process can be labelled *executive delegation*. EU legislators (ministers of the Council and, where involved, members of the European Parliament, MEPs) confer powers upon bureaucrats via secondary legislation according to the EU legislative procedures. The beneficiaries are the European Commission, other EU-level agencies and national administrations. Control mechanisms are also set up in these circumstances to ensure faithful implementation.

The theory of delegation has been a powerful vehicle to understand these processes and, more generally, EU institutional design. In this chapter, I first review three works on delegation in the European Union. Although the literature is expanding rapidly, I limit the analysis to Moravcsik (1998), Pollack (2003b) and, somewhat immodestly, Franchino (2004a), because I consider these studies as those that most explicitly test the expectations of the theory and use a considerable amount of data and information. Member states, acting through the ICGs or the Council of Ministers, are the key actors in these studies. In the following section, I address a lingering dispute about the relative importance of credibility and rule-preference interactions in explaining delegation outcomes in the European Union. Next, I shift the focus to the European Parliament and executive delegation. I test a hypothesis about the revealed preference of this institution with regard to delegation and control. The Parliament deserves attention because it plays an increasingly important role in shaping the delegation of powers in the European Union. I show that it systematically prefers less discretion of national administrations than the Council. Finally, and with the purpose of at least partially rebalancing the selective literature review, I consider future avenues of research by reviewing briefly the most recent works, especially in light of EU enlargement. I concentrate only on those studies that refer explicitly to the theory of delegation. Due to length constraints, I focus more on the European Commission than on the other supranational institutions or national administrations and mostly disregard how agents exercise their delegated powers.

Three works on delegation in the IGCS and the Council of Ministers

Moravcsik's (1998) well known contribution is based on a three-stage approach to analysis of the outcome of negotiations at the European level. A process of formation of preferences on substantive policies and institutional design underpins the negotiating stance of each member state in the supranational arena. Factors such as the best alternative to the negotiated agreement, the possibility of unilateral action and coalition alternatives shape the pattern of mutual concessions and compromises at the negotiating table. Finally, the need to bolster the credibility of policy commitments is the strongest determinant of institutional choices such as the pooling of sovereignty (i.e. shift from unanimity to qualified majority voting in the Council of Ministers) and the delegation of powers to supranational institutions.

Since the inability to write complete contracts and incentives for defection create problems of time consistency, pooling and delegation facilitate commitment to policy objectives. Shifts to majority voting enhance credibility especially where there is a perceived risk of *ex post* obstruction to the adoption of implementing measures of an agreed policy. Delegation performs a similar function where there are concerns about state compliance to policy objectives.[1] In five case studies spanning almost forty years of European integration, Moravcsik finds strong evidence in support of this proposition, such as the shift to majority voting in commercial and agricultural policy and the delegation of agenda-setting and enforcement powers to the Commission. However, Moravcsik also recognizes a secondary and significant role to pro-European ideology or federalism, for instance with regard to the quasi-constitutional design of the European Union.

Pollack's (2003b) work is an extended application of the arguments in his path-breaking article on delegation (Pollack, 1997) and is the most systematic attempt yet at applying agency theory to the European Union. Pollack uses the literature on international regimes and on legislative organization to predict the functions that are likely to be delegated to supranational institutions: monitoring compliance, filling incomplete contracts, providing expert and credible regulation, and setting the formal legislative agenda. He then reviews the various types of mechanisms adopted by the principals to control agency behaviour and how their establishment is motivated by policy conflict and by underlying demands for expertise and credibility. The discretion that agents enjoy in the exercise of those delegated functions should vary with different degrees of informational and distributive pressures.

Pollack reviews cross-policy and issue-specific powers and control mechanisms of the Commission, the Court of Justice and the Parliament, which are primarily specified in Treaty provisions. He finds that the expectations are strongly corroborated with regard to the first two supranational institutions, while only the Parliament's supervisory power over the Commission could be explained in such terms (i.e. as an institutional check). Norms of democratic legitimacy account for the delegation of budgetary and legislative functions. However, the considerable cross-policy variance in the exercise of those powers reveals the careful calculation made by member states of the consequences of such delegation decisions.

In Franchino (2004a), I select a sample of 158 major secondary laws to test expectations about delegation in the European Union. Measures of the Commission and national executive discretion are developed following the coding principles of Epstein and O'Halloran (1999). Results suggest that the Council of Ministers delegates greater policy authority to national institutions if legislation is adopted unanimously or in issue areas that require specialist and technical knowledge, while it relies to a greater extent on the Commission when acts are adopted by qualified majority voting or require general managerial skills at the supranational level. Additionally, evidence shows that national administrators are the main providers of policy expertise, while the informational role of the Commission is secondary, but not negligible.

Lingering issues and controversies: credibility and decision rules

There are points of commonality and disagreement in these three works. They share similar expectations of how policy complexity and principal–agent conflict shape the EU politics of delegation. The scholars broadly agree that complexity should lead to more delegation of powers and greater discretion. This is hardly a contentious view, as it goes back to Weber's (1946) writings on bureaucracy. Moravcsik (1998) argues that national administrations are well equipped to provide expert knowledge and that there is no evidence that delegation to supranational institutions is motivated by the need to rely on expert supranational technocrats. This view is broadly shared by both Pollack (2003b) and Franchino (2004a). They qualify it only marginally. They see some delegation to the Commission reflecting a demand for 'speedy and efficient decision-making' (Pollack, 2003b: 153) or 'general managerial skills' (Franchino, 2004a: 449). As far as preferences of actors are concerned, these authors also broadly agree, in line with the expectations of agency theory, that conflict between governments and the Commission should lead to less delegation or lower discretion for the Commission. Moravcsik (1998: 75) and Pollack (2003b: 26–34) also suggests that the Commission's discretion should decrease with more intense conflict within the Council. However, no systematic evidence is provided in support of these propositions (see more below in the section on the research agenda).

What sets these works more clearly apart is the relative importance that they give to the problem of commitment and to decision rules in determining choices of delegation. Moravcsik and Pollack maintain that the overriding reason for the delegation of powers to the Commission is to bolster the credibility of commitment to the underlying policy objectives. These works are predominantly centred on Treaty delegation, where there is no variance in terms of decision rules.

My study instead focuses solely on executive delegation and disregards the problem of commitment. Moreover, since national administrations are the main actors in charge of implementing EU policies, I pay greater attention to how EU law constrains national administrations (see more below also on this point). I produce my expectations based on the consideration that a Commission aiming to maximize its own executive discretion and minimize national discretionary authority will find it easier to achieve these objectives under qualified majority voting than unanimity (if the Council is internally divided).[2]

However, there is no *prima facie* reason to expect that credibility should not also play an important role in executive delegation. But, equally, it would be unreasonable to expect that different decision rules would not lead to different delegation outcomes. In this section, I will try to disentangle the impact on discretion of the commitment problem from the impact of decision rules.

In a narrow sense, majority voting is an indication of underlying credibility problems and a functional equivalent of delegation. For instance, Moravcsik (1998: 73) argues that

> unanimity, pooling and delegation [strike] different balances between the efficiency of common decisions and the desire of individual countries to reduce political risks by retaining a veto. As compare to unanimity voting, ... QMV and *to an even greater extent* delegation reduce the bargaining power of potential opponents.
>
> (Moravcsik, 1998: 75, emphasis added)

In other words, as the severity of the commitment problem increases, one should see first pooling and then delegation of policy authority. In addition to functional equivalence, the empirical results in Franchino (2004a: 449) could suggest complementarity. Qualified majority voting works as an indirect commitment technology by facilitating the adoption of legislation that increases the discretion of the Commission and constrains national authorities.

There are two problems with this interpretation. First, majority voting is extended to entire policy areas but, within them, each issue, or even each policy-specific act, has both informational and distributive components that vary in relevance and are difficult to separate (Epstein and O'Halloran, 1999: 216–219). Decision rules are imperfect indicators of the problem of commitment, which is only of a distributive nature. Second, and more important, the strategic interactions that result from different decision rules and preference configurations suggest that rules gauge something that is qualitatively and theoretically different from the problem of commitment. A discretion-maximizing Commission should systematically be able to exploit conflict within the Council to acquire more powers in qualified majority voting, *regardless of member states' need to pre-commit to specific policy objectives*. Similarly, if the Council is internally divided, a Commission that wants to minimize national discretion would also be more likely to succeed in cases of majority voting *regardless of the need to pre-commit*. Thus, decision rules capture both the severity of the commitment problem (imperfectly) and the strategic dynamics of EU decision making.

However, this conclusion is also controversial. Powers are delegated to the Commission for credibility reasons under unanimity, as Moravcsik (1998) and Pollack (2003b) clearly show. Delegation and majority voting could be functional substitutes. Hence, decision rules are not only an imperfect but also a partial indicator of the problem of commitment.

Thus, we have two theories of delegation, one based on the problem of commitment and the other on decision rules. Because of how credibility, majority voting and delegation interact, these theories are *non-nested*. One cannot be expressed as a restriction of the other by setting some coefficients to zero. Following Moravcsik (1998) and considering the discretion outcomes that are most likely to result from qualified majority voting, this decision rule is, at least, a partial indicator of the problem of commitment facing legislators. If majority voting is a simple functional complement to delegation, the commitment theory deserves theoretical primacy. The indicator's partiality is due to the fact that (1) powers are also delegated by unanimous vote (delegation and majority voting may be functional substitutes), (2) the distributive is only one of at least two components of a specific measure at hand and (3) the strategic dynamics of majority voting produces outcomes that cannot be simply explained by the need to bolster credibility. In sum, the decision rule theory may add significant additional information to the commitment theory or it may be entirely *encompassed* by it.

In order to test this, I run a series of additional tests on the data set I collected for my work in Franchino (2004a) where I have produced measures of *Commission Discretion*, *National Discretion* and *Relative Discretion*.[3] The key independent variable of one theory is *Decision Rule*, taking the value of one if an act is adopted in the Council by qualified majority voting. The independent variable of the other model should gauge the severity of the commitment problem. Hence, I have produced a variable *Commitment* that takes the value of one when the law at hand imposes concentrated costs in return for diffuse benefits. Many scholars have argued that, in policy areas that generate benefits for large, diffuse groups who face high costs of ongoing political participation whilst concentrating costs on small and resourceful groups who are able to sustain participation, the problem of commitment is particularly acute. In these circumstances, legislators can protect the durability of the deal by reducing the scope of delegated authority or by delegating that authority to an independent agent (Horn, 1995: 16–19; Majone, 1996: 71–78; Moravcsik, 1998; Pollack, 2003b: 29–31).

However, the operationalization of *Commitment* is not as straightforward as it seems. According to Majone (1996: 77), social and environmental regulation has these features.[4] Competition, transport (state aid), commercial policy (anti-dumping and illicit practices)[5] and consumer protection should also fall within this category. On the other hand, policy areas where benefits are concentrated include agriculture, fisheries, regional policy and some competition (exemptions), taxation and transport measures. Since most single-market legislation favours intra-EU export-oriented industries at the expense of import-competing ones, benefits (and costs) are concentrated, even though there are substantial gains for consumers too.[6] The same can be said for some liberalizing commercial policy measures (common rules and customs). For the remaining policies, it is harder to assess the distributive impact, though both costs and benefits appear (relatively) diffuse.[7] Interestingly, *Commitment* is uncorrelated with *Decision Rule* (the correlation coefficient is -0.0682).

I use Davidson and MacKinnon's (1981) J-tests to compare the two models $Y = f(X)$ and $Y = f(Z)$. The procedure consists of estimating the first (alternative) model $Y = f(X)$ and saving the predictions $\hat{Y}$. The (null) second model is then estimated $Y = f(Z, \hat{Y})$, and added to the first model prediction. If the coefficient of $\hat{Y}$ is significant, $Y = f(X)$ rejects $Y = f(Z)$. The procedure continues by reversing the order of two models, treating $Y = f(X)$ as the null model. The aim of the exercise is to see whether a null model encompasses the alternative. A significant coefficient of $\hat{Y}$ means the alternative model contains empirical information that is not entirely covered by the null model. The results are conclusive only if $Y = f(X)$ rejects $Y = f(Z)$ and is not rejected by $Y = f(Z)$, or vice versa. If the models reject each other, each adds significant additional information to the other. In case of failure to reject in both directions, neither model is uniquely informative.

Table 10.1 lists the t-statistics and significance levels of the coefficient of the alternative model predicted values. As explained above, it has been generated by adding these values to the regression of the null model.[8] I have used OLS regressions with Huber–White heteroscedasticity-consistent standard errors. Moreover, since the Commission is not delegated power in a relatively large number of observations, *Commission Discretion* may be left censored at zero. Hence, I have also run a Tobit regression in this circumstance. The results are quite interesting.

In the case of *National Discretion* (model 1), the data show that the decision rule model clearly encompasses the commitment model (i.e. the null hypothesis is rejected), while the converse is rejected. In other words, the decision rule model adds significant new information to the commitment model, while the commitment model does *not* add much unique information to the decision rule model. With regard to *Commission Discretion* (models 2 and 3), neither model strongly incorporates the other and each is uniquely informative. The same holds for *Relative Discretion*.

In conclusion, if we want to explain the scope of national executive discretion then a theory based on the interaction between preferences and decision rules appears to yield more convincing results and encompasses one based solely on the problem of commitment. This does not mean that achieving credibility is irrelevant. It means that the *Decision Rule* variable captures this problem *and* additional significant strategic interactions. However, when focusing on relative or Commission discretion, each theory appears to be powerful and to add significant new information to the other. Preference-rule interactions produce discretion outcomes that cannot be explained only by the need to bolster credibility. Equally, the problem of commitment adds significant new information to a theory

Table 10.1 J-tests for the *Commitment* and *Decision Rule* models

Model	Null: Commitment Alternative: Decision Rule		Null: Decision Rule Alternative: Commitment	
	t-statistics of $\hat{Y}$	p-levels	t-statistics of $\hat{Y}$	p-levels
1 National discretion	2.28	0.024	0.62	0.539
2 Commission discretion	2.24	0.027	2.70	0.008
3 Commission discretion (Tobit)	2.88	0.005	3.50	0.001
4 Relative discretion	2.06	0.041	2.03	0.045

Note
OLS regressions with Huber–White standard errors, except for model 3. $n = 158$. The full models are the same as in Franchino (2004).

merely based on preference-rule interactions. I move on now to an important new institution shaping the EU politics of delegation.

Delegation in the European Parliament

In November 1993 the Treaty of Maastricht came into force and a new major institution, the Parliament, entered the scene of EU legislative politics. Its powers had been moderately expanded in July 1987 with the cooperation procedure of the Single European Act. However, it was the codecision procedure of the Maastricht Treaty, later amended by the Amsterdam Treaty, which granted this institution law-making power on an equal footing with the Council.

Unsurprisingly, the Parliament has become the object of intense academic scrutiny over the last decade. Empirical studies on legislative behaviour have analysed the pattern of coalition formation under different procedures and the cohesion within the party groups of the Parliament. Other works have focused on the factors shaping voting behaviour of its members and on the main underlying voting dimensions. An equally large body of work has concentrated on inter-institutional legislative relations, predominantly with the aim of assessing whether parliamentary amendments are incorporated into EU statutes.

However, these works do not analyse the underlying reasons that induce the Parliament to propose specific changes to the legislative proposals. Hence, this section looks at the role of the Parliament in the legislative politics of the Union from a different perspective. Instead of assessing the circumstances under which its amendments are successful, it concentrates on how the Parliament uses its legislative power to exercise control over the execution of EU statutes. In the well known expression of McCubbins *et al.* (1987, 1989), my interest lies in understanding how the Parliament shapes the 'structure and process' of EU policy implementation.

In the EU literature, Kelemen (2002), Hix (2000) and Pollack (2003a, 2003b: 114–145) follow this theoretical tradition. Kelemen shows how, from 1995 onwards, the Parliament has used its budgetary powers to extend its control on the established European agencies and its legislative powers to shape the design of the new agencies, such as the European Food Safety Authority. Hix and Pollack review the attempts by the Parliament to change the administrative procedures of the so-called comitology system for the execution of common policies. Their work builds on the important earlier contributions of Bradley (1997) and Dogan (1997), which, however, have weaker theoretical underpinnings. The Parliament has generally held the view that the comitology system undermines its oversight role and sought to introduce more permissive procedures in the legislation. Its efforts were rewarded with a reform which repealed the most restrictive features of the system and enhanced its role in the policy process.[9]

This section tests one hypothesis about the revealed preferences of the Parliament with regard to the 'structure and process' of EU statutes.

A well established body of literature, predominantly studying the US Congress, has analysed the mechanisms used by legislators to exert influence on the bureaucracy, in response to views that delegation of policy authority to the bureaucracy was the equivalent of abdication of legislative prerogatives. It is beyond the scope of this section to discuss these contributions in detail. I will focus on only two control strategies: statutory control and ongoing non-statutory oversight.[10] The former refers to the reliance on statutes to ensure faithful and correct execution by the bureaucracy and the latter to the other non-statutory instruments available to legislators to ensure bureaucratic compliance.

For our purposes, it is relevant to consider how discretion preferences are informed by the environment where the political actors operate. For instance, Bawn (1997) argues that US Congress legislators that do not sit on the committee in charge of overseeing implementation are more likely to insert control provisions into the statutes than members of such committee. The cost of ongoing non-statutory oversight is higher for these legislators; hence they prefer more statutory control. In her study on the adoption in the US Senate of two bills delegating powers to the Environmental Protection Agency, she shows that amendments sponsored by non-committee members are significantly more likely to increase statutory control. Similarly, Huber and Shipan (2002) argue that the availability of a legislative veto, a non-statutory control tool, reduces the need for statutory control. They show that, in the US states, legislatures with a veto are less likely to rely on detailed Medicaid laws. The same underlying rationale operates in parliamentary systems. Huber and Shipan illustrate how, for labour legislation, the greater availability of ongoing control mechanisms in non-federal, corporatist and civil law systems allows legislators to confer more discretion on the bureaucracy, without compromising a correct execution.

In the European Union, since most policies are executed by national administrations, MEPs have a systematic disadvantage vis-à-vis the ministers of the Council with regard to the ability to exert ongoing control. The only mechanisms available to them are standard tools that are common to legislators in most political systems, such as questions, inquiries and hearings (e.g. Corbett *et al.* 1995: 257; Hix, 1999: 48–50). Instead, Council ministers, as heads of government departments and of their permanent representations within the Council administration, play an important role within national cabinets and legislatures in transposing and executing EU legislation. Although they may be constrained by cabinet institutions and decision rules, they enjoy a wide array of resources and instruments for shaping policy, such as setting legislative agendas, adopting decrees and regulations, changing budgetary priorities, appointing personnel and reorganizing staff.

In conclusion, because of the peculiar institutional setting of the Union, preferences with regard to discretion should systematically vary between the Parliament and the Council regardless of whether there is conflict between them. Paraphrasing Bawn (1997), MEPs face higher costs of ongoing non-statutory oversight than Council ministers do, hence they should prefer lower-discretion statutes. An objection to this argument is that a Council minister in a specific member state is in the same position as the MEPs with regard to policy execution in another member state. The German environmental minister cannot oversee on an ongoing basis the implementation of an environmental directive in Spain. A minister will have to weigh the costs for her own department of a low-discretion statute with the benefits of more controlled execution in the other states. The key difference is that the cost element that will be factored in is likely to be larger for the ministers than for the MEPs because ministers value policy autonomy for themselves and their departments much more than MEPs do. Thus, we should expect *the Parliament to prefer less discretion of national administrations than the Council.*

Methodology and data set

This hypothesis will be tested with a statistical analysis of the amendments proposed by the Parliament in the second reading of the codecision procedure. In this procedure, after a proposal from the Commission and a first parliamentary reading, the Council adopts, by qualified majority voting, a common position confirming or amending the proposal and incorporating or rejecting the Parliament's amendments. In the second reading, the Parliament may approve the common position by simple majority or may amend or reject it by absolute majority, namely a majority of the Parliament's component members. If necessary, the Parliament and the Council can convene a conciliation committee to reach an agreement in a third reading.

The second parliamentary reading provides the best environment to test the hypothesis for four reasons. First, since first-reading amendments are to the Commission proposal they may not reveal clearly differences in preferences between the Council and the Parliament, even though there is likely to be a certain degree of anticipation. Second, information is likely to be incomplete or asymmetrically distributed in the first reading. In complex policy areas, important issues may have been unintentionally disregarded in the initial proposal or the Commission may have failed to read clearly the positions of the Parliament and the Council. In the second reading, much of the 'noise' due to incomplete information is likely to have disappeared and amendments would reveal more clearly the political conflict between the Council and the Parliament. Third, in the second readings the odds are heavily stacked against the rejection of the null hypothesis. The Council may have incorporated amendments in its common position anticipating that it has to concede eventually to the Parliament's position. Moreover, in order to have more disciplined MEPs, rule 80 of the Parliament's rules of procedure states that amendments to the common position arc admissible only if they are germane to the first-reading amendments, amend a text that differs from the Commission proposal or take account of a new fact arisen since the first reading. Even as a concession to the Council, the Parliament may nevertheless decline to reintroduce an amendment. Finally, with regard to the third reading, it is more difficult to separate clearly the preferences of the Council and those of the Parliament because the output from this reading is likely to be the result of mutual concessions within the conciliation committee.

Online searches of the Parliament's legislative observatory[11] conducted between May and July 2003 have revealed that the Commission had initiated 414 proposals for directives or regulations under the codecision procedure.[12] A large majority, 300 of them, have become law; six were waiting for the second reading by the Council while fifty-six were waiting for the Council to adopt a common position. A significant percentage however, the remaining fifty-two proposals, lapsed or were withdrawn by the Commission. Of this group, the Parliament has rejected the joint text adopted by the conciliation committee in two cases, in another two instances the committee failed to reach an agreement, while in the remaining forty-eight cases the proposals did not even reach the second-reading stage. The initial data set for the statistical analysis includes the 310 proposals that became law or have been amended by the Parliament in the second reading. However, data on second-reading amendments were available only up to the end of November 2002, which brings the figure down to 270 observations and 1,445 second-reading amendments.

Operationalization of discretion of national administrations

Parliamentary amendments are not conducive to the type of operationalization of discretion that I carried out in Franchino (2004a) because that method was designed for entire legislative acts. This complication arises from the difficulty in translating amendments into meaningful measures of discretion and of its components (i.e. delegating and constraining provisions). Instead, I will take the lead from the work of Huber and Shipan (2002). These scholars argue that legislative statutes are blueprints for policy making and that policy-specific, rather than procedural, language plays a more important role in constraining implementation (Huber and Shipan, 2002: 77).

I would argue that this reasoning also applies to the European Union, especially when focusing on parliamentary amendments and national implementation. Consider the following two cases of labour and environmental legislation. The objective of codecision proposal 2000/0142 was to improve the legislation on equal treatment for men and women at work, taking into account Treaty amendments and judgements of the Court of Justice. It included additional definitions of discrimination, reinforced the protection system for victims, clarified the circumstances for the application of derogations, acknowledged the right of women to return to the same workplace after maternity leave and the right of member states to adopt positive action measures. In the second reading the Parliament adopted fourteen amendments to the Council common position. Table 10.2 provides extracts from some of them.

A few amendments improved the clarity, coherence and precision of the definitions. Amendment 4 provides a more precise definition of *harassment* and *sexual harassment*. Amendments 5–7 make specific reference to the actions that violate directives such as harassment, general exclusions to work activities and unequal treatment related to pregnancy or parenthood. The remaining amendments, such as number 11, are mostly aimed at reinforcing implementation.

Proposal 1992/0436 introduced a harmonized approach to the management of packaging and packaging waste with the objective of reducing the overall volume of packaging and preventing the creation of waste. The proposal set targets for the recovery and recycling of packaging and essential requirements for packaging. It stipulated measures to encourage reuse and recycling and established a system of marking, identification and information of packaging. The nineteen amendments adopted by the Parliament in the second reading dealt with various issues (see some extracts in Table 10.3).

The four amendments spelt out in greater detail and with more precision the definitions of *packaging, reuse, organic recycling* and *economic operators*. The term *packaging* includes non-returnable items and *economic operators* includes public authorities and statutory organizations, while landfill is not considered a form of *organic recycling*. Amendments 29 and 30 call for harmonized databases on packaging and packaging waste and specify in greater detail the information to be included. Finally, amendment 15 requires the Council to adopt the instruments to promote the objective of the act. National measures may be taken only in the absence of Community measures and are subject to strict conditions of no discrimination and respect for the principle that the 'polluter pays' (for a fuller discussion on both measures see Franchino, 2004b).

If we compare the columns on the left-hand and right-hand sides of tables 10.2 and 10.3, it is clear that the language inserted by the Parliament is designed to provide more detailed instructions for policy execution. It reveals a desire to describe with greater accuracy and precision the scope and objectives of the relevant act and the specific policy measures that need to be taken. Therefore, it shows the need to exercise greater control on the actions of national administrations, the key actors in charge of EU policy implementation. Moreover, the changes put forward by the Parliament are related mostly to the policy-specific sections of the proposals. This is illustrated clearly in Table 10.4.

Table 10.2 Amendments in Equal Treatment legislation

Council common position	Amendments by Parliament
Amendment 4 (*definitions*) *Harassment shall be deemed to be discrimination within the meaning of the first subparagraph when* an unwanted conduct related to the sex of a person *takes place* with the purpose or effect of violating the dignity of a person *and* of creating an intimidating, hostile, degrading, humiliating or offensive environment. *Sexual harassment, which manifests itself as unwanted conduct of a sexual nature expressed physically, verbally or non-verbally, constitutes a specific form of harassment*	Harassment: *the situation where* an unwanted conduct related to the sex of a person *on the occasion of access to or at the place of employment, occupation or training* with the purpose or effect of violating the dignity of a person *or* of creating an intimidating, hostile, degrading, humiliating or offensive environment Sexual harassment: *the situation where any form of verbal, non-verbal or physical conduct of a sexual nature occurs, which the perpetrator knows, or is under a legal obligation to know, to have the purpose or effect of violating, the dignity of a person or of creating an intimidating, hostile, degrading, humiliating or offensive environment.*
Amendment 6 (*actions violating the law*)	*Any general exclusion of, or restriction on, one sex having access to any kind of professional activity or to the training required to gain access to such an activity shall constitute discrimination within the meaning of this Directive*
Amendment 11 (*collective action*) Member States shall ensure that associations, organizations or other legal entities which have, *in accordance with the criteria laid down by their national law,* a legitimate interest in ensuring *that* the provisions of this Directive *are complied with,* may engage, either on behalf or in support of the complainants, with *his or her* approval, in any judicial and/or administrative procedure provided for the enforcement of obligations under this Directive	Member States shall ensure that associations, organizations or other legal entities which have a legitimate interest in ensuring *compliance* with the provisions of this Directive: *(a)* may engage, either on behalf or in support of the complainant(s), with her, *his or their approval, in any judicial and/or administrative procedure provided for the enforcement of obligations under this Directive,* *(b) may, where national law so permits, bring a collective action, in any judicial and/or administrative procedure, on their own initiative and aside from the particular circumstances of an individual case, in order to determine whether or not the principle of equal treatment for men and women is applied*

Sources: European Parliament legislative resolution on the Council common position. *OJ*, 9 May 2002, Series C 112, pp. 169–174. Further details can be found in the EP Report A5-0358/2001. The final act is Directive 2002/73/EC.

Table 10.3 Amendments in environmental legislation

Council common position	Amendments by Parliament
Amendments 40 and 19 (*definitions*) 1 'packaging' means all products made of any materials of any nature to be used for the containment, protection, handling, delivery and presentation of goods, from raw materials to processed goods, from the producer to the user or the consumer. 9 'composting' means the aerobic or anaerobic treatment of the *organic* parts of packaging waste, which produces stabilized organic residues.	1 'packaging' means all products made of any materials of any nature to be used for the containment, protection, handling, delivery and presentation of goods, from raw materials to processed goods, from the producer to the user or the consumer. *'Non-returnable' items used for the same purposes shall also be considered to constitute packaging* 9 *'organic recycling'* means the aerobic (*composting*) or anaerobic (*biomethanization*) treatment, *under controlled conditions and using micro-organisms*, of the *biodegradable* parts of packaging waste, which produces stabilized organic residues *or methane. Landfill shall not be considered a form of organic recycling.* . . .
Amendments 29 and 30 (*harmonized databases*) 1 Member states shall take the necessary measures to ensure that databases on packaging and packaging waste are established, where not already in place, ... 2 To this effect, the databases shall provide in particular information on the magnitude, characteristics and evolution of the packaging and packaging waste flows at the level of individual member states.	1 Member states shall take the necessary measures to ensure that databases on packaging and packaging waste are established, where not already in place, *on an harmonized basis.* . . 2 To this effect, the databases shall provide in particular information on the magnitude, characteristics and evolution of the packaging and packaging waste flows (*including information on the toxicity or danger of packaging materials and components used for their manufacture*) at the level of individual member states.
Amendment 15 (*economic instruments*) Member state may adopt *economic instruments*, in accordance with the provisions of the Treaty, to promote the objectives of this Directive.	*The Council, on the basis of a request from the Commission, shall adopt economic instruments. In absence of Community measures, member states may adopt measures, in accordance with the provisions of the Treaty, to promote the objectives of this Directive.* *Such economic instruments, adopted in accordance with the 'polluter pays' principle, shall not lead to distortion of competition, obstruct the free movement of goods or discriminate against imported goods.*

Sources: European Parliament legislative resolution on the Council common position. *OJ*, 9 May 2002, Series C 112, pp. 169–174. Further details can be found in the **EP Report A5-0358/2001**. The final act is Directive 2002/73/EC.

Table 10.4 Descriptive statistics on second reading amendments

Amendments to	No.	Word changes (absolute values)	% (word changes)	% (laws)
Recitals	327	11,486	21.63	36.30
Articles	924	35,004	65.92	45.93
Annexes	194	6,609	12.45	16.67
Total	1,445	53,099	100	50.74

A straightforward method, applicable across policy areas, to separate general from specific language is to consider the three sections that make up any legislative proposal: introductory recitals, articles and, if any, annexes. Recitals are general statements of purpose, articles enumerate in detail the specific legal requirements, while annexes are used for a variety of reasons but they are generally even more specific than the articles. Articles and annexes are thus used for detailed policy instructions. As Table 10.4 clearly shows, about 80 per cent of the amendments are to the policy-specific sections of the proposals. A similar percentage of the changes in wording, in absolute terms, belong to these sections. The last column shows that the Parliament has introduced amendments in the second reading to half the proposed laws. In about 45 per cent of the cases, at least one amendment relates to the articles, while more than 35 per cent of the proposed laws has at least one amendment to the recital section. This implies that, whilst the likelihood of amending recitals and the likelihood of amending articles do not differ much, the changes proposed by the Parliament to the articles are considerably more substantial. Moreover, amendments to procedural language are limited in number, especially in the second reading, and generally attached to specific policy requirements.

In conclusion, the addition of words by the Parliament to the Council common position tends to reflect willingness to reduce the discretion of the national agents in charge of policy execution. A substantial part of the second-reading amendments adopted by the Parliament are related to the policy-specific sections of the proposals. Changes to the general policy section are less frequent and substantial and procedural amendments are considerably less common. These considerations are similar to those of Huber and Shipan (2002). These scholars measure discretion as either the number of new words introduced by the legislature or the standardized page length of statutes (Huber and Shipan, 2002: 140–146, 176–183). I will measure *Discretion* of national administrations as the changes in word count resulting from parliamentary amendments divided by the total word count of the Council common position (in order to control for the length of the proposal). Positive values reveal a preference of the Parliament for less discretion. However, since recitals include mostly general language, an increase in word count may not imply necessarily a desire to increase statutory control. Moreover, annexes vary widely. Some are lists of items, others are tables and even figures. Hence, changes are harder to interpret and compare. Therefore, I will employ a broad measure of *Discretion* (I) that includes all the changes and a narrow measure (II) that counts only changes to the article part of the proposal, divided by the word count of only the article section of the common position.

Analysis of results

According to the hypothesis, we should expect that the second-reading amendments of the Parliament systematically add words to the Council common position as a sign of the greater willingness of this institution to reduce discretion and exercise statutory control. I have performed two tests to assess the validity of this claim. The results are displayed in Table 10.5.

The one-sample t-tests reveal that the sample mean is greater than zero at a high level of significance. In the regression analysis, I add two control variables[13] and compute two sets of regressions with Huber–White standard errors. The expectation is also corroborated in this case, because the constants of the regressions are significantly greater than zero. The Parliament increases by between 3.32 per cent and 5.46 per cent (equivalent to 156 and 100 words respectively) the length of each Council common position that reaches the second-reading stage. The average (4.39 per cent, or 128 words) is equivalent to the sum of amendments 11 and 14 of Table 10.2 on equal treatment legislation. Interestingly, the Parliament appears

Table 10.5 The impact of European Parliament second-reading amendments

	Dependent variable: discretion	
	I	II
One-sample t-test	5.611***	4.857***
n	270	270
	OLS regressions	
Constant	0.0332	0.0546
	(4.72)***	(2.99)***
Amending law	−0.0218	−0.0315
	(−2.24)**	(−1.81)*
Post-Amsterdam	0.0119	0.0040
	(1.20)	(0.22)
F	2.76*	2.21
Adjusted R^2	0.02	0.01
n	227	227

Notes
*$p \leq 0.1$; **$p \leq 0.05$; ***$p \leq 0.01$. Huber–White standard errors. There has been no second reading in forty-three cases; zero values have been entered in these cases for the t-tests, while they have been excluded from the regression because there is no value for the *Post-Amsterdam* variable.

to be relatively more active in trying to exert greater control in the more policy-specific article section of the proposal.

These changes do not lead to a radical revision of the common position. They tinker mostly at the margins of the legal requirements imposed on national authorities. Moreover, second reading amendments are less likely to be introduced in the final act (Kreppel, 1999, 2002). However, the ongoing and relentless activity of specifying policy instructions in greater detail and precision, revealing the systematic desire of the Parliament to reduce discretion, may lead to substantial cumulative changes in the design of EU statutes in the long term. Furthermore, second-reading amendments are likely to be the tip of the iceberg of an activity that starts immediately the Commission introduces a proposal.

The next section sets out a research agenda on the EU politics of delegation.

A research agenda

There are many additional factors that should be taken into consideration when studying choices of delegation in the European Union.

In line with traditional agency theory, *conflict between governments and the Commission* should lead to less delegation or lower discretion for the latter. Moravcsik (1998: 488) makes a relatively broad argument about Anglo-French ideological opposition to and German support of supranational delegation. Together with Pollack (2003b), they both show how control mechanisms are carefully designed to minimize agency losses, without, however, systematically mapping Council–Commission conflict on to delegation outcomes. In Franchino (2004a), the lack of available data prevented me from including a variable measuring this conflict.

On the other hand, Hug (2003: 60–65) shows that the member states who opposed delegation to the Commission on the third pillar, employment and foreign policy, during the Amsterdam intergovernmental conference were generally those most distant from the Commission's policy positions. Intensity of conflict between a government and the Parliament also explained the willingness to agree to some limited parliamentary involvement. Kelemen (2002) shows that conflict between EU legislators and the Commission has shaped the establishment and design of EU agencies. Yet, more research is also needed on this issue, because there are some alternative views. According to Majone (2001: 109–112), politician–bureaucrat conflict is a precondition for delegation to increase credibility.

A second important factor to consider is how *conflict among governments* affects delegation outcomes. Moravcsik (1998: 75) and Pollack (2003b: 26–34) suggest that the Commission's discretion should decrease with more intense conflict within the Council. In a formal model of delegation (Franchino, 2005), I argue exactly the opposite (and also for more constraints on national executive action), but only in case of majority voting.[14] We do not have systematic empirical evidence yet which would test these expectations, but, with the enlargement of the European Union, this is an important new avenue of research. In codecision, a related issue is to investigate how policy *conflict between the Parliament and the Council* shapes choices of delegation, especially the relative reliance on the Commission and national administrations.

Third, while delegation to supranational institutions is extensively analysed, the fact that *national administrations* are agents of EU legislators, and hence delegation theory could be applied, is less directly considered. Scholars are starting to address this issue (Franchino, 2001, 2004a; Kelemen, 2000, 2003; Tallberg, 2002, 2003), but we are only in the early stages.

Fourth, the chronic lack of *bureaucratic capacity* of the Commission should not be disregarded. This is a topic that formal scholars are increasingly paying attention to (Huber and McCarty, 2004, forthcoming) and its relevance is not purely speculative. Some students of EU regional policy have asserted that lack of capacity at the supranational level could explain partial renationalization (Bache, 1998). The latest reform to some key competences of competition policy is based on private litigation within the national judiciary systems. This partial renationalization has been proposed by the Commission to address a potential 'regulatory overload', namely the expected strain on its resources after enlargement (also considering the large body of existing case law and the convergence among states toward common policy principles which has progressively taken place since the mid 1980s) (Commission of the EC, 1999; Wilks, 2003).

We should also develop more systematic knowledge on the *dynamics of delegation*, or in other words, how past decisions of delegation condition new ones. There are many works on how the Commission uses its existing powers to shape EU policy outcomes (e.g. Bulmer, 1994; Sandholtz, 1998; Schmidt, 1996, 2000), but they rarely focus on the dependent variable of our interest, namely the distribution of power across EU institutions and levels of governance.

Finally, recent developments in formal delegation theory could also be of interest for potential application to the European Union, especially given their emphasis on bureaucratic capacity and compliance (Huber and McCarty, 2004, forthcoming; Huber and Shipan, 2002), simultaneous discretion and policy decisions (Volden, 2002), risk propensity, policy technology and multidimensionality (Bendor and Meirowitz, 2004), and conflict among legislators (Epstein and O'Halloran, in Chapter 4). For instance, an interesting implication from Huber and McCarty (2004) is that a low-capacity Commission is less likely to comply with EU statutes. Consequently, EU legislators delegating to it have to design laws that allow this bureaucracy more latitude to pursue its preferred policies rather than those of legislators. This decreases the incentives of European politicians to adopt new EU measures. A low-capacity Commission is an impediment to policies which would otherwise receive the support from Council ministers and MEPs.

Conclusion

The theory of delegation has contributed enormously to our understanding of the distribution of powers among EU institutions and across levels of governance. It has helped us sharpen our theoretical and methodological tools and guide our empirical investigations. Equally, the European Union has provided fertile empirical ground to improve our general understanding of international regimes and legislative–bureaucratic relations and guided us towards new theoretical avenues and empirical investigations for the theory of delegation.

In this chapter, I have briefly reviewed the main works on delegation in the EU, evaluated the explanatory power of alternative models, provided a first assessment of the role of the Parliament and suggested future avenues of research. Future research should be designed to further improve our understanding of the Union and to contribute to the more general theory of delegation.

Notes

Parts of this chapter have been presented at workshops at the University of Milan and the University of Bologna, at the EURATE workshop of the London School of Economics, and the ESRC Workshop on 'Principal–Agent and the Study of the European Union', Birkbeck College, University of London. I am indebted to all participants for their valuable comments. I am particularly grateful to Dietmar Braun, Fabrizio Gilardi and Marco Giuliani for a very thorough review.

1 This argument had been originally made by Gatsios and Seabright (1989: 49–50) and Majone (1994, 1996: 61–79).
2 For a formal proof see Franchino (forthcoming).
3 These measures are developed by adapting the procedure of Epstein and O'Halloran (1999) to the EU legislation. Discretion is the share of major provisions in an act delegating powers to a specific bureaucratic actor (Commission or national administrations), weighted by the constraints imposed on executive action. *Relative Discretion* is produced by subtracting the value of *Commission Discretion* from *National Discretion* for each act in the data set.
4 These include measures on safety and health, equal treatment, social policy, the organization of working time and environment and transport regulation (which encompasses social and health and safety provisions)
5 State aid and commercial policy measures should be interpreted as imposing costs on powerful groups because they limit the benefits they may gain at the expense of consumers and taxpayers. Note that these choices can all be criticized. Competition policy provides concentrated benefits to companies that are disadvantaged from restrictive practices and abuses of dominant positions. Even though an anti-dumping duty benefits extra-EU import-competing industries, it may also burden powerful importers. Companies competing with state aid beneficiaries are also burdened.

6 The areas are payments for services, technical standards, movement of capital, European Economic Interest Grouping, industrial and commercial property, credit and banking, insurance, public contracts, company law and transport (market conditions).

7 They are the adoption of ECU, qualifications and professions, establishment and services (movement of workers), international capital flows and taxation (VAT measures mostly). It is more arguable for movement of persons, social security and education, where costs may be concentrated on national administrations.

8 The following control variables for policy complexity are included in the regressions. Model 1: a *Programme Committee* variable that takes the value of 1 if either legal provisions of the relevant EU measure refer to action programmes *or* a committee is involved in an issue area or a single act. Models 2 and 3: a *Detailed Rules* variable measuring the number of major provisions in an act that call for 'detailed rules' to be adopted (*modalités d'application* in the French legislation). Model 4: *Programme Committee* and *Detailed Rules*. See Franchino (2004a) on the rationale for the use of these variables to measure policy complexity and for more details on the data set.

9 See Council Decision 1999/468 repealing Decision 87/373. But whether the reform will have the intended effects is open to question, see Ballmann *et al.* (2002: 571–1).

10 These were the tools mostly referred to by McCubbins and Schwartz (1984) and McCubbins *et al.* (1987, 1989) in their seminal work when taking issue with the abdication thesis.

11 The Web site link is http://www.europarl.eu.int/oeil/. Searches have been conducted first for the adopted laws (29 April 2003), then for lapsed or withdrawn proposals and for those waiting for the Council second reading (16 June 2003), finally for the proposals waiting for the Council common position (13 July 2003).

12 This figure includes only proposals that have been voted upon by the Parliament at least at the first reading. It includes ninety-six proposals that were originally proposed under a different procedure (ninety-one under cooperation and five under consultation). These were subsequently either confirmed or rejected by the Parliament under the codecision procedure.

13 *Amending Law* takes the value of 1 if the proposal amends previous EC legislation. In these circumstances, the default condition is the existing EU measure and adding words may not reflect the willingness to exercise greater control. *Amsterdam* takes the value of 1 if the Parliament has adopted the second reading amendments after 1 May 1999, when the Treaty of Amsterdam, and the reformed codecision procedure (codecision II), entered into force.

14 Similarly, in a model applied to the US separation of powers system, Volden (2002) finds that a moderate independent agency may enjoy greater discretion as conflict between an agenda-setting legislature and executive with veto power increases. The literature on central banking suggests that conflict among legislators may lead to more delegation if policy credibility is needed (e.g. Bernhard, 1998; Keefer and Stasavage, 2003).

References

Bache, I. (1998) *Politics of European Union Regional Policy: Multi-level Governance or Flexible Gatekeeping?* London: Routledge.

Ballmann, A., Epstein, D. and O'Halloran, S. (2002) 'Delegation, Comitology, and the Separation of Powers in the European Union', *International Organization*, 56: 551–574.

Bawn, K. (1997) 'Choosing Strategies to Control the Bureaucracy. Statutory Constraints, Oversight, and the Committee System', *Journal of Law, Economics, and Organization*, 13: 101–126.

Bendor, J. and Meirowitz, A. (2004) 'Spatial Models of Delegation', *American Political Science Review*, 98: 293–310.

Bernhard, W. T. (1998) 'A Political Explanation of Variations in Central Bank Independence', *American Political Science Review*, 92: 311–328.

Bradley, K. St-C. (1997) 'The European Parliament and Comitology: On the Road to Nowhere?' *European Law Journal*, 3: 230–254.

Bulmer, S. (1994) 'Institutions and Policy Change in the European Communities: The Case of Merger Control', *Public Administration*, 72: 423–444.

Commission of the EC (1999) *White Paper on Modernisation of the Rules Implementing Articles 85 and 86 of the EC Treaty*, Brussels: European Community.

Corbett, R., Jacobs, F. and Shackleton, M. (1995) *The European Parliament*, Catermill: Longman.

Davidson, R. and MacKinnon, J. G. (1981) 'Several Tests for Model Specification in the Presence of Alternative Hypotheses', *Econometrica*, 49: 781–793.

Dogan, R. (1997) 'Comitology: Little Procedures with Big Implications', *West European Politics*, 20: 31–60.

Epstein, D. and O'Halloran, S. (1999) *Delegating Powers: A Transaction Cost Politics Approach to Policy Making under Separate Powers*, Cambridge: Cambridge University Press.

Franchino, F. (2001) 'Delegation and Constraints in the National Execution of the EC Policies: A Longitudinal and Qualitative Analysis', *West European Politics*, 24: 169–192.

Franchino, F. (2004a) 'Delegating Powers in the European Community', *British Journal of Political Science*, 34: 449–476.

Franchino, F. (2005) 'A Formal Model of Delegation in the European Union', *Journal of Theoretical Politics*, 17: 219–249.

Franchino, F. (forthcoming) *The Powers of the Union: Delegation in the EU*, Cambridge, Cambridge University Press.

Gatsios, K. and Seabright, P. (1989) 'Regulation in the European Community', *Oxford Review of Economic Policy*, 5: 37–60.

Hix, S. (1999) *The Political System of the European Union*, London: Macmillan.

Hix, S. (2000) 'Parliamentary Oversight of Executive Power: What Role for the European Parliament in Comitology?' in Th. Christiansen and E. Kirchner (eds) *Europe in Change: Committee Governance in the European Union*, Manchester: Manchester University Press.

Horn, M. J. (1995) *The Political Economy of Public Administration*, New York: Cambridge University Press.

Huber, J. D. and McCarty, N. (2004) 'Bureaucratic Capacity, Delegation, and Political Reform', *American Political Science Review*, 98 (3): 481–494.

Huber, J. D. and McCarty, N. (forthcoming) 'Bureaucratic Capacity and Legislative Performance' in E. S. Adler and J. Lapinski (eds) *The Macropolitics of Congress*.

Huber, J. D. and Shipan, C. R. (2002) *Deliberate Discretion? The Institutional Foundations of Bureaucratic Autonomy*, Cambridge: Cambridge University Press.

Hug, S. (2003) 'Endogenous Preferences and Delegation in the European Union', *Comparative Political Studies*, 36: 41–74.

Keefer, P. and Stasavage, D. (2003) 'The Limits of Delegation: Veto Players,

Central Bank Independence, and the Credibility of Monetary Policy', *American Political Science Review*, 97: 407–423.

Kelemen, R. D. (2000) 'Regulatory Federalism: EU Environmental Regulation in Comparative Perspective', *Journal of Public Policy*, 20: 133–167.

Kelemen, R. D. (2002) 'The Politics of "Eurocratic" Structure and the New European Agencies', *West European Politics*, 25: 93–118.

Kelemen, R. D. (2003) 'The Structure and Dynamics of EU Federalism', *Comparative Political Studies*, 36: 184–208.

Kreppel, A. (1999) 'What Affects the European Parliament's Legislative Influence? An Analysis of the Success of EP Amendments', *Journal of Common Market Studies*, 37: 521–538.

Kreppel, A. (2002) 'Moving beyond Procedure: An Empirical Analysis of European Parliament Legislative Influence', *Comparative Political Studies*, 35: 784–813.

Majone, G. (1994) 'The Rise of the Regulatory State in Europe', *West European Politics*, 17: 77–101.

Majone, G. (1996) *Regulating Europe*, London: Routledge.

Majone, G. (2001) 'Two Logics of Delegation: Agency and Fiduciary Relations in EU Governance' *European Union Politics*, 2: 103–122.

McCubbins, M. D., Noll, R. G. and Weingast, B. R. (1987) 'Administrative Procedures as Instruments of Political Control', *Journal of Law, Economics, and Organization*, 3: 243–277.

McCubbins, M. D., Noll, R. G. and Weingast, B. R. (1989) 'Structure and Process, Politics and Policy: Administrative Arrangements and the Political Control of Agencies', *Virginia Law Review*, 75: 431–482.

McCubbins, M. D. and Schwartz, T. (1984) 'Congressional Oversight Overlooked: Police Patrols versus Fire Alarms', *American Journal of Political Science*, 28: 165–179.

Moravcsik, A. (1998) *The Choice for Europe: Social Purpose and State Power from Messina to Maastricht*, Ithaca NY: Cornell University Press.

Pollack, M. A. (1997) 'Delegation, Agency, and Agenda Setting in the European Community', *International Organization*, 51: 99–134.

Pollack, M. A. (2003a) 'Control Mechanism or Deliberative Democracy?: Two Images of Comitology', *Comparative Political Studies*, 36: 125–155.

Pollack, M. A. (2003b) *The Engines of European Integration: Delegation, Agency, and Agenda Setting in the EU*, Oxford: Oxford University Press.

Sandholtz, W. (1998) 'The Emergence of a Supranational Telecommunication Regime', in W. Sandholtz and A. S. Sweet (eds) *European Integration and Supranational Governance*, New York: Oxford University Press.

Schmidt, S. K. (1996) 'Sterile Debates and Dubious Generalisations: European Integration Theory tested by Telecommunications and Electricity', *Journal of Public Policy*, 16: 233–271.

Schmidt, S. K. (2000) 'Only an Agenda Setter? The European Commission's Power over the Council of Ministers', *European Union Politics*, 1: 37–61.

Tallberg, J. (2002) 'Paths to Compliance: Enforcement, Management, and the European Union', *International Organization*, 56: 609–643.

Tallberg, J. (2003) *European Governance and Supranational Institutions: Making States Comply*, London: Routledge.

Volden, C. (2002) 'A Formal Model of the Politics of Delegation in a Separation of Powers System', *American Journal of Political Science*, 46: 111–133.

Weber, M. (1946) 'Bureaucracy', in H. H. Gerth and C. W. Mills (eds) *Max Weber: Esseys in Sociology*, New York: Oxford University Press.

Wilks, S. (2003) 'Regulatory Overload: Collapse or Coherence in the Reform of European Competition Policy?' Paper presented at the New Governance of Markets, University College London, October.

11 Conclusion

Dietmar Braun and Fabrizio Gilardi

There are several modes of coordination to produce collective welfare by means of the state. Though delegation has been among these modes for a long time there has been no systematic and encompassing theory building similar to that which we find for other modes of coordination like hierarchy, market or networks. Democratic representation as one of the more obvious delegation structures in the political system was dealt with by normative political theory and the Weberian view of bureaucracy as a subordinate without discretion further prevented a more thorough reasoning on the essentials of political delegation. It needed public choice theory and particularly the work by Niskanen (1971) and Downs (1967) to prepare the grounds for such reasoning. Both authors contested the Weberian view and explained the oversized public sector in terms of selfish and opportunistic behaviour of bureaucrats that was often not consistent with policy-makers' objectives. The recognition of the possibility of divergence between the preferences of bureaucrats and policy makers made it possible to employ principal–agent theory to model the relationship between parliament, government and bureaucracy. New Public Management with its philosophy of contracting out public services to agents with procedural autonomy may have added another impetus to more sound reflection on delegation. These reflections have now reached a stage of considerable sophistication where empirical research becomes more and more important. The introduction to this book described several steps of theoretical refinement that have been taken in this respect.

In this book all the articles used principal–agent thought as their key framework for discussing delegation. The particularities of this approach, shared by the authors in this book, consist of anchoring it in bounded rationality, which invariably results in incomplete contracts between principals and agents; the assumption that principals do not have complete knowledge about what the agent does; and the possibility that agents are not trustworthy, i.e. that their preferences deviate from the ideal point of the principal. The relationship between principal and agent is regarded as a 'functional relationship', i.e. a division of labour which should have advantages for both sides (the principal gets information or work done that he cannot do by himself or only with considerable transaction costs and the agent gets resources he would not otherwise have) but which turns out to be subject to opportunistic behaviour and therefore to suboptimal outcomes. As there are never complete contracts, both the principal and the agent can deviate from the agreed contract. Much effort is therefore spent in reflecting on institutional constraints that keep both the principal and the agent as close as possible to the agreed objectives.

The advantage of having such a parsimonious and common framework is that until now separate issues in political science like democratic representation, elite theory, corporatism, the working of supranational institutions like the European Union (EU) or public administration can be viewed from a common angle. Though this angle is necessarily selective, it helps to reveal similar structures of political action that are found in each of these areas and therefore common problems, inefficiencies and dynamics. If this is so, encompassing remedies can be developed that may be applicable in all areas. Moreover, the common angle gives us the opportunity to make comparisons between areas of political science that until recently were disjointed. As far as we know there is no other theoretical offering at the moment that can compete in this respect with principal–agent theory, or rational choice theory more generally. This does not mean that one cannot try to integrate other theoretical approaches, but it is important to first have a common approach that motivates researchers to ask similar questions and test similar hypotheses.

We are aware, of course, that using principal–agent theory also has a price and that this price consists above all in its selectivity and in the loss of requisite variety. The 'economic approach' is based on methodological individualism, the assumption of opportunism and transaction cost economics which is in conflict with the constructivist approach and other more macro-societal approaches. The use of such an approach is much debated and evokes old discussions about the usefulness of parsimonious methods in general. It is clear that one can contest the usual assumptions of maximizing and opportunistic actors or the assumption that an action theory is the most adequate tool to understand political reality. Nevertheless, we think that the advantages of sticking to the principal–agent approach far outnumber the weaknesses: principal–agent theory allows rigorous theory building, comparison between unlikely cases, and above all empirical testing of hypotheses. It is the last point that allows necessary modifications and adaptations of the theory. In addition, in contrast to the neoclassical public choice approach, it integrates both the more realistic assumptions of bounded rationality and institutions as important constraints on action. It does not mean that it is the only interpretation of reality but it can claim to have a prominent and legitimate place among the theoretical options at our disposition.

In what follows we will try to summarize the major lessons we can draw from the various studies in this book. We will not pretend to develop a synthesis of the different 'building blocks' that have been used by authors and present a coherent and close-knit framework. Rather we would like to show that, despite the common framework used by the authors, its application in different institutional contexts still raises further questions that need to be treated in order to build a suitable theory of delegation.

Incentives to delegation

In order to justify a whole book on delegation as a primordial mode of coordination in state action, the question 'Why delegate?' seems to have high pertinence and is often raised in the studies of this book. Of course, the basic answer in principal–agent theory is that there is delegation because an actor has resources but not the ability to take certain actions. He then delegates to an agent with the appropriate capacity for taking such actions (Coleman, 1990). But what are these resources? Or in other words, what can the agent do that the principal cannot? The chapters of this book have covered several aspects, which we will discuss in turn.

The need for information as a crucial incentive to delegate has been stressed both in Epstein and O'Halloran's chapter on delegation to the executive and Christiansen and Norgaard's chapter on delegation to interest organizations. Epstein and O'Halloran see the need for delegation in the political system because policy makers require information only experts can deliver. Christiansen and Norgaard also recognize this need for information among policy makers, but instead place it in the context of the political struggle in a minority government system. They consider delegation to interest organizations as part of a governmental strategy to strengthen government's position vis-à-vis the parliament. By integrating otherwise hostile interest organizations into the context of policy-proposing committees they turn them into agents that work in the interests of the government. At the same time, these organizations become 'obstructive agents' of the parliamentary opposition. This observation demonstrates how important it is to place considerations of delegation in the political sphere in the context of democratic struggle and assess the motivations of the political principal in relation to his position within political competition.

The fact that policies may not be consistent over time is a second broad category of incentives to delegation, which has been discussed in a number of chapters. Time inconsistency occurs 'when a policy announced for some future period is no longer optimal when it is time to implement the policy' (Bernhard *et al.*, 2002: 705). In this context, Gilardi showed that a major incentive for delegation to independent regulatory agencies is the inability of governments to credibly commit to fair regulation, which stems from the fact that their preferences may change over time. Politicians may adopt a regulatory framework, but then seek to change it in the future. This is problematic when the goal of regulation is to shape an investor-friendly environment, as is the case in economic regulation (for example, utilities regulation). Through regulation to independent agencies, governments try to reduce the time inconsistency of regulation and thus increase its credibility for investors.

Time-inconsistent preferences also shape delegation arrangements in other domains, such as the relationship between politicians and bureaucrats. As Lapuente argues, in order to motivate bureaucrats politicians need to be able to credibly commit to appropriately rewarding their work, for example in terms of promotion or higher salary. However, time-inconsistent preferences make this difficult because politicians may promise a reward but then renege on the commitment once the job is done. Rational bureaucrats anticipate this and may thus refuse to cooperate fully in the first place, making the situation worse for everyone. Lapuente's argument is that politicians have solved this problem by delegating the management of public employees to independent institutions such as Civil Service Commissions, which increases the credibility of their commitment to bureaucrats, who will then be more willing to cooperate.

Franchino has identified similar phenomena in the EU institutional setting, where the credibility problem operates at two levels. The first is the Treaty level. Member states cannot credibly commit to respecting the provisions laid down in treaties and, as a result, may not be willing to sign, fearing that other member states will not abide by the rules. In this context, delegation of powers to the Commission is a means of increasing the credibility of the pact, since the Commission can sanction infringements of the Treaties. The second level at which credibility problems exist in the European Union is the Council of Ministers. The situation here is very similar to that of regulatory policies: the Council may have time-inconsistent preferences and thus lack the capacity to credibly commit to a course of action. Again, delegating powers to the Commission improves the credibility of policy commitments.

Time-inconsistent preferences and the credibility problems seem to be an important component of the incentives that lead political principals to delegate powers to agents. Further work in this direction thus seems warranted. In this volume, Gilardi has argued that at least three distinct phenomena can lead decision-makers to have preferences that change over time[1]. First, new and unforeseen contingencies may lead a decision maker to revise their original choice. The context often changes between time t and time t + 1, and so can decisions. Second, the strategic anticipation of other actors may be a necessary condition for time-inconsistent preferences. Even if nothing changes in the context, actors that are targets of the policy may anticipate the decision makers' time inconsistency and act accordingly, thus forcing them to revise their choice at time t + 1. Third, time inconsistency may arise simply because of the shape of discount functions. Temporary preference reversals may occur if decision makers, as experimental studies suggest, discount the future hyperbolically.

These are three distinct sources of time-inconsistent preferences, which are therefore sources of credibility problems, and which therefore create incentives to delegate. How incentives to delegate vary across these different forms of time inconsistency is unclear. The central bank literature, for example, which has studied in detail the consequences of time inconsistency, has not devoted the same attention to its sources, and has largely neglected the role of hyperbolic discounting. Does it matter for delegation whether credibility problems are due to the anticipation of actors rather than to changes in the context? Are delegation arrangements different if time-inconsistent behaviour is due essentially to the shape of the discount function of decision makers rather than to their sensitivity to changes in the decision-making context? These are some broad questions that future work should address.

Incentives to delegate may also be created by political uncertainty. As Gilardi has shown, one reason for governments to delegate to independent regulatory agencies is the fact that new governments can change previous decisions. From this view, delegation is a means of giving policies a longer life despite political turnover in government. Of course, changes in the political composition of executives is also a source of credibility problems, since policies are likely to be less stable if there is governmental instability. Therefore, although the credibility and political uncertainty problems are conceptually distinct as causes of delegation, in practice their effects may be tightly entangled. Two tasks for future work follow from this. First, theories of delegation should integrate both problems into a coherent framework. Existing work is either focused on only one of the two issues (e.g. De Figueiredo, 2002, who studies only political uncertainty) or puts them side by side without linking them (e.g. Gilardi in Chapter 6). Second, empirical work should devise strategies and techniques to distinguish the relative impact of credibility and political uncertainty on delegation – admittedly a difficult task, as the two problems are closely related. Existing work has relied on rudimentary operationalizations (e.g. Gilardi in Chapter 6), and more work is clearly needed.

Delegation, as both Braun and Lapuente have argued, may also be linked to a more fundamental 'trust game' between policy makers and target groups. In such a game both the principal and the agent – or the trustor and the trustee – have an interest in maintaining trust, while opportunistic behaviour might disturb such a relationship. Delegation is one of the possible options for maintaining trust in the system. For Lapuente delegation to independent committees responsible for the promotion of public employees is one way to ensure that public employees have a stable environment and, therefore, their chances of promotion are protected. This is necessary to maintain the trust of public employees, encourage their best efforts and gain their loyalty. In the case of no delegation and a powerful government, the replacement risk would destabilize the trust relationship between government and public employees. For Braun delegation to funding agencies in research policies is an important mechanism to maintain the belief of policy makers in the trustworthiness of scientists, while at the same time it can protect the scientists' interests vis-à-vis policy makers. This is important for the belief of scientists in the credible commitment of policy makers.

Taken together, these findings demonstrate that the motivation for political delegation cannot be adequately explained simply by an abstract referral to the principal's need for information. The political context and strategies of power, the willingness to embark on long-term commitments and to stabilize trust relationships with target groups play an important role in delegation.

Discretion and control

How much discretion should be given to the agent, and, conversely, how much control should the principal keep? This is the question most often dealt with in these chapters. Braun links the degree of discretion directly to the uncertainty of decision makers in a policy field and the possibility of policy makers defining policy objectives. High uncertainty is a good reason – in this he confirms Epstein and O'Halloran – to give large discretion to agents. Uncertainty is therefore an explanatory factor not only for the decision when to delegate but also for the degree of discretion. Similarly, another reflection from Epstein and O'Halloran holds in this context: the distance between the preferences of the principal and those of the agent influences not only when to delegate but also the discretion granted. This demonstrates that the constraining factors mentioned above have both an influence on the decision when to delegate and how to delegate, i.e. the degree of discretion.

This also holds for Franchino's study of the European Union. Decision rules and the underlying consensus or conflict decide not only when to delegate, but also how. When unanimity rules are adopted that enforce an internal consensus, then less discretion is given to the European Commission. In contrast, the more majority rules count, and therefore conflicts are possible, the more discretion the agent may receive. Franchino also links the degree of discretion to the availability of control procedures when he discusses the strategies of the European Parliament. The less one disposes of 'non-statutory *ex post* oversight procedures' the less one is inclined to give discretion and the more one is inclined to depend on detailed statutory procedures. The availability of '*ex post* oversight' procedures is important; when principals have an *ex post* veto, they have sufficient guarantees to intervene in case of the defection of the agent and this also provides support for them to take the risk of giving agents a lot of discretion.

The studies in this volume have also shown that that there is a link between the degree of discretion and control procedures. It is not often that one finds complete discretion if there are no control possibilities for the principal. But even this is not excluded, as the example of research policies presented by Braun has shown. Here, the fundamental uncertainty about knowledge production has resulted in high discretion to basic research agencies without the existence of functioning control procedures of policy makers. Braun demonstrates, however, that the lack of control procedures does not mean complete liberty for agencies. The fundamental dependence on government money means that all funding agencies must find a point on or within the indifference curve of political principals to survive in the long term. This can be considered a substitute for control, as agencies are constrained by the ideal point of preferences of the principal and do not have complete leeway.

Control has also been a major topic in the reflections on the 'chain of delegation'. In fact, in democracies the accountability of representatives to the voter plays a primordial role and discussion about how to control the action of representatives is central. Strøm *et al.* demonstrate that the main problem here is one of informational asymmetry; voters are not very likely to be able to control representatives themselves. It needs separate intermediary organizations like parties – that are not seen as agents themselves – to compensate for this. As an alternative, institutional features like checks and balances in the presidential system of the United States might offer control possibilities, because voters can make effective use of multiple agents. In parliamentary systems such control completely depends on parties. The analysis by Strøm *et al.* is not too encouraging, as it seems that parties are not able to control moral hazard but are, on the contrary, increasing the chance of moral hazard of representatives because of party discipline (at least in Westminster models). In addition, *ex post* oversight is less feasible in parliamentary systems than in a presidential system. The parliamentary majority has no interest in oversight of the government. This problem is worse in small parliamentary democracies, as discussed by Dumont and Varone. Small constituencies require representatives in parliaments to spend more time in contact with voters instead of using their time to control the government. The lack of specialization in small parliaments gives an additional advantage to government in this respect.

These examples demonstrate that, again, we do not find an unequivocal answer to when and how to use control procedures. The literature on the chain of democracy raises the problem of accountability linked to the availability of control and sketches a negative image for parliamentary democracies of the Westminster type. This gives us an opportunity to reflect further on how to use control procedures better. The recent trend, mentioned in Epstein and O'Halloran's chapter, that parliaments in the United Kingdom are starting to make more regular use of their own parliamentary committees is seen by the authors as a response to a resurgent conflict between parliament and government. One can also interpret it as a new tendency to make parliament more independent of parties and take control problems seriously. In this way, the control function of parliament might be strengthened in the future.

The institutional context of delegation

A common finding of most contributors in this volume is that the institutional context is important for delegation arrangements. Institutions are generally seen as constraints influencing the incentives of actors. Depending on the kind of institutional environment we have, we may therefore develop different expectations about the choices actors will make. This enriches the discussion and adds variety and, in addition, it allows comparison between countries or systems.

Epstein and O'Halloran discuss the organization of the relationship between parliament and government, and its influence on the decision of delegation. They see a clear difference between the presidential system in the United States and the parliamentary system in Europe. In the former case, the checks-and-balances system gives an incentive to Congress to delegate to external agencies 'and blur the distinction between legislation and implementation', while parliaments in Europe, in cases of conflict with the government, may rely on the internal production of expertise. Strøm *et al.* demonstrate the importance of regime types on the capacity to avoid adverse selection and moral hazard, while Christiansen and Norgaard evoke the particular distribution of power in minority government systems to explain the delegation strategies of minority governments.

Gilardi points to the fact that veto players are functional equivalents of delegation for increasing credible-commitment capacity. Veto players do not make preferences less time-inconsistent, but they do prevent changing preferences from leading to policy change. By increasing policy stability, veto players make policies less sensitive to changes in preferences and therefore more credible. Since one of the advantages of delegation can be increasing policy credibility, veto players are a functional equivalent of delegation in this respect. Lapuente comes to the same conclusion in his study of credibility problems between politicians and bureaucracy. He argues that politicians' promises to reward cooperative bureaucrats may not be credible, and shows that the situation can be improved by delegating the management of public employees to an independent authority. The problem, however, is less severe when politicians are constrained in their behaviour, in which case there are fewer incentives to delegate. In other words, constraints on decision making are a functional equivalent of delegation for increasing the credibility of politicians' commitments vis-à-vis bureaucrats.

These views are far from uncontroversial. In particular, the central bank literature has come to the opposite conclusion, namely that constraints on decision making, such as many veto players, are a precondition for credible delegation, and not a functional equivalent of it (see e.g.

Keefer and Stasavage 2003). The argument is that delegated powers can, in principle, be withdrawn as easily as they are granted. As a result, delegation itself is subject to a credibility problem, unless there are constraints on decision making. Since both views are theoretically informed and empirically grounded, we are faced with an unresolved puzzle – why do the same institutions have different effects on different types of delegation? This is a question that clearly deserves more attention.

The ambiguous effects of institutions on delegation arrangements also appear in Franchino's chapter, where the role of different decision rules (unanimity versus qualified majority vote (QMV) is discussed. Franchino stresses that the literature on delegation in the European Union sees QMV as a functional equivalent of delegation for the credibility of agreements. One key dimension of credibility in the European Union is linked to the strategic interactions among member states. A member state may promise to abide by the jointly agreed rules at time t, but renege on the commitment at time $t + 1$. If other member states anticipate this, there may be a failure to reach an agreement in the first place, hence the need to establish credibility-enhancing devices. Delegation to the Commission is a possible solution, of which QMV is seen as a functional equivalent, since it reduces the bargaining power of member states that are tempted to disrespect the rules. The effects of QMV, however, seem more ambiguous than suggested in the literature. On one hand, QMV facilitates the adoption of secondary legislation so that policy objectives set out in the Treaty are credibly achieved. On the other hand, QMV facilitates the overruling of the Commission's decisions (whose role, in this situation, is ensuring the credibility of commitments), which creates a credibility problem.[2]

In addition, there is a further complication over the effects of institutional structure on delegation in the European Union. In his chapter, Franchino differentiates between two types of credibility problem. The first has just been discussed, and involves member states. The second is different because it involves member states, on the one hand, and the target groups of policies on the other, similar to the situations discussed by Kydland and Prescott (1977), in the central bank literature and in Gilardi's chapter. The Council of Ministers makes promises to the group that it may not be able to keep because of time-inconsistent preferences. While QMV, for the reasons discussed above, can be a functional equivalent of delegation when credibility problems arise among member states, in this context it increases policy change capacity and therefore exacerbates time inconsistency and credibility problems. QMV makes policy change easier and therefore the promise less credible. Conversely, under unanimity policy change is more difficult. As a result, under QMV there is a greater need for delegation than under unanimity if credibility is sought. Therefore, in this context QMV is an institutional condition that exacerbates credibility problems.

To sum up, the chapters of this volume point to the fact that further work is needed on the role of the institutional context in shaping delegation arrangements. There is consensus on the fact that institutions matter, but the conditions under which institutions affecting policy stability constitute functional equivalents of delegation or, rather, preconditions for credible delegation remain poorly understood. More generally, this volume has made a first comparative inventory of important institutional distinctions. An important task for future work will be to try to develop clear empirical measures for how to distinguish different institutional types. Until now, there is still a mix of propositions that use traditional regime types (parliamentary and presidential systems (Epstein and O'Halloran; Strøm *et al.*) and a more general distinction between 'power separation' and 'power concentration' systems, based on veto players (Lapuente). This needs further clarification.

Accountability and legitimacy

The accountability of agents is another key theme that has been discussed in this book. If democratic representatives fail to be accountable to voters then the legitimacy of the political order may be in question. Recent debates on decreasing trust in politicians in many parliamentary democracies demonstrate that failing accountability procedures and failing control are major problems. If, as Strøm *et al.* suggest, one cannot avoid agency losses by control procedures – regardless of the institutional solutions we might have at hand – then parliamentary democracy is indeed in danger. This is one of the most disturbing conclusions, also reiterated by Epstein and O'Halloran. For them, though it is linked not to government and parliament but to the relationship of parliament and bureaucracy, there is no perfect control of agents, and agency losses can be expected everywhere. No contract or institution can be conceived that will solve this problem fully. Of course, it is worth while to reflect on good contracts in order to minimize these losses. The strength of the delegation approach is to have a rigorous framework at hand that can help to do this.

The interesting point is that the question of accountability and legitimacy is linked not only to the 'input legitimacy' of parliamentary democracy but also to those institutions of delegation that are usually considered to be on the side of 'output legitimacy', i.e. independent agencies. This is highlighted in Sosay's chapter, where she raises a fundamental problem, seldom discussed in the delegation literature, that independent regulatory agencies cannot be taken out of the 'democratic chain of delegation' and claim a special statute. Welfare efficiency cannot be taken as sufficient legitimization to accept these institutions, as the notion of welfare efficiency is itself contested and therefore part of the political struggle. If this is the case one needs to reflect on how to legitimize IRAs in terms of 'input legitimacy'. The accountability of IRAs is a problem that will remain if the trend towards more and more delegation of public tasks to such agencies continues and the first clear problems of accountability or shirking become visible.

Legitimacy is therefore a problem both for delegation in democratic representation (input legitimacy) and for delegation to independent agencies (output legitimacy). The problem of delegation to independent agencies is different from delegation to bureaucracies because bureaucracies are indirectly legitimated by their integration into the democratic chain of delegation. Bureaucrats are responsible to ministers, who are responsible to the government, which is responsible to parliament, which is responsible to the public. Therefore, legitimacy appears to be less of a problem and is seldom discussed in the literature on delegation to bureaucracies.

It seems to be of great importance to further integrate these reflections on accountability and legitimacy into the work on delegation. It would also strengthen the value and acceptability of the theory because such an important notion of political science, legitimacy, can be integrated within the theory. Further reflections on how to solve this problem also seem to be of utmost importance, as we still lack a thorough 'design' about legitimacy aspects in delegation.

Binary or more compound delegation relationships?

Should we conceptualize delegation as a binary or a compound relationship? The principal–agent tradition has until recently conceptualized delegation in terms of a dyadic relationship where principal and agent are involved in organizing a public task. The notion of the chain of delegation and the integration of democratic representation into principal–agent theory has led to more profound reflections on this. However, principal–agent theory has already offered some openings to more complex configurations, including multiple agents or multiple principals. Strøm *et al.* use this knowledge to classify the presidential system in the United States, for example, as a case of multiple agents, with evident advantages for the voters as principals (comparison of performance, control, transparency, etc.). They clarify that this concept of multiple agencies does not exactly fit the parliamentary model, at least in its Westminster form. The chain of democracy is a chain of linear, sequential and binary relations. This means that the usual lessons from principal–agent theory can be applied at each step, but it also adds something qualitatively new, as the different steps are interlinked and, as Dumont and Varone show, there can be 'short cuts' between different steps. The length of the chain also demonstrates particular problems for accountability. It is therefore worth while to discuss the 'chain' as a concept in much more detail in order to assess its implications for theorizing in terms of principal–agent. This still has to be done. The chapter about 'size' by Dumont and Varone offers a major contribution in this respect, as it tries to discuss in a rigorous way the relationship of size and the organization of the chain of delegation. Considering various forms of parliamentary democracy could enrich the discussion on the chain of delegation. Strøm *et al.* focus on the Westminster model, but it may also be interesting to integrate consensus democracies more explicitly here.

The notion of a chain is one indication that the existing binary principal–agent model may be too simple for understanding the more complex political processes. This point has already been raised above, that reasons for deciding to delegate depend on more complex figurations of democratic struggle. Other chapters offer further evidence for this. Epstein and O'Halloran in their 'compound model of delegation' develop a more complex situation in which Congress representatives have to choose, as they need to take into account the preference points of both internal experts and external agencies. Other actors must therefore be integrated in explaining delegation. Braun explicitly positions independent agencies in the distributive policy arena between 'trustor' and 'trustee' and demonstrates that these agencies cannot freely choose their ideal points outside the indifference curves of both actors. In order to understand delegation, he suggests a triadic configuration that still needs to be elaborated in more detail. Finally, Sosay brings in the public as the first principal in judging the legitimacy of independent agencies.

All this demonstrates that opening the notion of delegation to more compound relationships seems to be useful if we want to understand political delegation. The attempts to do so are not yet interlinked and systematized and much further work needs to be done, above all at the conceptual level.

The diffusion of delegation arrangements

Finally, we find it worth while to enlarge our vision of delegation. Most studies, not only in this volume, implicitly assume that the choice of delegation arrangements made in one country is independent from the choices made in other countries. In fact, this is a simplification that is routinely made in comparative politics, despite the fact that the so-called 'Galton's problem', namely the fact that observations may not be independent, has been recognized for a long time (see e.g. Ross and Homer, 1976). In this volume, Gilardi has shown that the interdependences among countries may influence delegation, and in particular the establishment of independent regulatory agencies. More specifically, Gilardi has shown that regulatory agencies have been created not only as a reaction to the pressures created by the credibility and political uncertainty problems, but also because they have progressively been taken for granted as an appropriate organizational form for regulators, independently from the actual functions they perform.

This result is specific to the case of regulatory agencies and cannot be easily generalized to other delegation steps. All delegation arrangements are not equally flexible; therefore, diffusion processes in this field should not be expected to be homogeneous. Delegation to regulatory agencies can surely spread more easily than delegation arrangements that involve a more radical change in the constitutional structure of the state. None the less, the main point remains relevant; what happens in one country is influenced by what happens in other countries. In other words, the study of delegation would benefit from taking into account these interdependences rather than making the unrealistic assumption that each country chooses delegation arrangements in isolation.

Conclusion

This conclusion has shown that the common principal–agent framework adopted in this book does not yet constitute a coherent theory on delegation. The different fields of application have served in the first instance as a heuristic exercise to find relevant variables to be used in further research. The advantage of the common framework is that it has disciplined authors to ask the same questions and use the same conceptual tools. The answers are a function of requisite variety; they depend on the different institutional contexts and need further analysis and empirical research to go from heuristics to systematic and empirically informed theory.

Notes

1 For a more detailed discussion see Gilardi (2004: chapter 4).
2 These arguments are taken from e-mail exchanges with Fabio Franchino.

References

Bernhard, W., Broz, J. L. and Clark, W. R. (2002) 'The Political Economy of Monetary Institutions', *International Organization*, 56 (4): 693–723.

Coleman, James S. (1990) *Foundations of Social Theory*, Cambridge MA: The Belknap Press of Harvard University Press.

De Figueiredo, R. J. P. (2002) 'Electoral Competition, Political Uncertainty, and Policy Insulation', *American Political Science Review*, 96 (2): 321–333.

Downs, A. (1967) *Inside Bureaucracy*, Boston MA: Little Brown.

Gilardi, F. (2004) 'Delegation in the Regulatory State. Origins and Diffusion of Independent Regulatory Agencies in Western Europe', PhD dissertation, Université de Lausanne.

Keefer, P. and Stasavage, D. (2003) 'The Limits of Delegation: Veto Players, Central Bank Independence, and the Credibility of Monetary Policy', *American Political Science Review*, 97 (3): 407–423.

Kydland, F. E. and Prescott, E. C. (1977) 'Rules rather than Discretion: The Inconsistency of Optimal Plans', *Journal of Political Economy*, 85 (3): 473–491.

Niskanen, William A. (1971) *Bureaucracy and Representative Government*, Chicago: Aldine.

Ross, M. H. and Homer, E. (1976) 'Galton's Problem in Cross-national Research', *World Politics*, 29 (1): 1–28.

Index

LaVergne, TN USA
16 October 2010

201016LV00002B/10/P